The Trainer's Handbook

The Trainer's Handbook

The AMA Guide to Effective Training

Garry Mitchell

American Management Association

This book is available at a special
discount when ordered in bulk quantities.
For information, contact Special Sales Department,
AMACOM, a division of American Management Association,
135 West 50th Street, New York, NY 10020.

Library of Congress Cataloging-in-Publication Data

Mitchell, Garry.
   The trainer's handbook.

   Includes index.
   1. Employees, Training of. I. Title.
HF5549.5.T7M58 1987   658.3′124   86-47819
ISBN 0-8144-5875-0

Printing number

10 9 8 7 6 5 4

TO
Val and Heather

Acknowledgments

KNOWLEDGE and skill are inseparable from the training that engendered them, no less for me than for all who read this book. So I must express my gratitude to my trainer Beverly Hyman, who has taught me much of what is written here. My four-year degree in education from the University of Alberta, Canada, gave me a basic framework that made 20 years of teaching everything from grade 4 to postgraduate seminars meaningful. But it was not until I met Beverly that I learned about training. It was she who taught me the power of Socratic dialogue; it was she who taught me the value of training objectives; and it was she who taught me program design. I can no longer separate what else I've learned from her, what I brought already formed to our professional relationship, and what I've learned from the thousands of trainers, secretaries, salespeople, and executives that I've trained in the past six years. I do know, however, that Beverly remains my model — the best trainer I know. Thanks, Bev. And thanks to Chris Nystrom for bringing us together.

Every book starts with an idea and for that I am grateful to my editor Philip Henry, who first sought me out and then helped to shape the structure, direction, and content of the book. Julia Goodwin took on the massive job of deciphering and typing almost two thousand pages of hand written manuscript and justly deserves my heartfelt thanks. I'd like to thank, too, Barbara Horowitz, my managing editor, and Richard Gatjens who got the book into print; and Carole Berglie who tackled the Herculean task of copy-editing the typed manuscript.

Finally, for the pleasure of working with them and learning from them, I'd like to thank all of my trainees, past and future.

Contents

Introduction

EVERY book has a purpose. Some entertain, some teach, some act as references, and some make excellent doorstops, shelf fillers, and booster seats. This book is a desktop reference, meaning that I envisioned it as a book to be kept beside the dictionary on a trainer's desk—that it would be an immediate and constant source of information.

It is possible to read this book from beginning to end (it was written that way, after all) and everything will make perfect sense. However, the basic structure is not sequential, nor is it climactic. Instead, it is centered around three major functions of the trainer: the face-to-face act of training other people, the planning for that training, and the management of training facilities, personnel, and operations. Part I, The Nature of Training, covers the essential interaction skills required of a trainer—skills such as maintaining leadership, creating learning associations, planning lessons, controlling training groups, analyzing trainees, and establishing credibility. It outlines the steps in handling resistance to training and for building environments that encourage a change in trainee behavior. In essence, Part I provides a perspective on, a methodology for, and a rationale for the role of training in the organization.

Part II, Planning and Preparing for Training, details the day-to-day steps involved in performing needs analyses, writing training programs, and conducting evaluations. It also covers the preparation of task analyses and evaluations of outside sources, such as off-the-shelf training packages, consultants, and commercial seminar organizations. Finally, it addresses the care, uses, and creation of audiovisual aids. In short, Part II provides detailed, step-by-step descriptions of how to carry out the basics of training.

Part III is about management concerns, not in general terms but,

1

rather, in those matters germane to training. It deals with the task of marketing and selling internal training programs as well as the usually neglected areas of writing skills, negotiation techniques, financial management and budgeting, and human resource development.

A word of warning is necessary. This book is not intended to be the benchmark of training against which all other efforts must be measured. Instead, I've provided a compendium of workable solutions to most training problems. At no time should you view these solutions as necessarily the *only* answer to a problem. Training is in large measure an art form. As in any art, there are many ways to approach a problem; some are better than others. All the ideas presented here are effective, well worn by years of use. If you haven't already found a solution of your own, try one of these.

Finally, as befits the principle of redundancy, concepts are presented in two forms: once in detail within each chapter, and once in a brief summary at the end of each chapter. Many key ideas are also repeated for emphasis in checklists, figures, and sidebars. Experienced trainers should first read the summary to see what is covered in the chapter. If they are familiar with the material or have no problems in that particular area, they should move on. If readers desire somewhat more detail, they should then skim the chapter and peruse the figures and checklists, which present, in a quick-to-read fashion, the basic precepts and guidelines of the training process. Those who need a thorough treatment of the topic should read the entire chapter to consider the subject in detail. Yet another help to readers is the table of contents. A glance at the breakdown of chapters by major headings will give a good overview of the various areas covered.

Once you have read the book, or portions of it, you'll find the table of contents will help you refresh your memory. Once again the chapter summaries will be helpful, and the checklists and figures throughout will bring back to mind the important procedures and techniques.

This book is also intended as a skills manual for the training of trainers. A training manager can assign readings from it and build practical experiences around its various topics. When the book is used for training such practical assignments are vital. The emphasis here is on detailing the procedures; it is not on theory or even skills mastery. Intended as a backup when mastery of skills is incomplete, the book allows those who are as yet unskilled in any of these areas to tackle unfamiliar tasks with proven techniques.

This is a book for trainers at all levels. For the novice, it is a daily procedural manual. For the expert trainer newly appointed to a management position, it is the practical guide to new perspectives on familiar material. And for the experienced training manager, it is the field reference for getting back to basics, keeping on track, refreshing your knowledge, training new trainers, and developing new managers.

PART I

The Nature of Training

Introduction to Part I

PART I is the most theoretical of the three major parts of this book. That is not to say it isn't practical. This first part gives you an orientation to the theory behind training and also introduces you to many of its practices. Chapter 1 establishes the role of the trainer as a change agent — an agent for structuring change and growth in a company. It is this concept that sets the tone for the rest of the book, so for those learning the craft, this beginning chapter is essential for grounding all other necessary skills solidly within the corporate culture. In addition, Chapter 1 gives the experienced trainer a detailed set of instructions for analyzing the needs for change in an organization, as well as provides steps to be taken to effect those changes and a format for long-range planning. In short, this chapter provides an overview of some of the functions and issues of training.

Chapter 2 encompasses the basics of adult learning theory, how to cope with resistance to learning, and the dynamics of group behavior. The person or group to be trained is the focus here, with a discussion of how people learn, the role senses play in receiving input, differences in learning ability, and ways to discover what trainees know and what they want and need to know. Also included are some effective techniques for handling groups, including the roles members assume and how decisions are made.

Chapter 3 examines the structure of training. We look at the bedrock of training — objectives. We examine the need culturally for live training and discuss the importance of maintaining a learning dialogue and patterns of redundancy. Structural patterns are examined and, finally, the four basic steps to creating effective lessons are discussed.

In Chapter 4, the function of the trainer is examined, especially with regard to personal skills. We look at the ways a trainer can assume a leadership role and we consider the various tasks a training leader must perform. We explain ways of controlling distractions in the classroom, including difficult trainees. There are also specific instructions on improving your listening skills and heightening and varying your question-forming abilities. We provide guidelines for making effective responses to other people's questions and give tips on projecting a positive nonverbal image. Credibility is discussed, including how to establish it and how to use it effectively.

Part I is, therefore, both a compendium of solid training techniques and a theoretical underpinning for the novice or the expert; indeed, it is for anyone who wants to better understand the nature of training.

CHAPTER 1

The Function of
Training

WHY would a company hire a trainer? You can probably think of a dozen or so specific problems that a company might try to solve by setting up a training program. But no matter how many you might think of, all of these problems can be condensed into one basic reason: A company hires a trainer to produce a *change* in its operation. The singular function of training is to produce change.

Training can bring about changes that solve a variety of problems, but it is not an economic cure-all. In 1981 the United States began to feel the pinch of a major recession. Before it ended, we suffered from the highest inflation rates and the greatest unemployment figures since the Great Depression of the 1930s. During the first eight months of this recent recession, there was a tremendous boom in training, as company after company felt the need to do something about the economic slowdown and negative growth. Train people! Get them to perform better! Turn the economy around! Stop the recession!

Of course training alone couldn't stop a recession. No matter how much employee performance was improved, with no market there would be no growth. When managers all over the country realized this, they pulled the plug. Training budgets shrank faster than the economy. The training had failed to produce the necessary improvements, so it was cut back. Remember, the function of training in the corporation is to produce change. When it does, it is successful; when it doesn't, it fails. Regardless of other results a trainer or training manager may accomplish, the bottom line is the measurable change in performance. The trainer is an agent for change, and this book concentrates on the ways of achieving that change.

The Nature of Change

No one wants to change. We would all happily have others change to suit our needs or habits or desires. None of us, not even the managers who demand the change, wants to change how we do things. Our society pays great lip service to change. We call ourselves the most progressive and advanced society. Indeed, technologically we are advanced. But if that technology causes us to change the way we do things, we resist it (unless, of course, it palpably makes them easier). We want to think faster and work more efficiently, but not if that means having to learn how to program a computer. We like creating new jobs and rapidly developing new industries, but not if they mean having to move or change the face of our cities. We like to earn more money, but we don't want to learn new, higher-paying jobs. People love the *status quo*. It's a very human trait. To change is to risk losing what we already have, and few people are willing to run that risk.

Of course there are exceptions. Many people welcome change in any direction. But most people are, at best, concerned with what the future may bring, and when learning new job skills, they are apprehensive about their ability to make the change. They resist the required change, often in subtle ways, and it is this resistance that the trainer must anticipate, recognize, and reduce.

The Motivation to Change

Change is neither good nor bad, only constant. Individuals respond constantly to various combinations of elements in the environment. These elements can be as diverse as pressure from a family or peer group, the temperature of the room, a recent illness, traffic conditions, a working situation, feelings of indigestion, attitudes about age, concerns about inflation, or fears for the world economic condition. Or these elements can be a host of other factors that affect us. We are constantly adjusting to a shifting environment, changing to meet new demands. Thus, it is the environment that actually creates change.

Trainers cannot create change, but they can guide it. Obviously no trainer can control or even influence most of the conditions that create change. Conditions constantly form and re-form, and individuals learn to cope with those conditions they perceive as needing a response. It is this perception that is the key. Because we are reluctant to change, we alter only those behaviors we perceive as needing change, and then we change as little as possible.

Educators talk a great deal about motivation—the desire to learn—but in the end, an individual either does or does not want to learn. An instructor cannot create motivation where none exists. We are all familiar with the old saying, "you can lead a horse to water but you can't make it drink." What can be done, however, is to work the horse hard before leading it to the water, so that it will be much more likely to want a drink. In other words, a trainer shapes the environment to make it conducive to learning. The how-to's of this book are all directed toward shaping and controlling the learning environment to facilitate change.

Three Steps for Changing People's Behavior

Anyone who has ever tried to diet or to stop smoking knows how difficult it can be to break a habit. Yet no change can take place until the old way is given up. Thus, the first step in making a change is to "un-freeze" the present habit. Once the habit is broken, the second step is to replace it with a new one, that is, to change the behavior. The third step is to "re-freeze" the new behavior, usually through a reward system. The reward helps you perceive a benefit in the change and makes you feel good about it.

One of the most successful applications of this three-step method is the U.S. Marine Corps induction system. New recruits are taken to a place where they have never been, talked to in a manner to which they have never been subjected before, stripped of their old wardrobe and given an ill-fitting new one (including underwear). They receive a closer-than-close haircut; must sleep in narrow, public conditions; are denied all contact with old friends and family; and must submit to complete control over their vital functions such as sleeping, eating, exercising, and so on. In effect, the Marine Corps disposes of all old habits. Life as it was known before induction into the corps is completely "un-frozen." The recruits have no choice but to change.

Now the Marine Corps creates its change. In six weeks, recruits learn an entirely new way of life. They lose weight, become much more physically fit, learn detailed new skills, obey instructions, experience group living, and take on a host of other behaviors necessary to survive in that organization. As each step is mastered, recruits are rewarded with a sense

---

10 Steps to Making Effective Changes

1. Assess the corporate *status quo.* Determine the climate for change.
2. Define the objectives of your proposed change in terms of end result, not method.
3. Devise methods for "un-freezing" present procedures.
4. Develop methods for teaching the new, desired procedures.
5. Devise methods for rewarding ("re-freezing") the new procedures.
6. Put the methods you devised in step 3 into practice.
7. Implement the training planned in step 4.
8. Utilize the methods devised in step 5.
9. Evaluate the effectiveness of your changes so far. Make necessary adjustments.
10. Repeat the process until you achieve your desired results.

---

of pride, accomplishment, and self-worth that "re-freezes" the new behavior, making it seem right, proper, and worthwhile. In my experience, most marines remain loyal to the corps and value its training for the rest of their lives.

Three Stages for Controlling the Training Program

The Marine Corps (and the other branches of the armed services) has a singular advantage over industrial training programs: It has complete control over almost every element of the learner's environment. The depth and impact of any change to be achieved relates directly to the degree of control a trainer has over the learning environment. The object, then, is to gain as much control as possible over the environmental elements that affect the learning experience.

There are three stages during which the environment has an impact: pretraining, training, and posttraining. Control of the actual training environment is easiest, but to be fully effective, a trainer must control to some extent all three environments. Let's consider each stage, with its respective requirements.

The Pretraining Stage

To gain some control over the environment prior to training, a trainer needs to become active in three areas: needs analysis, in-house networking, and company-wide public relations. Each of these areas is discussed in greater detail elsewhere in the book: needs analysis in Chapter 5; in-house networking in Chapters 4, 8, and 13; and public relations in Chapter 13. At this point, we need look only briefly at each area.

Needs Analysis

Most frequently, management institutes training as an answer to a perceived need. It is often rushed into operation because few managers have the foresight to perceive and solve future problems outside their regular responsibilities. As a result, too often the trainer has little say in the initial demand for training or even the shape it takes. A needs analysis is one way to anticipate future needs and avoid this situation.

Training needs arise traditionally from one or more of five areas: government regulation, labor, management planning, customer responses, and technological advances. By monitoring all, or at least the most applicable of these, you can gain greater control over the pretraining process by anticipating and preparing for new training thrusts. Indeed, you might even become the agent who defines for management the need for training, and so gain even more control over the nature of training in the organization.

In-House Networking

Networking is simply a process by which you can keep your finger on the pulse of the organization. It means not only cultivating existing contacts in the departments you train for, but regularly meeting with all of the managers and supervisors to define your function, to determine what they want their people to learn, and to explore how you can best produce results for them. It is particularly important to sit down with those supervisors and managers who normally oppose training and resist your efforts. By sounding out the people to whom your trainees will report, you will find out where the training should lead, and you'll gain the opportunity to shape their expectations and build their support. These discussions will ultimately give you greater control over the pretraining stage of your work.

Public Relations

Perhaps the most important pretraining step is to create a company-wide public relations effort. If those to be trained will perceive it as a good thing, a strong company benefit, and something of which to be proud, you'll diminish much of the resistance to learning. The only way for your trainees to develop that pretraining perception is for you to tell them, through active public relations. To build a strong positive image for training, you can try the following:

- Seek out the editor of the in-house magazine or newspaper and offer to write articles and take pictures for the paper. Become a regular reporter on what is happening in the training programs. Create a high profile. Make it a regular column, if possible.
- Give awards for completion of training. Certificates are good; lapel pins and badges are better. Every new employee will see the certificate or badge and realize that training is something the company is proud of.
- Offer to speak at conventions, meetings, or other employee gatherings. Blow your own horn a bit.
- Make friends with company public relations people and let them know the important work you are doing and what your plans are for the future. Publicity sells training.
- If none is in place, develop a regular system for advertising training programs. This is particularly vital if you offer optional courses.
- Become a public speaker for other departments. Acquaint yourself with available consultants and speakers, and when a division wants a guest speaker, arrange it. Their entertainment becomes a part of training, too, and they begin to look on your function as a positive one.
- Bring in outside speakers to train in key generic areas such as management communication, technical writing, sales skills, telephone skills, office etiquette, negotiation techniques, and so on. If you don't have a budget for this, get one; it adds glamour to the training function and makes your role even more important.
- Take a "pro-active" stance (see Chapter 5). Memos don't have to be one-way. Every time you complete a training unit, send memos to key managers, the CEO's office, or others to inform them of the results — for example, describe the number trained, in what skills, anticipated follow-up, and so on. This gives training a high profile, and gains you importance in the company.

The Training Stage

There are four aspects you can control during this stage: the agenda, personal leadership, methodology, and physical space. Each of these is discussed in greater detail elsewhere; agenda is explained in Chapters 3 and 8; personal leadership is covered in Chapters 2 and 4; methodology is presented in Chapters 2, 3, 8, 9, and 11; and the physical environment is explored in Chapter 10. Here is an overview of these environmental factors.

Agenda

Setting the agenda gives you control over time. All of us are governed by our personal sense of time. In fact, the efficient management of time is one of the key skills any executive must master. Language is full of expressions about time and how we respond to it. We "kill time," "make time," "waste time," "run out the clock," have a "good time," enjoy "the best time," and so forth. By setting and sticking to your agenda (that is, deciding what is to be covered, when it is to be covered, and in what order), you take control of the time your trainees will spend with you. You begin and end the lesson, you set the subject, you say when the lunch break begins and ends, and you decide how long other breaks will be. Time exerts subtle control over us, yet mostly we are unaware of it. Simply by setting the agenda, you take control of this vital aspect of the learning environment.

Personal Leadership

Think back to your schooling. Which teachers were most effective? Which taught you the least? Your most effective ones were able to lead you to the learning you acquired—the least effective ones simply were not.

People need to feel they are in good hands. Every parent knows that children challenge authority from time to time to discover the boundaries of their freedom. If they find no boundaries, children usually become very insecure and frightened. But when they learn the limits they are allowed, children gain a sense of security they can rely on. In effect, they see and respond to good leadership.

Were you ever in a classroom when a student challenged the authority of the teacher? If the teacher handled the situation with a strong, positive, and confident response, how did the class react? If the teacher failed to react with confidence or, worse, allowed the challenge to pass unanswered, then what happened? The obstreperous student simply became *more* obstreperous, pushing to find the limits of his or her freedom. If there were no limits, the student became the leader and took over the class. Learning (at least formal learning) stopped, and few students appreciated it. I have seen even the most difficult students become active, avid learners once they find a teacher they can look up to. People need to know they are being led with confidence.

Leadership, however, is not a heavy-handed action. A too-firm hand of leadership is oppressive, whereas good leadership simply fulfills the expectations of those being led. It is a subtle form of control, not a coercive one. For example, we expect when we board a bus that the driver will drive it, and we put ourselves in that driver's hands without a thought, unless for some reason he or she loses our confidence. Only when leadership is questioned is there a problem. Exercised consistently, with confidence, sound leadership can exert a powerful and subtle control over the learning environment.

Methodology

It is not what you say but how you say it that carries the impact. Comedian Norm Crosby has made a career of uttering double-talk with such conviction that people swear he must be saying something. Lewis Carroll's "Jabberwocky"[1] is the ultimate literary example. Educator Marshall McLuhan identified this important element of human communication with his realization that "the medium is the message."[2] In short, the method you use to teach something is far more important than the content you are trying to teach. The method that fails hinders learning rather than helps it. After all, it is the method you use that either stimulates or fails to stimulate the learner to take hold of the new material and master it. The method becomes even more critical when you realize that the average adult attention span is only 20 to 30 minutes. And that's for college graduates; if you train minimally educated people, their ability to pay attention to what you say will be even less. This means that no matter how good a particular method is, too much of it becomes boring. Few people can concentrate for very long on one subject, presented in one manner. Fortunately there are a great variety of methods you can use. By carefully blending the methodology and by matching the appropriate method to the material to be covered, you will gain tremendous control over the learning environment.

Physical Space

I once taught a college course in a military barracks that had been built as a temporary structure 35 years earlier. The floor was a dull, industrial brown linoleum, badly worn and stained. The walls had once been an institutional green but were now splotched with smoke stains, soda pop spills, hair oil smudges, and other unidentifiable things. The building was used largely for showing films, so all the windows were painted over in black, though resourceful students had scratched numerous peepholes to relieve the darkness. The building was so old that when the wind blew, the walls moved and creaked. Finally, because it looked so poor, generations of students had treated it poorly. The floors were spotted with cigarette burns and covered with ashes and butts, the desks were broken, and graffiti was everywhere. To this day I don't know how really effective my teaching was in that room, but I remember dreading having to teach there. I can only imagine how the students must have felt.

Physical environment plays a greater role in teaching than is usually suspected. The surroundings cannot guarantee learning, nor do they prevent it. At least one of my students in that barracks classroom earned and maintained honors status and became a lifelong fan of my teaching. But the environment does have an intangible effect on how the learning is perceived.

Physical environment is, to a great degree, under your personal control. Certainly the way you set up the room, what kinds of audiovisual aids you use, the room's furnishings, and to some extent even the lighting all are in your domain. Furthermore, if you have control over budgets and suppliers, you can choose comfortable chairs (a vital element), the color of the room, lighting patterns, acoustical properties and—the most vital element—the temperature. All these factors allow you to shape an environment in which your trainees will want to learn.

The Posttraining Stage

Of the three stages, the posttraining environment is the most difficult to control. Planning, networking, and personal leadership all impact directly on the training program, but once the training is finished, how can you continue to exert your influence? How can you effect changes in what has already taken place?

Of course you cannot, but by evaluating your performance you can monitor your own effectiveness in creating change for future training programs. You cannot control what people do with what you have taught them, but you can continually adapt your training methods so they produce the desired results in the future.

There are three ways you can control the posttraining environment: formal evaluations, evaluation sessions, and additional public relations. Evaluations are covered in detail in Chapter 6, evaluation sessions are covered in Chapter 12, and public relations are partly discussed in the pretraining section earlier in this chapter as well as in Chapter 13.

Formal Evaluation

When he was campaigning for election, New York City Mayor Ed Koch used to interrupt television newspeople and even his own speeches to ask, "How'm I doin'?" At best, progress is random without some form of monitoring. With sufficient feedback, however, the person in charge can steer toward a goal. This is never more true than in training. Once you've created your training program, you need to measure how successful you've been in meeting your objective.

For trainers, this measuring is never a simple matter, because there are so many variables that can impact on the results. At the very least, however, there are two ways in which results need to be monitored:

- Short term. This is the easiest. For the short term, use regular formal tests, projects, or assignments to learn whether the trainees are (1) understanding what you're teaching, (2) learning the material (at least for the time being), and (3) keeping up with the material.
- Long term. How long do your trainees remember or practice what you've taught them? You need to develop several long-term measuring devices (such as, follow-up surveys, advanced levels of training, key variables to monitor, all of which are detailed in Chapter 6) to check against each other, against your short-term evaluators, and against the impressions you get from discussions with superiors and supervisors.

In any kind of trainee evaluation, there are two types of results to look for: cognitive and affective. Let's look at the nature of each:

Cognitive results. In both short- and long-term evaluations, look for concrete learning. What skills or knowledge did the trainees gain by attending your seminars or workshops? The answer to this question provides an evaluation of the cognitive results.

Affective results. Much harder to evaluate, affective results are a measure of how the trainees feel about what you've taught them. Remember, you want to create a positive predisposition toward training. At the completion of training ask them to evaluate you. This gives you an immediate affective response. To gauge the long-term affective response, set up a measurement program that reveals attitude changes and general company *esprit de corps.* There are some specific formats for doing this in Chapter 6.

It is important to recognize that evaluations of the long-term, affective results are key elements of good training. How much the trainees retain and how they feel about what they've learned are the elements that either promote or destroy your effectiveness as a change agent.

Evaluation Sessions

An important part of the posttraining stage is convincing the organization for whom you work of the worth of your services. Seek out the supervisors and managers of the employees you have trained and ask them for input. Ask them to evaluate the training you've done so far. In this way you create a climate for change, you develop internal support for that change, and you gain leverage to increase your effectiveness in the future.

In addition, keep those above you in the hierarchy informed of your results. Solicit their input. Set up a schedule for providing regular reports, by memo or through face-to-face meetings. These managers will be the ones to support your efforts in the future. You want to create an image of responsiveness, so that the company sees your training programs as a service that gets results — results they want. This image will establish your credibility and strengthen your position.

Public Relations

As mentioned in connection with the pretraining stage, public relations is largely a matter of letting people know you're there; it is developing and keeping a high profile. To do this, you must create, maintain, and monitor an information dissemination network. Make it easy for people to hear about and attend your seminars. If you find that people are not getting the message, supplement or change your methods of getting out the information. Use bulletin boards and in-house newspapers or magazines. Announce the training sessions at company social events, meetings (sales, quality circles, union, and so on), and coffee breaks (ask if you can place a poster on the coffee wagon). Post notices in cafeterias, have handouts at the exits, circulate news by word of mouth — use any creative outlets you have. Use your imagination, but get the word out!

Of course maintaining a high profile also makes you competitive, so be prepared for some resistance. If your campaign starts to gain attention, some managers who feel threatened may resist the change. If necessary, negotiate for your high profile (see Chapter 14 for guidelines). You are in a strong bargaining position because your business is to train their employees. Show them how you can get results for them, and give them the opportunity to shape (within reason) the training you'll do for them.

One final, necessary step to solidify your image is to prepare a formal report on every session you teach, every activity you perform. It can be a written or a face-to-face verbal report (followed by a written summary for the record) and should include as much data as possible. For guidelines on how to prepare such a report, see Chapter 13. Don't confuse these reports with the public relations promotions we've just discussed, which are for advertising. Formal reports are for the record and intended to create a solid image of both you and your training.

Long-Range Planning

As a trainer, you are concerned with bringing about changes in the present way of doing things. An integral part of your function is long-range planning. There are four phases to planning a change. The first is to analyze the climate for change that presently exists in the company. The next phase is to analyze your goals and determine how you are going to utilize the organizational climate to achieve them. The third phase is to put your plan into action by drawing up a needs analysis, writing proposals, giving the actual training, and so on. The final phase is to set in motion the evaluation and feedback systems that will allow you to update and fine-tune your efforts.

Analyzing the Climate for Change

To analyze the present situation, you need to define your organizational culture and determine how it responds to change. There are five dimensions for measuring change in an organization: rate, bias, magnitude, structure, and power.[3] Let's explore each.

Rate

How fast has change taken place in the past and how long do you think it will take to make the changes you propose? Ask yourself these questions.

1. What changes in management are imminent? What happens when management personnel are replaced?
2. When was the last senior-level reorganization? What management changes resulted? How did those changes impact on the rest of the organization?
3. Which new ideas have been accepted into the organization during the past 18 months?
4. What current ideas have yet to take effect? How long have they been in the offing?

Then choose an innovation (such as a new procedure begun by a new manager) and track it until it is in universal use. These findings will lead you to make some conclusions about the rate of change.

Bias

Changes in operation are shaped considerably by the biases of those people in power. In fact, any change you plan will have to be modified to flow in the direction of bias in your organization. To discover such leanings, you will need to ask yourself these questions:

1. How do things get done in the organization? You are not asking *what* is being done but rather *how*. (This is a question of style, and it therefore indicates bias.)
2. How does management style differ among the most powerful people?
3. Within the last two years, have any middle- or upper-level managers left the organization because of differences in style? (This is another question of style — how things get done, not what gets done.)
4. What past training programs have failed despite initial management support and enthusiasm?

Then compare the educational, ethnic, familial, social, and professional backgrounds of three or four of the most powerful middle managers. Do the same for some in the top management team. Compare the results to predict potential friction or compatibility. This information will give you an idea of the underlying management biases and whether they will continue into the future.

Magnitude

What kind of change has succeeded or failed historically in the organization? If only major changes succeed, you'll have to build a major change very carefully. Otherwise it may be wiser to subtly ease in the smaller changes you want. To determine which approach to use, you will need to know the answers to these questions:

1. What apparently sound ideas in the past five years have failed to take hold?
2. Which pet projects of top management have been sidetracked by middle management's failure to implement them effectively?
3. Which past training programs succeeded in bringing about change?
4. Have any proposed changes been dropped or simply forgotten because of resistance from the rank and file?
5. What is the largest major change that has taken place under the present management? How was it managed?

These answers will give you an idea of how receptive management will be to either large or small changes in operations.

Structure

How a proposed change is packaged usually becomes a major factor in its ultimate success. Advertising agencies, for example, spend much creative time determining how to present a new product so as to make it most appealing. New ideas in the corporate culture are no different. There are two forces that come into play when presenting a new idea: formal corporate channels of communication and informal routes such as the grapevine, friends in key positions, and the like. Anyone familiar with the military or government agencies knows the difference between the two as well as the powers and limits of each. Corporate cultures are the same, and the channel you choose to bring about a change impacts heavily on how well the change succeeds. To map your corporate structure you will need to answer the following questions:

1. What are the formal channels of communication in your organization?
2. What are the informal channels of communication and how are they approached?
3. Who, regardless of position, are the people most effective at packaging ideas and selling them to top and middle management? How do they package what they want done?
4. Who, regardless of position, are the people with reputations for getting things done? And what channels do they use to do so?
5. What new procedures or ideas have been extremely successful in recent months? Who originated them? Who sponsored them? Who packaged them? How were they eased through the organization?

These answers should provide some ideas for packaging your proposals so they are accepted and ultimately succeed.

Power

Who holds the real power in the company? That is, who will the rank and file follow? That person is not always the designated leader, as you'll see in Chapters 2 and 4. The real power is in the hands of the person on whom the group bestows its trust. In fact, power is often the most important of the five factors mentioned here. Certainly, a powerful person is a great ally in making changes, and you are doomed to almost certain failure if that person openly opposes you. In identifying where the power lies, you must find the answers to these questions:

1. How has top or middle management used the company grape-vine? Do they fight it or do they promote it? Does the grapevine ignore them?
2. Who in the company, regardless of position, defers to the senior secretary?
3. Who does the organization's senior secretary report to?
4. Who has inordinate power for the position he or she holds?
5. Who gets things done? Who are the people always powerless to achieve their ends?

These answers will point you in the direction of where the power is that can help you achieve your goals. The answers to all these questions should provide you with an effective map of your corporate culture. Use the map to plot the route for reaching your goals as an agent of change in the company.

Summary

The ideas in this opening chapter oriented you to the basic premise of this book: that the purpose of training is to produce change, and the role of the trainer is first and foremost that of an agent for change. There is a strong human tendency to resist change, so a crucial part of training must be to motivate trainees to learn. Motivation is done by creating an environment conducive to learning, in which existing behavior must be "un-frozen" then changed and "re-frozen" as new behavior.

To be fully effective, the trainer must control the pretraining, training, and posttraining environments. Gaining control of pretraining involves a formal needs analysis, in-house networking, and company-wide publicity. Controlling training incorporates personal leadership, planning, methodology, and an effective physical environment. Maintaining control of posttraining calls for formal evaluations, assessment sessions, and additional public relations. Lastly, since changes seldom come about suddenly the chapter included a format for assembling long-range plans for changes and described how to determine the corporate climate for change.

CHAPTER 2

The Object of Training

CHANGE is a constant; it is always with us. It happens to us all, all the time. As writer Alvin Toffler has pointed out, not only is change continuing to happen, but the rate of change is increasing and will continue to increase well into the 21st century or longer. As was discussed in the preceding chapter, most people tend to resist change unless they can perceive an immediate, definable benefit. For trainers, the process of change is further complicated by the fact that training alone cannot accomplish most organizational changes. But training can help. What a trainer changes is skills, and insofar as new skills bring about the desired changes in an organization, training can achieve far-ranging results. Training itself cannot motivate a work force. It cannot change the economic system. But training can and should be—indeed *must* be—an important part of any organization.

Even on the most basic, straightforward skills level, learners will tend to resist change. Whether their training is part of an overall corporate change or an entry-level assessment, they will not want to change unless that change is both easy and attractive. As was discussed in Chapter 1, trainees need to be motivated to learn. You as trainer must set up an environment that is conducive to change. And to ensure that such an environment is conducive, you must organize your training sessions around the following basic principles of learning.

The Principles of Adult Learning

In the early 1900s, Edward L. Thorndike did some of the most definitive work on learning. He concluded that there are three laws which govern how we learn:[1]

The Law of Readiness. Simply stated, the Law of Readiness means we only learn when we are ready to learn. "Readiness" includes seeing a need to learn, feeling a desire to learn, being interested in the subject, and having sufficient skills to both comprehend and utilize the new information.

The Law of Effect. Nothing succeeds like success. This law points out that the more success we feel in learning, the more excited we get about learning. We need to gain pleasure from our learning, and the successful performance of a formerly difficult task is one of life's greatest pleasures.

The Law of Exercise. In essence, practice makes perfect. This means that hands-on drill is necessary. It also means that the more personally we are involved in learning—that is, the harder we work at it—the more it engages us and the more we learn.

So, to take advantage of Thorndike's findings, you must ask yourself the following questions and evaluate your training methods accordingly:

1. Are the trainees ready to learn the material? This question really has two parts: (1) Are they motivated to learn it? If not, what can I do or say to move them? If so, how can I best encourage that desire and align my material with it? (2) Do they have sufficient background to understand and proficiency to perform the new skills? If not, how can I best bring them to the readiness level? If so, how can I utilize the material to be studied so they will be both challenged and able to perform the new skills?
2. Have I provided sufficient opportunities for them to succeed? Have I created enough feedback mechanisms for them to be able to see their success? Have I created opportunities for constructive failure? Can those failures be transformed effectively into successes?
3. Have I built in sufficient practice phases? Is each group given hands-on practice? Is there a practice drill to ensure skills improvement? Have I created enough practice and built enough conceptual bridges to engage and hold their interest?

If your answer is no to any of these questions, you need to familiarize yourself with the elements of learning. There are ten recognized principles of adult education.

How Adults Learn

When planning your lessons, build them around the following concepts:

1. People learn only what they are ready to learn.
2. People learn best what they actually perform.
3. People learn from their mistakes.
4. People learn easiest what is familiar to them.
5. People favor different senses for learning.
6. People learn methodically and, in our culture, systematically.
7. People cannot learn what they cannot understand.
8. People learn through practice.
9. People learn better when they can see their own progress.
10. People respond best when what they are to learn is presented uniquely for them. Each of us is different.

Each of these principles is a complex idea, of critical importance to your training objectives. In the pages that follow, these topics are discussed, with special attention to how they relate to the training situation.

Readiness and Resistance

As mentioned earlier, little or no positive learning takes place without a readiness to learn. In fact, the learner merely learns how to resist more effectively, and the training becomes confrontational and ineffective. The first step in responding to resistance is to ventilate it, encourage the trainees to express their resistance. Once you know what form their resistance is taking, you can respond to it. According to Dr. Beverly Hyman, there are seven sources of resistance to training:[2]

1. *Parochial self-interest.* This is a "what's in it for me?" attitude. Trainees ask, "Why should we learn this?" Your best response is to sell them on the idea of what the training will do for them. Don't be coercive (unless the training is intentionally punitive) but, rather, structure your response in positive terms. Empathize with their resistance, but show them how they will benefit from the training. Give them reasons for wanting to at least try to learn.

2. *Lack of trust.* You, as the trainer, are always perceived as management and so your motives will be suspect if employees are in any way suspicious of management. Again, sell them on the benefits of the training. This may mean redefining the purpose of training. For instance, suppose a trainee's supervisor said, "Get in there and get trained or else!" The trainee might feel you are there merely to evaluate him or her, so you

---

The Seven Forms of Resistance

1. Parochial self-interest
2. Lack of trust
3. Different assessments of different information
4. Low tolerance for change
5. Fear of losing face
6. Peer-group pressure
7. Mistaken first impressions

---

will have to earn that employee's trust. To gain the trust, be frank and open, talk about the trainee's resistance, and ask questions. Listen to the answers, then sell the benefits of the program. Incidentally, any promises you make *must* be kept if you want to maintain that trust.

3. *Different assessments of different information.* In this case, the trainee is resisting because he or she perceives the purpose or value of the training to be quite different from what you propose. If you carefully define your plan and explain the purpose right at the beginning, it should ease this form of resistance. You may have to redefine why they are there, choosing your words with care to allay any fears or misgivings. Again, it is vital to talk over the resistance and get them to explain how they feel before you begin clarifying the situation for them. I have found this to be the most common form of resistance to training and one of the easiest to deal with.

4. *Low tolerance for change.* This form of resistance is common in shy people, people with a low self-opinion, and those who are slow learners. It is a hopeless attitude, not usually expressed openly but, rather, indirectly through nonverbal attitudes, lack of participation, shrugs, nervous behavior, uncertain laughter, and so on. These people simply are afraid they lack the skills or correct behavior patterns to learn the new material. To ease such resistance, give them something they will succeed at right away, something they *will* be able to do. Show them that they can do it, and build on each success. Go slowly. Let them gain self-confidence.

5. *Fear of losing face.* This is a much stronger fear than the previous one. No one wants to look foolish, and it takes a lot of courage to perform an about-face to admit having been wrong. Most of us are reluctant. To deal with the fear of losing face, you must build bridges that allow such people to modify their former opinions. Avoid either-or formulations. Define the terms so that everyone agrees on the end result, and shape that end result so that it is within the parameters of their original position. In other words, give them large opportunities to save face.

6. *Peer-group pressure.* This, too, is a powerful source of resistance.

Despite Thoreau's admiration for those who do, it is very hard to march openly to the sound of a different drummer. Most of us do not want to look foolish in front of our peers. This is particularly true for those who define themselves socially. They see themselves as a part of an ethnic group, labor union, community, religious group, sexual minority, and so on. "What will they think of me?" becomes a powerful motivator. If peer-group opinion is against you, you have a hard task. To handle such resistance, you must win over the group rather than the individual. To do that, you will need to persuade the group leader (s) of the value of the training. Again, ventilate the problem first, then work out a joint solution with the key group influencer (s). Finally, sell the entire group on the merits and benefits of the training program.

7. *Mistaken first impressions.* According to Edward DeBono, a noted researcher on creativity, we tend to make snap judgments about new things and then invest all our energies defending those initial judgments.[3] If the judgment is against you, you have a problem. The best tactic to counter such an eventuality is to ensure a positive first impression. This means carefully "positioning" the training in your initial advertising or selection process. It also means having a positive physical environment and creating a good initial impression. If you fail to give a favorable first impression, then you'll have to ventilate the resistance, empathize with it, and negotiate a modus operandi for carrying on cooperatively despite the trainees' first impressions.

In all seven cases, the basic approach is to ventilate the resistance by bringing it out into the open, establish a low-threat environment by empathizing with that resistance, then sell them on the need for training. Stress the innovation and indicate the benefits they will reap from what you plan to train them to do.

Active vs. Passive Learning

We learn by doing. Recall how you learned to drive a car. You learned by actually driving it, didn't you? All the classroom work and book study couldn't really teach you to drive. Certainly no lecture could. You needed to get your hands on the wheel. In short, we need to get our hands on whatever it is we will learn. This is why 75 percent of the training in America takes place on the job.

To take advantage of this basic principle in your training, remember two things: (1) minimize passive learning experiences such as lectures, films, slides, video presentations, or demonstrations; and (2) maximize active learning experiences such as case studies, workshops, projects, panel discussions, hands-on activities, and so on. Without active sessions to lock in the learning, people will not transfer that information — that is, they will not put the new learning to work on the job.

We retain roughly 10 percent of what we read, 20 percent of what we hear, 30 percent of what we see, and 50 percent of what we both see and hear. But if we become active, those percentages jump to 70 percent of what we say and 90 percent of what we both say and do. Get your trainees to report back to you what they've learned. After all, the best way to master a skill is to teach it.

Trial and Error

We learn best by making mistakes. Edward Thorndike's Law of Effect, which was discussed earlier, tells us that nothing succeeds like success. Success motivates us and makes us want to learn more, but it is the errors we make that we remember and learn to correct. To learn we must have a chance — indeed, several chances — to fail (or succeed). The problem is that errors on the production line or in the field can be very costly; this is why training facilities exist. The training climate must allow for errors and invite challenges. Medical technicians practice on plastic dummies, airline pilots polish their skills in cockpit simulators, and lawyers hold formal debates and mock trials in law school. Our errors teach us far more than our successes. Build the chance for errors into your training.

Association

Training doesn't take place in a vacuum. No one comes to your session with an empty mind waiting to be filled. We learn by connecting the new material we meet with the things we know already. Each person learns the same things differently because he or she brings a different background to the learning. When learning fails to take place, often the learner had no internal reference with which to connect the new material. He or she failed to understand because the context in which the material was presented did not strike a responsive chord in his or her memory.

The core skill of training is building bridges that relate new material to the familiar. Few people can make a quantum leap into the unknown. We must relate new information to the known in order to understand it at all. The trainer, by discovering what trainees already know, can build upon that knowledge. (This is discussed further in Chapter 5, in connection with needs analysis.) However, you can ask questions of the trainees early in the seminar so you can zero in on key elements they already know and on how they feel about the material to be learned. In addition, pretests reveal a great deal of what trainees know. Among the best ways to begin is with a group exercise or management game so that all trainees have a common experience to draw upon later. Teach by using stories or parables and personal examples; give each individual a reference point to which he or she can relate new material.

Multisensory Input

All of our senses are sources of learning. Everything we know comes to us through one or more of them. Yet, as industrial psychologist Jard DeVille points out, we are a product of the traits we inherit, the experiences we receive through our senses, and the choices we make throughout our lives.[4] These last two factors combine to produce sensory biases —that is, each of us tends to favor (choose) one sense and make it dominant for learning. The other senses continue to function, but the dominant one is our preferred way to learn.

Let's review the sensory biases, and how they affect learning.

Sight

Many cannot follow a complicated description but can instantly grasp the same process when it is diagrammed. This is why computer software manufacturers stress the ability of their systems to generate graphs and charts. The old saying, "a picture is worth a thousand words," is true for many of us. Architects not only describe and draw schematic diagrams but also construct scale models and sketch representational perspectives for what they plan to build. Our eyes inform us greatly.

Hearing

We learn of others' experiences because they tell us about them. The sense of hearing is a particularly important one because it relates back to the distant (and sometimes not so distant) heritage of all peoples. All human cultures were at some time oral. That is, they did not have a written language or, if they did, it was only for an elite few and was not used extensively. Many cultures today still have a predominantly oral tradition. In such oral cultures, sound and language play huge roles. Spoken communication is oral and repetitive; memory becomes paramount. Ballads, poems, and legends abound. Social events and rituals take on deeper meanings. In modern America, we retain at least two major vestiges of our oral past: religion and education. We like to learn by hearing others (teachers) speak to us, and we like to worship communally. The oral tradition is the deep-rooted, powerful learning tool you use in creating learning through discourse. (Note that it is *discourse* that teaches, not lectures. We need to hear the sound of our own voices in order to learn.)

Touch

Through touch we understand the size, shape, smoothness or roughness, texture, and temperature of objects. Touch is our measure of physical comfort, and therefore it controls a potentially negative response to training. If the room is too hot (or cold) or the seats are too hard (or soft), such sensory input interferes with the learning environment and must be corrected.

Temp.

Kinesthesia

This sense is often confused with touch and, indeed, the two work together closely. Kinesthesia is the sense through which we determine the degree of hardness or softness of an object, the direction and amount of muscular movement, and the amount of effort we have to exert to move it. Manipulative skills depend heavily on this sense. It is kinesthesia that is involved directly in hands-on training. We use it to gauge where to move our fingers to strike the keys of a typewriter or computer, while at the same time, we use it to determine how much force to exert when lifting a tool or lever. This sense, when engaged in learning, is very powerful. Whenever possible, utilize the kinesthesic sense as a direct pathway to understanding and retention.

Smell

Though potent in creating memories, the sense of smell is not really vital to most training situations. It gives the learner a strong sense of being there—a sense of place. If trainees are working where odors are pervasive, capitalize on this aspect of the workplace and emphasize its positive nature to motivate them. Certainly anyone who has worked at sea or in a printing shop, furniture finishing room, coffee plant, or lumber mill will recognize the evocative power of odors to awaken and sharpen the memory. Of course, the same is true for negative smells. Once experienced, the odor of a building on fire can never be forgotten.

Taste

The sense of taste is, unfortunately, not very useful in training, except in the food and drug industries. Still, if it can be utilized, you can lock in learning as surely as with the other senses.

The three senses most commonly and most easily involved in training are sight, hearing, and kinesthesia. Work the following methods into your training, so you are using these senses to encourage learning:

Sight

Diagrams
Charts and graphs
Training manuals
Flip charts
Reference materials
Lists of parts or definitions
Sample transactions
Films
Slides
Actual situations to be observed
Demonstrations

Sound

Lectures
Discussions
Demonstrations
Question and answer sessions
Definitions
Panel discussions
Group projects
Films
Audiovisuals

Kinesthesia (Hands-on)

Supervised practice on the job
Simulations
Paper and pencil tests
Flowcharting
Case histories
Group projects
Role-playing

Create a variety of sensory input because what isn't clear when read by one sense often crystallizes through another. This is particularly true when you remember that people show a bias toward one sense as the easiest or most trustworthy.

One Thing at a Time

Most trainers have the dangerous tendency to overload their learners. As experts on the subject, we see all the problems and their ramifications. We forget that the learner is completely new to the subject and cannot grasp *all* of it. We tend to go too fast and to give trainees too much material at one time. When we do this, we lose them.

We want to rush ahead because we are under time constraints. But the trainees may not yet have grasped some key element. We cannot afford to lose them. Information overload is as critical a problem in training as it is in computers. Given more information than they can process, learners' minds simply shut down.

To prevent information overload, practice the slogan of the 1920s' Bauhaus School of Design: Less is More. The simpler you can make the material, the more effectively it can be learned. This means taking even the most complex technical material and breaking it into manageable chunks of instruction. Set up a simple structure or pattern or model, then build your lesson around the pattern you've created. Enhance the pattern with stories (parables), analogies to material with which they are already familiar, and audiovisual aids.

Understanding

Learning takes place only with understanding. This is why, even in a how-to book such as this, we must cover some key elements of theory. Learning by rote, with no understanding, produces inferior performance at best and very quick loss of memory and skills. On the other hand, if trainees can comprehend why they need to learn something and how that information fits into the overall picture, it will make a great deal more sense and be much easier to learn. Therefore, whenever possible, take your trainees with you on the road to understanding. Explain what they are doing and why. Give them a map of the territory, so they will know both where they have been and where they are headed. Use agendas, summaries, progressive diagrams, and flowcharts.

In addition, know in advance at what level of understanding you are aiming. When necessary, let the trainees know what level is required of them. As a rule, aim at one or all of the four most commonly recognized levels of understanding:

- Simple recognition—that is, do learners recognize the correct answer when they see it (as in a multiple-choice question)? Can they tell when something is wrong? Do they recognize the correct tool or the need for the step being taught?

- Specific recall — can learners describe the process involved? Can they delineate the step? Fill in the blanks? Repeat the formulas? Recite the uses?
- Discrimination — can learners pick the appropriate responses from among several choices (multiple choice)? Can they choose the correct method or response to match the situation (as in emergency training, budgeting, and so on)? Can they select an appropriate applicant? Recognize incorrect usages?
- Judgment — can learners use the material to solve problems? Case histories? Role-playing? Can they create new formats? Judge between two appropriate responses and analyze which would be preferable? Troubleshoot the system?

Practice

We all know the saying, "practice makes perfect." Always allow time for some form of practice. The more opportunity learners have to practice, the greater their retention rate will be. Practice should be as close to on-the-job situations as possible, and initially it should follow the instruction as closely as possible. Make practice sessions an integral part of learning.

Feedback

People need to know how they are doing. It is impossible to learn in a vacuum, yet testing newly acquired knowledge can also create problems. Many of us experienced test anxiety in school. We knew we would be judged, so we put great pressure on ourselves to do our best. If test anxiety is a problem for your learners, sell them on the idea (a true one for adult learning) that the purpose of the test is not for you to judge them but, rather, for them to evaluate what they have learned and compare it to what you expect them to learn. Tests are merely a form of feedback. They let the trainees know how they are doing.

You'll need other forms of feedback as well, though. Create lessons that invite dialogue. Provide opportunities for evaluating their work. And offer chances for trainees to make self-evaluations. This is particularly important for jobs in which trainees are unsupervised for part of the time. Help the trainees perfect the skill of self-evaluation.

Uniqueness

Individual differences are always a factor in learning. Each person is a unique individual, and each learns differently. People come to training with different backgrounds, abilities, skills, knowledge, and personalities. For your training to succeed, you need to recognize and respond positively to each individual's different perceptions, habits, and manners. Typical areas of difference include the following:

Sources and Kinds of Resistance

People resist learning for different reasons. We've already covered the seven forms of resistance and what to do about each. Remember, however, that until you've dealt with all the forms of resistance, the only learning that will take place is how to be an effective resistor. There may be several different forms of resistance among your trainees. You will have to recognize, ventilate, and deal with all of them in order to successfully train the group.

Personal Temperament

People vary. Some bubble with enthusiasm, others' tempers flare up easily; still others remain easy going and affable under all circumstances. As a rule, positive traits such as affability, enthusiasm, willingness to try, and so on are helpful and need encouragement whenever they appear. Negative traits and habits such as a quick temper, a complaining nature, gossiping, apathy, boredom, sloth, or suspicion hinder learning. Make every effort to avoid triggering these negative responses. In addition, you should:

1. Make suggestions rather than give orders. Telling people what to do implies a superior–inferior relationship, which can trigger negative responses. It is usually better with adults to lead by suggesting. If resistance occurs, ask what the problem is rather than polarize the situation by responding to what seems to be a challenge to your authority. Besides, asking is a courtesy most of us respect.
2. Sell the learners on the benefits of your training. Tell how they can grow and develop in their respective jobs by using the skills you are teaching. Even when there is no resistance, it is good to specify how they will benefit. Learning done with a personal purpose locks in more easily. Also, sell the idea that their work is improved with an understanding of the theory and concepts behind that work.
3. Define necessary strictures (rules for behavior) as regulations, not as punitive rules. Make it clear (if necessary) that some regulations are always necessary to allow a group to function. Otherwise

you'll have chaos and anarchy — fun, perhaps, but tedious after a while and very unproductive.

4. Maintain leadership. In essence, the group should be guided toward learning through clear directions, suggestions, agendas, questions, and focused instruction, rather than coercion.

As a trainer, you have no authoritarian right to control. The most punitive thing you can do is have an offending individual removed from your class. The second most authoritarian action is to report the individual to his or her boss. Outside of the military, there are limits to disciplinary action. If you use even these heavy-handed actions, you will lose the offenders as learners, the respect of the rest of the group, your effectiveness as a teacher, and, possibly, your own job. Force and coercion are simply not effective or even viable tools for training.

You must lead the group by winning its respect. You are dealing with adults, who demand to be treated as such. You may suggest, urge, persuade, even cajole, but if you command or try to dominate an individual or a situation, you risk losing far more than you gain. It is partly for this reason that I stress discussing any problems of resistance. If you ask the difficult person(s) to explain the problem, you create a forum for discussion. Summarily ordering them to behave creates a confrontation that you may lose.

In summary, you must be tolerant of individual differences and find ways to help those who need help. Utilize the good traits of others. Regard your trainees as colleagues rather than as subordinates. Build trust rather than resentment, even among those whose personalities lean toward mistrust or anger.

Background Experience and Level of Education

When you are faced with a relatively homogeneous group, simply follow your agenda. Watch for two variations: (1) any individual form of resistance and (2) any need for extra explanation or coaching. If either appears, respond appropriately (usually privately) and solve the problem.

On the other hand, when you have a group that varies in experience, education, and skills, you will need to consider one of these three steps:

1. If possible, use the more experienced people as part of your teaching team. Ask them to illustrate some of your points from their own experience; for instance, they can share their own war stories. Appoint them as skills resources for some practice exer-

cises so each becomes responsible for the practice of one or more novices. Create group projects in which experienced people function as expert resources for the rest of the group. Assign them to make presentations to the rest of the group in their areas of interest and expertise.

2. Divide the class into groups by level of experience and then give each group an assignment commensurate with its ability. This is the classic approach of the one-room schoolhouse. It's not as efficient, perhaps, as a giant consolidated urban system, but the method has been effective for more than 100 years.

3. Instruct each trainee individually. This tactic is necessary when you use the one-room schoolhouse approach, particularly when individual differences are very great. It is the most time consuming and, therefore, the most inefficient. It is, however, the most effective way to learn, which is why so much training in America takes place on the job. It is also the medieval guild system of training via apprenticeship to journeyman to master. Artists have always found this the best approach to excellence. They study with the masters.

Learning Ability

Although people learn at their own rate, it is usually convenient and useful to group trainees into three types: slow, regular, and fast. Most instruction is aimed at regular learners — the middle group. Even in a group of the most gifted learners, there will be some who are fastest, some who are slowest, and most who are just fast. Aim your lesson plans at the majority in the group. This will always leave a few for whom the work is easy and a few for whom the work is difficult. To be fully effective, you cannot ignore either extreme.

To help the slow learner keep pace, first diagnose what the difficulty is. All too often, it is merely a problem of finding a bridge — some connecting link between the new material and the old. The more familiar the material, the closer the parallel, and the more easily and quickly the learner will grasp the concept.

Another difficulty might stem from insufficient prior education. This can be approached two ways: (1) assign related remedial work to bring learning up to par and (2) provide extra attention or individual instruction.

Poor reading ability (or eyesight) may also be a problem. If the problem is reading ability, assign remedial work with minimum reading demand and maximum oral or manual involvement.

If the problem is simply that individuals are slow, give extra attention and individual instruction. Also, build confidence by asking them questions that can be answered easily. Show sincere interest in them and their work. Provide clear, vivid explanations in simple terms. Use visual aids whenever possible. Lastly, group slow learners with average learners rather than with fast ones.

When working with slow learners remember that they *are* capable of grasping concepts and improving skills. The problem is reaching the level of understanding they presently have and then building bridges to what they must learn, creating the necessary maps, and taking them at their own rate across those bridges over the solid groundwork they need to progress. Patience is vital.

To help superior learners, you must devise ways to challenge them. People who learn fast, who grasp concepts quickly, are often ahead of you and get bored or impatient. This situation lends itself to being criticized and evaluated, and you open the door to potential resistance.

You must engage and challenge superior learners. To engage them, create challenging assignments. Such assignments can be case histories, additional reading, or problem solving. Have fast learners complete specific research or design exercises that can be used by the entire group (such as developing a flowchart, devising specific figures to work through an example, creating critical-incident case histories, and so on). Have them become group facilitators or resource people; use them as group observers or evaluators. Have them prepare and present material to the rest of the group or participate in panel discussions and plan agendas. All of these give quick learners enough stimulation to keep them active in the learning environment.

In making special assignments, however, be careful they don't appear punitive or like mere busy work. Position the extra work as opportunities to expand learning for the adventurous, or as aids to you personally, or merely as a challenge, but never as added chores. Be careful, also, not to create animosity toward those you've assigned more challenging material. No one likes the idea of favored treatment, especially when they're not among the favored. Most people are reasonably tolerant of personality differences — such as the flamboyant learner who is always first to volunteer or the shy one who says little — and they extend their tolerance both to those who learn more quickly and to those who are slower. But minimize the differences and make everything as normal and low keyed as possible, because the range of tolerance is limited. Most people feel embarrassed by too much or too obvious special attention, and all people feel resentment when they perceive that someone else is getting more than they.

Whom Are You Training?

Whom you are going to train is far more important than what you are actually training them to do. Of course what you train people to do is your overall objective. If you are a change agent then your effectiveness is measured by the changes you bring about — in other words, what they learn. But before you can bring about those changes, you must establish a baseline — a point from which to start. If you don't, you'll have no way of measuring the changes you've caused, and so will create only chaos — change for its own sake, without direction or meaningful function. A major part of that baseline is who it is you are training.

Let us say that you are about to instruct a group of trainees in some rather technical skill. The skill is demanding, difficult to master, and yet not really intellectually challenging. It is something those who know how to do treat as routine, but people who first encounter it find it rather intimidating. Suppose you need to teach that group a new computer program. The course would be completely different, depending on who was in the group. Your learners could be a grade-7 science class, a grade-12 class of business majors, a college class in plasma physics, members of a doctoral research seminar, newly hired secretarial trainees, senior executive secretaries, recently hired robotics engineers, or 15-year production-floor veterans; each group would demand a completely different approach.

Remember, you cannot create learning. You can only create an environment that is conducive to learning. Each group of trainees just mentioned needs a different environment. The content — how to set up and run the new computer program — remains the same. But whether you succeed in bringing about a change ultimately is a function of how skillfully you have analyzed the group's makeup and its needs and how well you have created an environment that encourages them to learn. Therefore, who you train is as important, perhaps even more important, than what you are training them to do.

There is a fundamental question you should ask about a group before you begin training: "How will the group have changed because of this training?" After all, this is the question you were hired to answer. As you will see in Chapter 13, an important part of your job is ensuring that the company — workers, middle management, supervisors, support system people, senior management — recognizes that training gets results. If you don't remind them how effective your training is, you'll constantly be on the defensive, justifying every dollar you spend. Training is always on the wrong side of the ledger. To avoid being considered an expensive frill, use every opportunity to show the positive changes your training has brought about. Start, therefore, by answering the initial question. How will they have changed because of this training?

Once you begin thinking about it, you'll realize that the answer does not come quickly. In order to answer it, you need to ask three other questions:

1. What do they know about the subject?
2. What do they want to know about the subject?
3. What do they need to know about the subject?

Let's consider each of these questions.

What They Know

In accordance with one of the learning principles discussed earlier, you must move from the known to the unknown, from the familiar to the new. Begin by finding out what the group knows, so you can guide them from that place to where you want them to be.

Perform a formal needs analysis as described in Chapter 5. Ask the group for information about themselves and their experience. Conduct a preclass survey or give an assignment asking them to describe their personal objectives — what they'd like to get from the class. Give a pretest of the material at the beginning of the first class and study the results.

Engage the group in discussion, by asking questions about why they are in the class. Ask questions that establish a common ground. Open up the floor for a gripe session, or ask them to list things that bother them.*

Create or administer a game or event that you can use later as a common experience. This is one of the main uses for management games. Set a task for them to accomplish and evaluate their performance. Ask them to describe a critical incident that has just happened and then discuss it.

Any or all of these approaches will tell you a great deal about what the group knows. Of course, several of the techniques just listed can't be used in advance. Start with those that can be used in advance — for example, a needs analysis — then build your course around the results and later bring in the others to verify your original analysis. In any event, stay flexible and adapt your course to the level of knowledge you discover.

---

* I have had great success with this technique when training clerical staff in better communications and customer service techniques. Many participants tell me they are thrilled to find others have the same problems.

What They Want to Know

This question addresses the problems of motivation and resistance. Most of the techniques just mentioned also answer the question of what they want to know. In particular, the most effective techniques are performing a needs analysis (records and supervisors' input on each trainee), holding a gripe session, asking them for their objectives, taking a preclass survey, asking questions about why they are there, and using a critical incident.

What They Need to Know

Of course this has already been established by a subject matter expert (probably yourself), but it has been expressed only in terms of the end result—the change desired—not in terms of the starting place. What does this particular group need to know in relation to what they already know and in relation to what they want to learn? Combine what you know they need to know with what they already know and with the new material they are willing to learn. For example, if $N =$ the need to learn, $O =$ the desired change (your objective), $K =$ what they already know, and $W =$ what they want to learn:

$$N = O - K + W$$

The techniques for discovering the answer to this third question are all the previous ones used to answer the first two questions but in particular they are:

1. A needs analysis
2. Preclass surveys
3. A pretest
4. Management games
5. Discussion or role-playing of critical incident
6. A preclass assignment

Principles of Group Behavior

In this chapter we have been looking at elements that affect individual trainees. But you don't always train individuals. In fact, most trainers are involved in groups of people from three to three hundred at a time. There are some key training factors that involve group interaction, so we need to look at them, too.

Characteristics of a Group

In most group situations, people interact with those around them. But they also have the opportunity to act as a group. For example, strangers in an elevator or at a corner waiting for a stoplight, managers at a meeting, people in a movie theater, or trainees in a seminar can ignore the others and remain alone, can casually interact with one or more of the others, or can interact with all the others as a unit and create a group that behaves in several special ways.

Once a decision is made to interact as a group, several things happen. In training groups especially, these distinct features play an important role. The first distinction is that all groups have a purpose. Individuals can be purposeless, but a group without a purpose simply isn't a group. The feeling of being a group arises out of a sense of purpose, of what is to be done. Consequently, if you wish to create learning groups (a highly recommended tactic), break up any preexisting groups before establishing new ones. People who begin a class as a preexisting group tend to sit together, stay together, fulfill the purposes of their own group (some positive perhaps, some not), and tend to exclude others. They constitute an independent power base in the training room, and these functions are in no way conducive to a learning environment. At best they are irrelevant, at worst a detriment. Whenever possible, break up preexisting cliques by (1) assigning seats or seating people by a random alphabetical or numerical system, and (2) placing people in new learning groups.

All groups have norms. Norms are informal, often unspoken, rules of conduct. Some things are acceptable to the group, some things are not. It is usually advisable to ask for input in making procedural rules. This is particularly important in cross-cultural training situations where group norms may differ widely. To go against a norm is to create resistance, whereas to ally your purposes with the group's norms is to enhance the chances for cooperation and lessen resistance.

Frequently, the skills you are training may be perceived as norms. "That's the way we've always done it," is an all-too-frequent comment. If you arbitrarily dismiss such comment you will polarize the group and lessen or even negate the effectiveness of your training. It is essential that you understand the wants and habits of your trainees.

If you have to change their group norms, follow the procedures discussed in Chapter 1 concerning breaking habits. Also, there are key opinion- or norm-molders in any group. These are the people whose support you need to gain, whom you need to convince. They, in turn, will influence the rest of the group.

Three events occur in a sequence when a group is confronted with a problem and needs a decision. First, each member with status voices his or her opinion and tries to rally support for it. In a group dominated by one individual, this may be a very short discussion. In more loosely structured groups the discussion can go on interminably (as, for example, in congressional or parliamentary debates). Second, those who have been strongly opposed by one or more of the others will make an effort to rethink or adapt their positions to the majority or to those they perceive as most powerful; where they are not threatened, they will adopt what appears to them to be the most rational position. If they can accept the other position or persuade the others to accept some compromise, the decision is made and the group adopts the agreed-upon concept. If the concept proves successful or remains unchallenged, it will become a new norm for the group.

But there is a third step that occurs when no agreement can be reached. That is, both sides have tried to persuade each other, both have tried to re-evaluate and compromise, and both have failed. At this point one or both (or more, if there are more factions) will redefine the group. Each will exclude the other or, if that is not possible, each will agree only on the surface but will hold back privately. If the group does this to one individual, that one is ostracized, blackballed, made into a scapegoat. If the individual does it to the group, he or she simply goes another way, seeking some other affiliation but usually downgrading the value or the members of the group. When whole parts of the group exclude entire other parts, we get factionalism: splinter groups, fanatics, moderates, cliques, and so forth.

Change in Groups

Training creates change, as we have seen, and means "un-freezing" the old way. You do this in step one of the group process, but you must reach step two to cause them to rethink their current norms. You cannot push them to step three, or they will drop out and resist learning anything (a syndrome we have probably all observed in our high school days). The members of the group must be allowed to air their opinions in step one, or they will feel resentment at being force-fed a new way of doing things and will resist that, too. This is why building an environment that is conducive to learning (see Chapter 1) is so important.

You'll win the first part of the battle for learning when you reach the members' minds and give them cause to rethink their comfortable old ways. This is also why, as will be seen in Chapter 3, there must be an effort to prepare them for learning. It's why dealing with resistance is so important. Unless each trainee comes to realize the worth of the material you are teaching — that it is worth changing for — he or she will redefine the situation to exclude you from the group and will dismiss the norms of management in favor of the norms of whatever subgroups he or she can create or join. To be conducive to learning, the environment must:

1. Allow and encourage the airing of trainees' problems, habits, doubts, and so on.
2. Encourage interaction and the discovery of ideas.
3. Encourage testing of both opinions and skills so that people are motivated and learn from their mistakes.
4. Engage and challenge learners rather than bore them.
5. Stimulate thought, effort, discussion, and new ideas.
6. Encourage openness rather than private withdrawal.
7. Demand commitment through action.
8. Provide an abundance of practice and evaluation.

Obviously, some of us train groups that are prepared to learn, and so the task is easier. These groups already recognize the need to change. But with groups that are reluctant, you must deal with the three stages of group dynamics.

Roles Within the Group

There are several easily recognizable roles that members of a group may adopt. If you recognize these roles, you can move with them and lessen the amount of change required. To fight these naturally elected roles is to court resistance, but to engage them — by tailoring requests and assignments to the norms of the group — is to encourage and motivate members to learn.

Leader

In most groups the leadership emerges informally. Leadership is always present to some degree when a group of people is undecided about what to do. In a theater after a spectacular performance some people will lead a standing ovation, jumping spontaneously to their feet. Others will wait to follow their lead. A group of friends standing around with nothing to do always inspires suggestions for activity; those who suggest are bidding for leadership. In a classroom, if the trainer fails to arrive on time, sooner or later (usually after about 20 minutes) at least one person will appeal for support in doing something about it.

Such moves are bids for leadership. If several bids are made at once or early on, discussions and possibly arguments will occur until the members of the group go through the three steps outlined earlier. Then they choose to follow one leader or break into several factions. These bids for leadership are largely a result of the frustration level individuals can tolerate. Those who can least tolerate the frustration will move toward what they perceive as an easement.

Usually these early bidders will ask for support from others. If they get none, they will either act alone or capitulate, following someone else's bid for leadership. If they get some support, they will usually measure its strength by demanding immediate action or inviting discussion directly or indirectly. Eventually they gather their supporters, having gone through the argue, rethink, redefine cycle. Leadership usually grows from three actions: (1) suggesting or demanding courses of action, (2) monitoring progress, and (3) evaluating performance or other calls to action.

Authority – Reference – Advisor

Another almost mandatory position is that of the authority. This is the person everyone respects and listens to because of his or her experience or special expertise. In a group of strangers it is anyone who can gain credibility by appearing to know what he or she is talking about. Often the authority is self-proclaimed ("I read a book once . . . ," "I know a fellow who . . . ," "My uncle was once . . . ," and so on). This person can be appointed, but then must prove he or she is worthy of respect. The authority can bid for leadership but just as often maintains a power position by having prospective leaders seek his or her endorsement. The authorities in groups sometimes become the scheming force behind the leader.

Entertainer

We are all familiar with the quick wit who can make a funny remark about almost anything. Such people need an audience and readily find one in their social and business groups. They are important to their groups because their humor provides a relief from tension and often prevents a confrontation. Consequently, even the most serious groups will have a member who makes wry remarks.

Peacemaker

Peacemakers hate confrontation. They are often excellent facilitators or negotiators, and they strive to iron out difficulties among those bidding for leadership. They are harmonizers. They try to work out rational, mutually beneficial solutions to problems. In doing so, they sometimes end up in leadership roles themselves, sometimes effectively and sometimes not so effectively. This is particularly true in parliamentary systems such as are in Great Britain, Israel, and France, where coalition governments are led by prime ministers who, to keep the peace and get the job done, negotiate shaky compromises between fighting factions. In fact, this leadership option—the role of peacemaker—is available to the trainer even in the most difficult groups.

Worker–Follower

The workers are the people who carry out what the leaders, authorities, and peacemakers want done. They are the power base upon which leadership is based, and they are usually the majority in any group. Because they don't relish change and would rather go along with their friends than create an issue, they are easily swayed as a group. To change their opinions, persuade the leader and the group will follow. Such a statement may sound crass, but there is considerable evidence that it is true. In a series of studies done by psychologist Solomon Asch, after viewing a geometric figure projected on a screen a significant number of people would deny their own perceptions of the figure rather than disagree with a planted observer who intentionally lied about what he had seen. When there was more than one person disagreeing with them, an even larger number of individuals falsified their own observations to more closely align themselves with the distortions of others.[5] It seems that when we perceive ourselves to be part of a group, we have a strong urge to conform to what appears to be that group's norms—even if it means compromising our own beliefs.

Most people do not feel comfortable acting alone. If you can recognize the roles and patterns of group behavior, you can take advantage of such mental states. You can establish a learning environment that harmonizes with the natural behavior of the group to create a learning situation that leads to positive change. If you are unaware of a group's dynamics or intentionally at odds with it, you court friction, resistance, confrontation, and, ultimately, the likelihood that little will be learned.

Summary

In this chapter we looked at the trainee, both as an individual and as part of a group. We began with the realization that, while you, as a trainer, are a change agent, the changes you can bring about are largely limited to the skills you can train others to perform. In doing so, you are likely to face resistance because most people prefer to do things the way they've always done them. Resistance can take many forms, but it stems from seven basic causes, each of which you should recognize and deal with. Once you have uncovered the cause of resistance to change, you can eliminate it by ventilating the resistor's need and motivating the learner toward a desired change in behavior.

To deal with resistance, you must create an open environment that is conducive to the ventilation and discussion of the problem. To accomplish this, you must be aware of, and structure your learning sessions around, the psychological principles of adult learning. These principles are Thorndike's Law of Readiness, which states that people can learn only what they are ready to learn; the Law of Effect, which says that succeeding at a task motivates people to work still harder; and the Law of Exercise, which demands that people practice what they've learned. These laws brought us to the Ten Principles for Learning, which provide the basic framework for all training. We also covered in some detail how to create learning environments that use these fundamentals, particularly in handling resistance, using multisensory approaches, building conceptual bridges between old and new material, and handling individual differences among trainees.

To apply these principles to your training programs, you must recognize the needs of the group you are training. We examined ways of analyzing trainees to discover what they already know and what they need to know. Lastly, one of the vital aspects of understanding your trainees is recognizing the interactions of groups. We looked at group behavior and norms, and saw how groups handle change. We also outlined the roles that emerge in most groups, and concluded the chapter with comments on using group dynamics to foster an effective learning situation.

CHAPTER 3

The Structure of Training

WE have examined what the role of training is in the organization. We've looked at the aspects common to most trainee groups. We've studied the basic principles of learning, and stressed how who you teach is more important than what you teach. Now it is time to turn to content, and discuss how to prepare and structure training.

Training Objectives

The single most important action for a trainer is to set clear, action-oriented objectives. Once you've defined the learning population and established the present level of performance, you must decide where you want to go, that is, what change you want to bring about. Your objectives will govern what you teach and how you teach it, how that training is evaluated, and how management, ultimately, will gauge your success. Clear objectives are the bedrock of good training. Training cannot be effective without clearly defined and specific objectives.

Management Goals versus Training Objectives

First, let's distinguish between management goals and training objectives. A management goal is a statement of purpose. It names targets to be aimed at and acts as a guide in efforts to hit the targets. It is an informed estimate of future necessary performance levels. It is an extremely effective tool, but is limited to end results, not the means toward those ends.

A training objective, on the other hand, is both means and end. It states the end results (not of training, but of learning) by specifying what must be taught, how it will be taught, and how the learning will be evaluated. Because it describes the means, the end, and the evaluative feedback, the training objective is your single most important tool in training. Attaining your training objectives means reaching management goals, too. Each time you meet a training objective you've taken a step toward attaining management's goals.

Criteria of Objectives

To be effective, a training objective needs to meet four criteria:

1. The objective must describe an action the trainee will perform.
2. The action must be stated specifically and in detail.
3. The action must be evaluable.*
4. The action must be realistic.

Let's look at each of these.

Trainee Action

I have seen objectives such as, "I will teach the trainees to. . ." or "I will communicate the X principles of. . ." or "The trainer will instruct the trainees. . . ." These are descriptions of what the *trainer* plans to do. They describe teaching, not learning. Trainers can teach perfectly, yet trainees might not learn, and objectives can't be met unless learning takes place. Indeed, this is what often happens in schools. Students are taught at, rather than taught with.

The company hires a trainer to achieve a change in work behavior. It is concerned about the ultimate change, not what the trainer does to bring it about (within reason, of course). An objective that states what the trainer plans to do is beside the point and of no interest to management.

---

* The author uses "evaluable" to refer to actions that can be evaluated by various methods, including formal tests, performance measurement, simulations, on-the-job behavior, and trainee attitudes.

What the *trainees* will be able to do is the point, and it should be stated as the training objective.

The easiest way to write a trainee-oriented objective is to ask yourself, "If I teach them *XYZ*, what will they be able to do with it?" Concentrate on the verb that describes what they will be able to do, then construct a sentence or group of sentences that state clearly the objective using the verb that you've selected.

Personally, I like the simple phrase, "at the completion of this training, the trainee will be able to. . . ." Then I list all the things they will learn to do. You might prefer to list each action separately, or you can prepare a checklist of the skills, and as the trainee performs each one, you can check it off. An excellent variation on this idea is the evaluative checklist, which lets you rate the performance of each task as excellent, good, fair, or poor. As long as the objective is written in terms of tasks (active verbs) trainees must perform to show you that they have learned, the objective will be effective.

Specific Action

New trainers often fail to pin down the action in an objective. "The trainee will be able to operate the machine. . . " is too general. It is much more effective to say, "The trainee will perform the following tasks on the machine:. . . ." The objective is focused on the specific results to be accomplished, not on weak generalizations.

This approach is particularly effective when there are special conditions under which the tasks must be performed. In Coast Guard training, for instance, certain tasks must be completed under gale-force winds, in driving rain, with limited visibility, and on a pitching deck. It isn't enough to mention that special conditions may interfere with doing the tasks. In such cases, list the conditions as part of the objective.

If your training lesson is informational rather than strictly skill oriented, then state your objectives in terms of grades on tests. "The trainee will pass a final test with a grade of *X* or better." Passing the test is not enough; the objective should point to exact performance. Whenever possible, quantify the objective: "Trainee will perform *XYZ* within a 3 percent tolerance for error," ". . . with a 16 percent reduction in scrap," ". . . will perform eight tasks in running sequence with no errors in an allotted 4 1/2-minute time span under full open-factory floor conditions." Notice that when the conditions and criteria are spelled out carefully, the objective leaps into clear focus. Clear objectives give direction to the learners, the trainer, and management. They are businesslike because they are specific and action oriented. They are professional because stating a clear objective demands results.

Evaluable Action

There are common words that we believe we know the meaning of and assume that the people we talk to understand. We are right in both cases. The problem is the other people understand the word differently than we do and so they (and we) become confused or misled. These words are simply too abstract for everyone to share the same meaning. Such words frequently pop up in poorly phrased training objectives. Probably the worst are *understand, know,* and *feel,* as in "The trainees will be able to understand the XYZ. . . " or "The trainee will know how to. . . " or "The trainees will feel better about. . . ." Such words tell us nothing. They are too abstract. A word like *understand* means different things to different people, and besides, there is no way to really *know* that they understand except to test for understanding. In that case, the objective verb should be *demonstrate* or *show* an understanding by *passing* the test.

The verb that drives an objective needs not only to describe a specific action but it must also be evaluable in some way. "Knowing" and "understanding" are things that happen in the head. They are private. No trainer can see them happening. What a trainer can observe is behavior that indicates knowledge or understanding. The objective, therefore, must describe the behavior by which the trainer will recognize that the trainees have learned.

Avoiding nonmeasurable words is quite easy, fortunately. Ask yourself, "Is this measurable? How will I know they've learned?" If the answer isn't expressed by the verb you've used, change it until you get one that tells you just how you'll know they've learned. You will find that every objective contains the method for evaluating the training. Each training objective not only sets the goal, it also suggests how to reach it and how to measure it.

Evaluable Verbs for Writing Training Objectives

Compare	Make
Create	Perform
Defend	Present
Demonstrate	Program
Describe	Show
Discriminate	Solve
Explain	State
Identify	Use
List	Utilize

Realistic Action

Sometimes trainers set goals that are desirable but beyond the capacity of the learners to master in the available time. You build in frustration with an unrealistic objective, and with frequent frustration comes despair. So, in addition to describing a specific action, in evaluable terms, the objective must also be attainable.

In summary, then, to ensure that your objective meets the criteria stated earlier, answer the following questions:

1. How will trainees be able to use what I have taught?
2. What verb precisely describes this action?
3. Does the verb clearly state what the trainee will do?
4. What simple sentence can describe the desired result?
5. Does this sentence describe the specific activity and the conditions under which it must take place?
6. Is the means of evaluation implicit in this statement?
7. Does the statement ask for realistic action? Can the objectives be met in the given time?

Cognitive versus Affective Learning

So far we have been dealing with cognitive learning; that is, specific skills. Objectives for this learning tell us what tasks the trainees will know how to do. But there is another very important type of training objectives —affective ones. We are often called upon to change both skills and attitudes. As will be seen in this chapter and the next, you need to influence the attitude of your trainees to ensure their participation in the learning process. Objectives to describe affective learning are more abstract. You must decide how you want your trainees to feel as well as how you want them to think and act.

Your problem with affective objectives is that feelings are not specific and measurable. Yet you must try for as much precision as possible. Fortunately, feelings usually lead to actions. By specifying and quantifying the actions to observe, you can evaluate affective learning. Observable types of actions include:

Absenteeism
Lateness
Cleanliness in the workplace
Frequency of confrontational situations
Employee turnover rates
Customer complaints

Scrap rates
Safety records
Sales figures
Service calls
Numbers participating in company-sponsored community events
Numbers participating in voluntary company programs

These and many more actions are legitimate means for evaluating employee attitude. Therefore, affective learning is evaluable when objectives are tied to specific, observable behavior.

Learning Patterns

We think in chronological patterns largely because we have been trained to do so from early childhood. As soon as we begin to read we get locked into a linear pattern as well. In Western culture, printing goes from left to right, from top to bottom, in numbered sequence. The pattern becomes second nature, and since much of what we learn is through reading, we tend to think in that same linear pattern. So when it comes to training others, we find it natural to follow a linear, chronological approach. This is not always the best way to communicate a subject, however. In fact, it is frequently the worst way.

Once you have set your objectives, decide on the most effective structure for achieving those objectives. Because you know your subject, you will likely think of *what* you are going to teach first. As we've just observed, don't slip thoughtlessly into a chronological pattern. The chronological approach is dull. It is common in novels and movies and on television, but these have an element of suspense. Also, reality is compressed so you see only key, exciting parts. An unedited documentary is as lengthy and dull as life on a boring day. As a trainer you want to create an environment that makes learning easy, that motivates the trainees and

---

Training Patterns

1. Funnel—from broad concepts to specific skills.
2. Inverted funnel—from specific skills to broad concepts.
3. Tunnel—steady presentation of topics, needs strong substructure.
4. Spool—from initial concepts to specific skills back to broad concepts.

involves them in the subject. Without suspense or condensing, a chrono-logical pattern is de-motivating and makes learning difficult.

There are four basic patterns of presenting information: the funnel, the inverted funnel, the tunnel, and the spool. Try each one until you find the method that best suits your trainees, your subject, and your objectives. You are, in effect, creating a pattern for learning—a structure around which you will mold or model the content of your lesson.

Funnel Pattern

With the funnel pattern, you start with a broad concept and narrow it down until you are teaching the step-by-step how-to's of the subject. The effect is like a funnel, hence the name (see Figure 3-1).

For example, this is the overall structure of this book. We look first at the concepts—the why's of the topic—then proceed to the specifics. We follow this pattern when we learn from experience. It is the way we solve problems; design houses, clothing, and cars; make friends; and learn informally. Our interest is aroused by the concept of an idea, then we apply it to our specifics. It is the pattern of deductive reasoning.

Inverted Funnel Pattern

In the inverted funnel, you start with details and move gradually to the broad concept (see Figure 3-2). The inverted funnel is the pattern of traditional education. We begin with the ABC's and simple arithmetic and, as we gain proficiency, expand our understanding and tackle novels and essays, quantum mechanics and relative field theory. Or we learn the actual events of history, and as we begin to understand them, we move on to why they happened and how one thing leads to another. The inverted

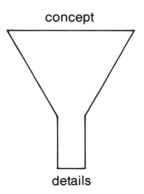

Figure 3-1. Model of funnel training pattern.

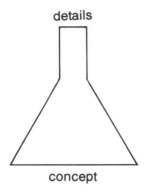

details

concept

Figure 3-2. Model of inverted funnel training pattern.

funnel is the traditional approach to skills training, too. It is the way we learn music, math, and motor mechanics. We start with the parts, then gradually work up to the whole. This is the pattern of inductive reasoning.

Tunnel Pattern

The third pattern is the tunnel. As its name suggests, this method is a straight progression. In effect it is a linear arrangement of information (see Figure 3-3).

We travel in a linear sequence. We view our lives in a linear way. We move from point A to point B as directly as possible. It is how we read. Computer programming is usually taught in a linear pattern. Following a recipe is a matter of moving from one step to the next. Concepts are either ignored or incidental, whereas the movement through a time frame is the vital activity.

Spool Pattern

Each of these patterns has its application and you must decide which works for your group, your material, and your objective. For mastery of practical skills, the tunnel is likely to be efficient. If you are developing long-range planning abilities—for example, progressive management

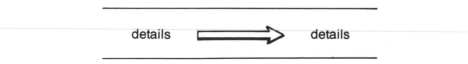

details ⟹ details

Figure 3-3. Model of tunnel training pattern.

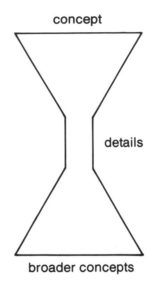

concept

details

broader concepts

Figure 3-4.   Model of spool training pattern.

skills for future senior executives — the inverted funnel provides a grow-ing sequence of challenges. The problem with these patterns, however, is that with the tunnel there is no motivation unless it's brought in by the learner, while with the inverted funnel all the motivation is in the later phases. Anyone who has ever taken piano lessons knows the drudgery of the early lessons. Only the funnel method grabs the learner's mind at the start. It is most effective for creating a want-to-learn atmosphere.

As has been stressed throughout this book, you always need a want-to-learn atmosphere. It is inherent in any good training environment. The more appealing the learning, the more effective it will be. The ideal structure — extremely rare — is a combination of the three, which I call the spool pattern (see Figure 3-4).

With the spool pattern, the learner is grabbed instantly by the con-cepts, then learns the application of those concepts to reach a new thresh-old of yet broader concepts. Whenever possible, make the spool your basic approach.

Using the Learning Patterns

Ultimately, you will choose an approach that opens the initial funnel and motivates the trainee with a concept. You'll create bridges from what is already known to the new concept and then from the concept to specific skills. You'll break the skills into steps so learners can look back at the progress they've made. You'll challenge them with new ideas, and inter-weave concepts with skills at appropriate levels so that mastery of both produces independence and self-direction. In planning your lessons this way, you'll use seven organizing substructures to form your spool.

Problem/Solution

Few things motivate people more than tackling and solving problems. This format is one of the best for establishing concepts and setting a tone or environment for your training. Pose a problem and let the discussion lead to its solution, or present the training as an answer to a company problem. The closer you make the problem come to the trainees' personal needs, the more effective this format will be.

Cause and Effect

Another compelling format is cause and effect. People do not learn in a void. Cause-and-effect relationships are strong bridges between the known and unknown and between concepts and practices. They provide a rationale for learning. They are particularly effective because the cause/effect relationship of a known example can be paralleled with an unknown case to clarify it. As with problem/solution, this is a dynamic form. Usually a cause-and-effect relationship is more memorable than the parts separately, because that relationship is an action and engages the learner's mind. Finally, a cause-and-effect relationship can be verified—put to the test—so trainees learn by doing and seeing the outcome.

Logical

Another way to build mental bridges between the known and unknown is to create logical relationships between the elements. Both the funnel and the inverted funnel are classic patterns of logic. Other patterns may be combined to enhance and enliven your lessons. For instance, use a series of problems and solutions to lead the group to inductively or deductively find the solution to a much larger problem. Learning is exciting when logic is exercised.

Climactic

Everyone loves a story, and every culture is built on myths and stories. Simple chronology tends to be monotonous. Adding an anecdotal structure with a beginning and middle leading to a climax and denouement creates interest in the chronological format. The Judeo-Christian

---

Structural Planning

1. Choose the overall structure best suited to:
   a. Your trainees
   b. Your objectives
   c. Your material
2. Choose a substructure that will engage trainee performance.
3. Choose substructures that build bridges from the known concept to the needed skill.
4. Structure learning plateaus that enable you to measure progress.
5. Keep in mind that the end result is to produce mastery and self-direction, and choose structures accordingly.

---

heritage is built upon parables and life histories from which we draw lessons. So are the ethical and moral teachings of all of our predecessors and contemporaries. Most moral training is through parables, fables, myths, or legends. Everyone loves a story. Work them into your training. This is why case histories work. Parables, personal histories, war stories, and tales of the trail all serve to enlighten and enlarge us conceptually. When you need to work in concepts, use stories. They can be used to combine other relationships or patterns. A mystery is always fun — and effective. A joke (cause-and-effect relationship) is often dramatically effective for getting a point across. A case history transforms concepts into practical applications. Use stories, parables, and anecdotes to make your point memorable.

Topical

A topical pattern is a sequence of topics in some sort of order. Frequently the topics you need to cover are unrelated, which makes them hard to learn. If you have several only loosely related topics, look for — or create — similarities among them or link them by structure (stories, cause and effect, and so on). Acronyms are excellent. For instance, the four elements of a good training objective are made memorable with the sentence "*Two Awfully Silly Experts Resigned.*" The first letter of each word stands for *Trainee Action, Specific, Evaluable,* and *Realistic.*

The key here is "less is more," one of the ten Principles for Learning (see Chapter 2). Simplify. The more a learner thinks there is to learn, the harder it is to learn anything. It all seems overwhelming. Break up your material into consumable chunks. For instance, 28 steps for doing a particular task are very hard to remember; on the other hand, 7 steps, each with 4 substeps, are easier to remember and look far less intimidating. The more concentrated or complex the material, the more you should follow the "less is more" principle.

Chronological

The straightforward chronological approach has already been discussed. It is useful only when you can create some sort of suspense using the other structural tools. It is probably inescapable when an exact step-by-step sequence must be followed, as in teaching complex computer programming. Counter its limitations by frequently using problem/solution, cause and effect, and anecdotes to break the monotony. By incorporating other structures to keep it lively, you can use the chronological format to great effect when it suits your group, your objectives, and your material.

Spatial

You can organize your material in such a way as to work with the physical relationships of articles in a given space, say the room in which you are teaching. This method is excellent when your materials can be flowcharted or explained with large diagrams that let you walk from Point A to Point B. Charts, graphs, layouts, models, and the like are excellent for this. Also, use the literary device of allegory to develop a concept, endow it with symbolic names and characters, and then wander through a series of symbolic places to prove your point. People learn from such allegories and find them generally more interesting (and therefore easier to learn) than a dry recital of the facts themselves. Try to give straightforward but static material a spatial dimension. Diagrams do it well, allegories are a bit esoteric but fun, and case studies are even better.

Redundancy

Another structure essential to learning is repetition, or redundancy. In Chapter 2 we discussed briefly the effectiveness of oral behavior and its effect on our learning. We need now to take a more detailed look.

Human beings can talk. None of the animals around us seems to have the range, depth, or fluency of oral expression that we have. Many have surprisingly rich vocabularies but none appears to have as many as the more than 250,000 words in just the English language. Even so, as we all know, it's not what you say but how you say it that gets meaning across.

When our power to communicate orally was combined with our ability to design and use tools that shape and control our environment, a written language developed. Then came printed language. Writing was a "time binder" that solved the problem of remembering. If people wrote it down, they would always have it. Printing was a "space binder" that gave that initial time-binding ability to everyone anywhere who could learn to read and write. Writing — and ultimately printing — changed people's lives and livelihoods in every culture that adopted them. They are still doing so.

Cultural anthropologists are exploring the changes that occur when a culture makes the transition from an oral pattern to a literate one. They have found many changes, including a decline in the credibility of the spoken word. People in a literate culture don't believe something until they see it in print, hence the need for written legal contracts and the power of the press. Another change is that listening attention spans shrink. Even as recently as 100 years ago people in America would listen attentively to six hours of political debate. Today one hour seems far too long. Several radio stations have tried with no success to revive old radio plays, but they find that their listeners today need visual stimulation, too. It is too hard today to listen attentively. A third change is a result of the increasing dependence on writing. People begin to revere the written word and use it as the final arbiter of truth. A fourth change is that the language shrinks. Poetic devices, colorful words, precise expression — all of these diminish in frequency in spoken language. Compare the crackling dialogue of Shakespeare's semi-literate society with that of our own more literate one. Speech loses mnemonic devices and parables, rhymes, strong metaphors, and richly descriptive adverbs and adjectives.

But these changes are not universal, nor are they evident in all facets of a culture. In several areas people retain their oral traditions. One such area is education. Any subject you wish to learn is available in books (including this one, of course). Yet thousands of people attend training seminars, many of which are largely talk-fests. The public seminar business has become hugely successful in the United States and around the world. Despite strong leanings toward print, people still feel the need for oral stimulation when they wish to learn. Yet, nowadays people are less equipped to learn orally. They have shorter attention spans, weaker memories, no ability to create their own rich metaphors that bridge the gap between the old and the new. They are used to passive entertainment, not active engagement. They like a good show, but take little learning from it.

The trainer must compensate for culturally induced learner short-comings by returning some of the practices of oral culture. Redundancy is a key element in this return. In all myths and legends, the epic poems and genealogies of peoples of ancient times, repetition of names, events, messages, and morals is central. In surviving oral cultures today, there are patterns of redundancy in rituals, dances and songs, as well as in words and gestures. Anthropologists believe repetition enhances memory; it embeds learning in the subconscious. Therefore, repetition must become a part of any effective training lesson. Devise and use patterns of redundancy. They become the hooks on which to hang the memory.

Of course repetition doesn't mean simply repeating things over and over. That shortens the attention span and dulls the mind. There is an old rule for effective public speaking: "Tell 'em what you're gonna tell 'em, tell 'em, and then tell 'em what you told 'em." I like to shorten this to "Tell 'em.³" Metaphorically, it is telling them raised to the third power. As every math student knows, a number multiplied by itself three times is considerably larger than that same number multiplied by the number 3. The Tell 'em³ rule calls for forecasting the material, covering the material, and reviewing the material. Each repetition takes a different form and serves a different purpose. This is the recommended pattern for building redundancy into your lessons: forecast, teach, review. It is similar to old-fashioned writing drills in which you were asked to fill page after page with spirals.

Learning progress is like that: two steps forward and one step backward. Several tools are available for creating redundancy. Any way you can cover the same material from different perspectives will enhance learning. What we are doing is using the multisensory principle of learning to lock in what has been taught with memory hooks provided by redundancy. Build redundant patterns into your content, relate each of the patterns to one of the principles of learning discussed in Chapter 2.

1. Share your training objectives with the learners before beginning.
2. Review the agenda with the group before beginning to teach.
3. Use a "kick off" incident (for example, role-playing) to start a lesson, then refer back to it to draw out principles.
4. Assign material to be done and then go over it with the group.
5. Review what you have covered so far.
6. Summarize what has been taught.
7. Use visual aids (more than one where possible) to make your points clearer and to vary the presentation.
8. Devise practice sessions so trainees can apply what they have been taught.
9. Give both written and oral evaluation.
10. Administer tests and quizzes frequently.
11. Have refresher sessions.
12. Devise games in which material taught must be used to win.
13. Provide reading assignments that cover the same material from a different perspective.

Timing and Structure

There has long been controversy over whether first impressions (primacy) or most recent impressions (ultimacy) have the greater impact on an individual and are therefore more memorable. Currently, the consensus is that the first impression is stronger. In any event, both first and last impressions hold key positions for engaging the memory. One of your structural considerations, then, is the matter of primacy or ultimacy. Determine which key ideas need to be presented at points perceived to be starting places — first thing, first day, beginning of afternoon session, beginning of each day, first section after each break, and so on. Remember that the first impression the learner receives will govern whether there is resistance to it and will also shape the learner's readiness to learn. Make those initial impressions highly memorable and influential. Give careful thought to how you will introduce topics. This means that your start-off positions should be keyed to a motivator. Examples of such motivators are:

> Demonstrations
> Stories
> Exercises
> Visual aids (films, charts, and so on)
> Projects
> Discussions
> Challenges
> Lectures

Or use other methods so long as they engage the learners, have a degree of excitement (sales appeal), and set the stage for the material to come.

Timing also means making your strongest points first. There is an academic argument for approaching subjects chronologically and saving the big moment — for example, the solution to the problem — for last. It is a good approach, but remember the Tell 'em³ format. Tell them what the exciting solution is at the beginning to grab their attention, then work through the problem in good order until you reach the solution again, this time in context. Because the final thing said is the second most memorable, repeat what you told them before. You'll begin by grabbing attention and end by reinforcing the concept. This way you will be taking advantage of both primacy and ultimacy.

Four Steps to a Good Lesson Plan

After setting your objectives, choosing your structure, building in patterns of redundancy, and taking advantage of the primacy-ultimacy

Sample Lesson Plan

Population: Customer service personnel
Time: 1 1/2 hours
Objectives: Upon completion of this lesson trainees will be able to:

- Define their own need to change their telephone responses.
- Describe the four characteristics of professionalism on the telephone.
- Create a telephone log.
- Diagnose their own key problem calls from that log.
- Script a response to each of the types of calls they receive.

Preparation:

1. Ventilate resistance by explaining that the class is a chance to self evaluate and polish personal skills. Instructor only provides the critical standards of professionalism.
2. Assign participants to list two things they hate that customers do on the phone.
3. Debrief with volunteers and solve some problems.
4. Conclude with overhead projection on human relations and the need to change. Discuss.
5. Conduct Socratic discussion about fear and comfort as de-motivators.
6. Lead hand-clasping exercise.
7. Discuss hypothetical situation of job where the employees hate the boss, and discuss the three changeable variables.
8. Ask for conclusion: The trainees must change to get the callers to change.

Presentation:

1. On flip chart (refer them to page in workbook):
   A. Introduce the four aspects of professionalism.
      1. What/When/How
      2. Unflappable
      3. Handle it
      4. Make it easy
   B. Draw each of the principles out through examples, stories, and Socratic questions.

2. Explain that these are the agenda for the course and that the rest of the morning will be spent on What/When/How.
3. Turn to page in workbook and project it overhead to describe a telephone log and its uses.
4. Assign the log for two weeks and describe how to use the data collected to prioritize calls and trouble-shoot calls.
5. Describe scripting format using workbook page and overhead projection.

Practice:

Assign groups of five to discuss their problem calls and then select two as a group to solve. They should write a script using the morning's lesson as a model.

Evaluation:

Ask each group to role play one of its solutions. Working with the entire class, work through the solution. Everyone helps to critique and fine tune each group's efforts.

---

phenomenon, you are ready to work on the specific content — the lesson plan itself.

Every learning sequence should be a separate lesson. It is usually convenient to break up the material into natural blocks of time, so each lesson corresponds to a time chunk, such as from the beginning of the day to the first break. The four step lesson plan is the most effective method for structuring these blocks of time and topics: Preparation, Presentation, Practice, and Evaluation. Let's look at each step.

Preparation

In the academic world, *preparation* refers to something the teacher does. Not so in training. Certainly the trainer also prepares, but in this book that activity is part of the Ten Principles of Learning discussed in Chapter 2. And as mentioned in that earlier chapter, people cannot learn unless they are ready to learn. They must be prepared to learn — which is the meaning of the term *preparation* in the training context. The preparation you choose depends on your learners, your objectives, and your content. Even if the group is already motivated, their learning will be made easier, will be better focused, and will be more dynamic if you prepare them. If they are not motivated, the preparation will lay the groundwork for positive learning. Ways of handling the preparation stage are as follows:

1. *List the objectives to be learned.* When learners are already motivated and have come prepared to learn, this is an effective preparation. It puts the learning into perspective; it gives the learners a map to follow so they can build mental bridges for themselves between what they already know and what they will learn. In addition, it is the first part of the Tell 'em³ formula.

2. *Ventilate resistance.* If you are concerned that there might be resistance to learning, it must be ventilated before learning can take place. Preparing them means getting rid of negative steam. Depending on what form the resistance takes, you can explain how they will benefit from the training and why they should learn. If the problem is lack of trust or misunderstanding, explain why you are there by describing your purpose as you see it. If the group has a different assessment of the training, explain management's goals or redefine your goals as discussed in Chapter 6.

If the resistance stems from a low tolerance for change, express confidence in the group and its ability to master the subject. Make it seem not hard at all. If there is a fear of losing face, again redefine the purposes to allow room for others to save face. If the problem is peer pressure, there is little you can do in this preparation phase. Allow group leaders to save face by keeping the options open.

Create a strong first impression with positive nonverbal behavior and enthusiasm. Make the surrounding environment attractive, and start your lesson with a "grabber."

3. *Ask challenging or engaging questions.* Start the group thinking and discussing. Good questions cause them to build mental bridges to the new material. They call for immediate active participation and help direct understanding. In addition, questions allow each participant to adjust uniquely to the learning environment.

4. *Administer a pretest.* Or have the group perform some skill (role-playing, for example). If you think some people feel they already know the material, the pretest tells them they don't know as much as they thought they did.

5. *Begin with an exercise or management game.* These games engage the group and create curiosity about what they are to learn. The activities are bridges made from common experience. They also foster group feelings early in the training. Furthermore, they can be fun; people love to play.

6. *Tell a story or set up a mystery.* Both draw people in, establish a common ground, and help to meld the trainees into a group. Of course,

the story or mystery must make a point and must direct them to some element of the subject.

7. *Ask them for their objectives.* What would they like to gain from the session? This forces them to think about the program, to apply it to their unique situations. It also allows you to repeat your training objectives and to focus the group's attention on learning. Lastly, it provides them with a learning map of the course.

Presentation

There are two approaches to presenting information, each hundreds of years old. By far the most common was presented by 17th-century English philosopher John Locke, who described the mind as a *tabula rasa,* which means "blank slate." In effect, the trainer assumes the learner knows nothing and proceeds to fill that mind with ideas and learning in much the same way one fills a chalkboard with writing or diagrams. The blank slate approach assumes that the learner knows nothing and the trainer knows all and transmits the information to the learner, usually through words.

The other approach is called the Socratic Method, after the fifth-century B.C. Greek philosopher Socrates, and made famous by the writings of his pupil, Plato. Socrates didn't define his method, but Plato illustrated it by reporting the learning dialogues in which Socrates engaged. Socrates never voiced a point of view but, rather, challenged learners by asking them questions. The dialogue led the learner to discover for himself the truth that Socrates was teaching. The Socratic Method assumes that the learner knows a great deal and can be guided by questioning to reach new understandings.

If we examine each approach in the light of the Ten Principles of Learning (see Chapter 2) it is obvious that the Socratic Method engages far more of them than does the blank-slate method. It is, therefore, the more effective approach to learning. Yet it is much less common. This is because when we are asked to "teach" someone, our first approach is simply to tell what we know. Leading a person to information through questioning is much more demanding. Besides, if a learner doesn't know the subject, how can he or she answer questions about it? We trust ourselves to know the material, but it is very hard to trust others to know it, especially when we assume that because they are in training they need to learn. Furthermore, the bulk of our own education came to us by the blank-slate method, which makes it seem the natural way to teach.

We will discuss other benefits of the Socratic Method and illustrate how to structure Socratic interactions in Chapter 4 when we discuss

Applying the Ten Principles of Learning to the Lesson Plan

1. *Readiness and resistance.* The preparation stage. Use funnel and inverted funnel patterns to structure the lesson. Ventilate resistance. Share objectives, use substructure formats to engage the learners.

2. *Active versus passive learning.* The practice stage. Set action-oriented, trainee-centered objectives for training. Use questions to introduce material. Include dynamic substructures (problems and solutions, cause and effect, and the like).

3. *Trial and error.* The practice and evaluation stages. Provide hands-on practice to reinforce learning and provide a means for evaluation.

4. *Association.* The preparation, presentation, and evaluation stages. Use questions to prepare learners and introduce material, repetition to reinforce learning, and practice sessions to provide a basis for evaluation.

5. *Multisensory input.* The presentation and practice stages. Use integrated Socratic Method and lecture approach with audio and visual aids in patterns of redundancy.

6. *One thing at a time.* The four-step method is applied by topic for discrete time periods. Following the "less is more" principle, guard against information overload. Use acronyms, numbers, simplified chunks of topics, and patterns of redundancy.

7. *Understanding.* The preparation, presentation, practice, and evaluation stages. Set clearly defined, specific training objectives, which specify the level of understanding and learning you will demand. Use questions to prepare the group for learning. Following the "less is more" principle, introduce material in sequences. Use repetition to reinforce learning.

8. *Practice.* The practice stage. Set action-oriented, trainee-centered objectives. Use repetition to reinforce learning. Provide hands-on practice, simulations, and so forth.

9. *Feedback.* The practice and evaluation stages. Use Socratic questions, explain corrections, analyze errors, and provide learning maps.

10. *Uniqueness.* The preparation stage. Use questions to bring out individual differences. Ventilate resistance. Engage the more advanced to help you work with those who need help. Use panels, projects, special assignments, and so forth.

leadership. For now, it is important to recognize that, despite the effectiveness of the Socratic Method, both approaches are usually necessary. In highly technical fields learners cannot know what has not been explained to them, though even with this type of training the more Socratic you can be, the better the learning. A blending of active participation (Socratic) with passive absorption of information (blank-slate) will likely constitute the presentation stage of your lesson. Therefore, plan the method(s) you will use to inform or lead your trainees to the learning you've defined in your objectives. You might use any of the following:

1. Socratic Method of posing questions and leading the group to reach their own conclusions.
2. Straight lecture (remember that the average adult attention span is less than 20 minutes—keep it short).
3. Participative lecture, wherein you create dialogue and perhaps physical activities as you go along.
4. Panel discussion, using the best informed of your learners.
5. Film, video, slides, or audiotapes.
6. Stories, games, and exercises to vary the presentation.
7. Demonstration or simulation to illustrate the practical application of concepts.

In using any of these, remember: less is more, one thing at a time, and association. Build bridges for their understanding to cross to new knowledge.

Practice

People learn by doing. All the instruction in the world will not lock in learning. Only practice makes learning happen. Consequently, to teach only content, no matter how skillfully, is to waste your time unless you also structure in practice. Hands-on experience is the best way to learn, so help them by creating chances to practice.

Every lesson must include time for practice. We are all pressured to complete training in as short a time as possible. But if you offer only content (which many public seminars do), you lessen your effectiveness, deprive your trainees of the opportunity to really learn, and fail to bring about the changes you have been hired to achieve. Without the practice stage training becomes a pleasant and interesting way to pass the time, but nothing more.

There are many ways to challenge your group to practice. Among them are:

Socratic reviews
Written exams
Oral tests
Role-playing
Problem-solving exercises
Case histories
Projects and assignments
Simulations
Hands-on practice sessions and practice under simulated conditions

All of these methods (detailed in Chapter 6) allow learners to practice what has just been taught. Whichever method you choose, carefully relate the activity to the skills. If you demand too little, you de-motivate and hinder learning. If you demand too much, you frustrate and discourage. If mastery of the skill is a requirement of the training, then more practice is needed. If, on the other hand, trainees are expected to perfect their skills in the field, then the practice phase should merely introduce the new skills and provide a chance to try them out.

Evaluation

Your objectives will have stated what level of learning is needed and how it will be evaluated. We will cover specific methods of evaluation in Chapter 6. Do recognize, however, that we are talking about evaluation, not grading. Evaluation is detailed feedback to the trainee to help him or her measure progress. Grading is largely an administrative and, secondly, a competitive instrument useful for screening people. Grading in the business world may be used for assessing training among fast-tracking executives or for selecting new employees. It is a legitimate function of some training; however, it is not essential to learning. Evaluation, however, is an integral part of learning. People must know how they are doing. Evaluation capitalizes on the Law of Effect by providing feedback, by fostering a nonthreatening climate in which error can occur, by addressing each learner individually, and by providing, in retrospect, a clear map of what has been learned. Evaluation is vital to all levels of understanding.

Evaluation is frequently not a separate step and is often integrated into the practice step. But it must be planned for, so it is included here as a separate step of lesson planning.

Some ways to create opportunities for evaluation are:

Socratic dialogue
Written or oral responses to projects

Tests (written or oral)
Problem-solving projects
Practice in simulated circumstances
Case histories
Role-playing and other performances
Hands-on practice sessions
On-the-job training
Personal counseling

The four parts to a lesson plan are integral. Once you have broken down the material you are going to teach into individual units of instruction (using the less is more principle to divide your subject into topical units), each unit should have all four steps. Create a preparation session, a presentation phase, practice session, and outline how you will evaluate each topical/instructional unit. If each step is complete you will be presenting your material in the most effective manner possible. It will be harder for your trainees to not learn than to learn.

Summary

This chapter was about planning an effective lesson. We began with the single most important step in training: writing the training objectives. It was pointed out that an objective is not so much a statement of desired results as a map of how to achieve them. It has four components: (1) it must describe what skills the trainees will be able to perform, (2) it must be specific in describing those skills and the conditions under which they are to be performed, (3) it must detail criteria to be met or specify how the trainees will be evaluated, and (4) it must be realistic.

Two types of objectives were discussed: cognitive and affective. Though affective learning is much harder to measure, the same format for objectives applies. The measure of performance, however, becomes more subjective.

Once you have defined your objectives, structure becomes more important than content. There are several ways of structuring learning. The way you choose will depend on who you are training, what your objectives are, and what it is you are teaching.

The basic structures are: (1) a funnel, (2) an inverted funnel, (3) a tunnel, and (4) a spool. These are given life by dynamic substructures, such as problem solution, cause and effect, logic, climax, topics, time, and space. The patterns of redundancy were discussed, including how to build such necessary repetition into your lessons. Timing, or when to teach your most important material, was explored within the concepts of primacy and ultimacy. We also looked at the less is more concept as a means of simplifying complex material.

We concluded the chapter with the four steps of a good lesson plan. You must prepare the trainees to learn, present the material, give them an opportunity to practice it, and provide evaluation (feedback) for them. With all of these elements of structure weighed and incorporated, and using the four-step method as your guide, you are ready to write your training program, which will be covered in Chapter 8.

CHAPTER 4

===

The Role of the Trainer

IN the early 1950s a psychologist, Stanley Milgram, carried out some startling experiments at Yale University.[1] He was interested in how people respond to authority. He wanted to know what conditions would incline people to be obedient. His results were quite disturbing.

A majority of the participants in Milgram's experiment (limited to men) inflicted what they thought was severe, possibly life-threatening pain on another man merely because they were told to do so by someone they believed to be an authority. These were volunteers who thought they were participating in a learning experiment. They were told to ask a series of questions of another person (who was, in reality, an actor pretending his responses). For every wrong answer, the volunteer was told to administer an increasingly severe electric shock. As the shocks became more intense, the actor's reaction was greater, until he begged not to continue. The investigator, a man in a white lab coat with no other sign of authority, calmly insisted that the volunteer continue. Sixty-two percent of the volunteers administered shocks up to the highest level possible, despite a warning sign on the equipment that clearly stated the top voltage was dangerous.

Milgram tried several variations on this experiment. In one such variation, 90 percent of the volunteers went all the way, despite warnings, beggings, and apparent agony of the man being given the shocks.

Milgram was very surprised. So was the rest of the psychological community, who had predicted fewer than 20 percent of the participants would even come close to going all the way. From his results Milgram drew some important conclusions that relate to training:

- People tend to concentrate on the narrow technical aspects of an assigned task. This is particularly true for unpleasant tasks. It is as if they simply put their ears back and do the job just to get it done, without worrying about its consequences. Many are even proud of the way they do unthinkable jobs. In other words, people tend to have a very narrow focus when obeying an authority.
- People believe that an authority is totally responsible for what happens. They place this trust (and the consequent blame, if it proves wrong) on that person alone. They abdicate their own sense of responsibility.
- People sense that whatever is institutional or formal is bigger than themselves. They obey someone as an authority representing that institution rather than as an individual.
- People are bound by three personal factors: (1) a sense of politeness or propriety (the right way to behave); (2) a sense of commitment (once they say they will do it, they have to keep their word; once they begin, it's too late to stop); and (3) a fear of open confrontation, especially with an authority figure.

All of these conditions are present in the training seminar! Like it or not, you are the authority figure representing the institution. This is so merely by your assuming the physical space of the leader whenever you are in the room. The power over people's tendency to obey is in your hands. Even if you don't feel comfortable about it or are opposed ideologically to such a role, the group of learners gives you this power. You must assume it; you have no choice.

In Chapter 2 it was explained how leadership arises naturally in any group. Because people perceive the start of a training session as a formal, institutional situation that involves some structured activity, all of their expectations demand an authority figure. That authority figure will tell them what to do, where to begin, what they will learn, how they will proceed, and so on. People need someone onto whom they can shift responsibility for the training. These conclusions are borne out by Milgram's findings. In an institutional situation, people choose someone to be the leader and to assume responsibility.

What other psychologists have discovered is that if no one assumes the authority, the group selects someone and gives the power to that person. If you do not assume the leadership role, someone else will and your training will be undermined.

We are not talking here of autocratic leadership. The point is that trainees come with built-in expectations to be taught, that is, to be told what to do and how to do it. If you fail to fulfill that expectation, you will be alienated from the group and will leave a vacuum to be filled by someone who has come to the session reluctantly or who shows great resistance. It is an invitation to mischief. I cannot stress enough how important, indeed vital, it is to accept the mantle of leadership from the very first moment on.

The Roles of Leadership

There are a number of ways for a trainer to assume the role of leader. This chapter is about how to accomplish that. To begin, consider the ten roles of a leader:

1. Setting the agenda and keeping track of time.
2. Maintaining training objectives.
3. Protecting the rights of all participants.
4. Listening.
5. Summarizing the material.
6. Reviewing.
7. Focusing the attention of the group.
8. Handling challenges to your authority.
9. Involving silent members.
10. Providing a modus operandi.

Let's examine the impact of each of these functions on your training.

Agenda

One of the responsibilities that trainees push onto the trainer is determining what will be covered and when. Time after time I've observed trainees in great discomfort while they wait for the trainer to call a break. Milgram's observations explain why they wait until they are desperate or until the trainer lets them go. It is your function as leader to set the agenda for learning and to conclude learning at appropriate times.

To assume leadership by setting an agenda, follow the full instructions and considerations discussed in Chapter 8. Write your training objectives, structure your lessons following the patterns described in Chapter 3, and use the four steps of preparation, presentation, practice, and evaluation. Also consider time; remember that attention spans are relatively short. Shift your methodology at least once an hour, more if need be. Whenever possible, schedule a practice session once an hour.

Make sure there are numerous, regular breaks. If you have a lengthy lecture or discussion session, plan on frequent short breaks. If you have a balanced presentation of discussion, lecture, practice session, and so forth, fewer breaks are necessary. You are in charge of the time and the topic.

Objectives

A good trainer keeps the course on track. Be on guard for both external and internal distractions. Outside distractions are the reason most good training rooms are windowless. Spectacular scenery can be very distracting. So can the activities of grounds personnel, animals, lovers, and passing traffic. If you have windows, arrange the seating so trainees face away from the action outside.

Internal distractions can be very frustrating, too. I once had to conduct a public seminar in a hotel room that remained below 40° F. Needless to say, learning was minimal. We had to take breaks every 15 minutes just to warm up. Of course the hotel finally provided a better room, but the damage was already done.

Poor seating, inadequate lighting, uncomfortable temperature, poor visibility, noise, interruptions, smoking, and so on, are all conditions you need to protect your trainees from in order to maintain a clear focus on the subject being taught. These issues are discussed further in Chapter 10. In this context, however, review the following list of potential distractions.

1. Seating — Is it comfortable?
2. Lighting — Is it dim? Is it too bright?
3. Temperature — Is the room too warm? Is it too cold?
4. Sightlines — Can everyone see you? Can they all see your charts and other visual aids?
5. Messages — Is there a system for handling them without interrupting the class?
6. Smoking — Can you set aside a section for smokers? Also, make rules about when and where smoking is allowed.
7. Breaks — Schedule at least one every 90 minutes.
8. Windows — Cover them, close blinds, or arrange seating to minimize distractions.

In addition to physical distractions, there are other ways your teaching objectives can be waylaid. Many times you will have garrulous participants who try to share too many, often irrelevant, tales. These tales take the group away from the main point. Curb these "asides" and bring the group back on track. You might get a participant who has a hidden personal agenda—someone who tries to challenge your leadership or distract the class with humor, practical jokes, or questions. Deal effectively and quickly with such people and get back to your objective. (Handling such participants is discussed in detail later in this chapter.)

When a discussion gets going, it's often hard to stop. But if the discussion sidetracks, you especially need to intervene and get things back on course. This is especially so when an argument develops between participants. To handle such an event, choose the most appropriate action, as follows:

1. Intervene aggressively by interrupting the discussion and preventing further debate (or comments).
2. Offer to discuss or solve the problem at the break.
3. Remind the participants, and everyone else, that everyone is there for the purpose of learning, not fighting.
4. Point out that, in the interests of everyone, it's time to go on with the lesson. This usually allows you to proceed because most people in a confrontation are happy to stop at any excuse that saves face.

Perhaps the single most common source of sidetracking is the trainer. All instructors like to illustrate their points with stories, jokes, and examples. If a point is particularly important, some will beat it to death. Whenever anyone asks a question (often an irrelevant one), they spring to answer it. None of these is good practice. A trainer needs self-discipline to maintain the training objective. When you find yourself running overtime, you probably are guilty of one of these sins.

There is in itself nothing wrong with using stories to illustrate points or answering questions when they come up. In fact, each is an important teaching tool. It is only when you overdo it by telling one story too many or making an irrelevant joke, or, in the interest of being perfectly clear, run a topic into the ground that they are detrimental. When you answer every question, no matter how irrelevant, you don't maintain your own objectives. Keep a constant check on yourself. Ask yourself every day if you are guilty of straying from your objectives. Ultimately, your trainees will thank you for it.

Fairness

When groups form, as described in Chapter 2, they reject those who don't agree with the group. Sometimes the excluded ones become scapegoats; sometimes they remain loners. Often the excluded ones are silent and go largely unnoticed. As leader of a training group, you must be fair to all. You must also remain equally accessible to all. The group has given you the power of justice, but if you abuse it, they will take it away and undermine your authority. Don't allow others to be used as scapegoats, don't tolerate abusive language, and don't let one person dominate the group to the exclusion of others. Be aware of the political climate so you can be responsive to the needs of each member. It is not fair to let either the majority or the minority control others.

Listening

Often you hear a leader say, "my door is always open." This means people can bring the leader their problems and he or she will listen. Good leadership listens to the group. Keep yourself open and attentive. Don't interrupt participants when they speak; let them have their say. If they are wrong, explain why. If they are right, go with them.

Unfortunately, listening is a difficult skill. Our minds race ahead of the speaker and fill with our own comments. If we say them, we interrupt the other person and are not listening anymore. Your mind is capable of processing information faster than others can speak, so you can easily be distracted from listening. To listen well you need to give your mind something to challenge it rather than let it drift off or plan retorts. Fortunately, there is a way that you can improve your listening ability (even the best listeners can improve); it is called *active listening*.

There are three steps to active listening:

1. As you listen, summarize in your mind what the other person is saying. It's like taking notes, but in your head. As the talk goes on, keep a running summary of it.
2. When you reach capacity—that is, when you begin to have difficulty remembering what the first point was—interrupt by saying something like, "So let me see if I understand you correctly. You're saying . . . ."
3. Feed your mental summary back to the speaker so you clear your mind to listen to his or her response.

When you practice active listening you gain several important things at the same time. First, you give your mind the necessary challenge to keep it focused. It will still want to wander, but having a specific task to perform makes it easier to keep it on track. Second, you remember what was said much better because you are experiencing it three times: you hear it, you structure it, and you repeat it. Third, you win friends. Most people are very flattered by the interruption because it tells them you are very

---

Improving Your Listening Skills

Active Listening

1. Mentally summarize what's being said.
2. At capacity (when you start to forget what's been said), interrupt by saying, "So if I understand you. . ." or "Let me see if I've got this straight. . . ."
3. Feed your summary back to the person speaking.

Advanced Active Listening

1. Mentally summarize what's being said.
2. Look for the essence, the core of what is meant.
3. When you have the essence, interrupt and ask a single question about this item.

---

interested in what they are saying and that you want to make sure you get it right. Fourth, the method practically eliminates all misunderstanding. It is the perfect feedback loop. If you have not understood correctly, the speaker will say so. If you have, there is no problem.

Practice active listening to hone your skills and make yourself a truly fine listener. It only happens if you practice, however. Active listening is not natural, and you may find it quite difficult at first. Persevere; it pays off when you master it.

Once you have mastered the basic form of active listening, you can move on to my extended technique. When someone is speaking, continue to summarize what's being said but don't feed it back. Instead, look for the essence — the core — of what's being said. Most people speak around a subject, in phrases, stumbles, and spurts. They have things to say, but unless they have thought them out ahead, they seldom express them directly. Look for the essence, the heart, of the matter.

When you've targeted it, interrupt the speaker, or step into a pause, and ask a single question about that essential point. When you do this, the speaker will light up. It clarifies that person's thinking and makes him or her feel successful in communicating. The speaker sees you as a great listener, which indeed you will be when you've mastered this advanced active listening skill.

Summarizing

People like to perceive things in relation to other, usually larger, things. So they mark off the halfway point on a journey or for a task. They look at things as half empty (or half full), half over, and so on. At certain points in your instruction you need to stop and show how far you've come. Do this by summarizing what's been covered so far. It gives the trainees a feeling of progress. In effect, you are setting up plateaus so learners can look back and see where they've been. These summaries provide a coherence to the learning, showing how each part connects and how each is a step in the progress toward the goal.

Reviewing

Reviewing material and summarizing it are rather closely related in concept but require quite different skills. Reviewing is also looking back, but in much more depth. It is not just a "see where we've come" device; it also provides measurable feedback that says "see what we've learned." Reviewing prepares learners for the next lesson by refreshing their understanding of prior material. You can review in several ways: (1) with quizzes and tests, (2) by asking questions that invite discussion, (3) by walking through the topics covered, and (4) by using a combination of these methods.

My favorite type of review is to ask the group, "What stands out in your memory from what we covered this morning (or yesterday, or whenever)?" This gets them to review the material in their own minds, causes each to be engaged in activity, saves my having to repeat myself, and allows me to add to or clarify any points that appear to need it.

Focusing

As leader, you must focus the attention of the group. Of course, you do so by referring to your agenda, which will highlight the topics, and by using visual aids to hold the group's attention. Group discussions, however, must be orchestrated to be effective learning devices. When you begin a discussion, remain as the moderator and control the speakers. If you have a guest speaker, gently take back control of the group when the speaker is finished by leading a question and answer period. For example, watch a presidential news conference to see how a leader can control the focus of a discussion. As leader of a training group, you tell them who to listen to when you select who is to speak. This is how you facilitate group discussion without losing control.

Challenges

One of your crucial tasks as leader is to maintain yourself as such in the eyes of the group. They trust you to perform the functions we've already discussed, and they look up to you as long as you handle those functions adequately. When your leadership is challenged, whether intentionally or not, you *must* meet that challenge to maintain your leadership. If you fail, the group will take away your leadership and bestow it on one of its members. Once again, you have no choice. By beginning the course, you put on the mantle of leadership. It is given to you, as we saw with the Milgram experiment, when you perform any or all of the functions of leadership. And you need to have it to train. But, you are also expected to defend that leadership role against all comers. You can't explain or rationalize the confrontation away. It must be responded to strongly and confidently.

The challenge may result from a participant's genuine doubt or disagreement, or it may be the need of a high-status participant to be recognized, or it can be a personal (usually irrelevant) attack. Perhaps the person feels he or she knows more about the subject than you do (or wants the group to think he or she does). Maybe the challenger is opposed to training, or is hoping to be dismissed by antagonizing all authority figures and wasting other workers' time. Whatever the reasons, you must deal with the problem.

Greet the challenge openly. Smile warmly, if possible. Walk toward the challenger. Never walk away or stand behind a desk, lectern, or projector. Smile warmly and, by moving in, tell the rest of the group that you are confident and in charge. It signals them to relax.

Begin to ventilate the resistance. Ask why, then ask for clarification, for details. Encourage the person to explain his or her position. If the issue is a genuine one, that quickly becomes apparent and you can use it as a learning situation, perhaps by drawing the group into the discussion or by providing a demonstration. If the challenger is a high-status participant, allow that person the floor for a moment to satisfy his or her need for recognition.

If the challenger becomes a self-proclaimed authority by questioning your agenda, when you ventilate his or her challenge through questions, it will quickly become apparent to the entire group that the person is alone, seeking some personal involvement. The group will side with you and join you in responding to the individual. If the challenger's complaint makes sense, or the person really does speak for the group, you will still command their respect by being open to the challenge. Respond to it warmly and move in while asking questions to clarify.

This is strong leadership behavior. It is also nonconfrontational. The troublemaker wins if you respond defensively or in an authoritarian manner. He or she will have succeeded in disrupting the class. You lose the group even if you win the battle. By responding openly with questions, you put the challenger on the defensive and force an explanation. And you win, no matter what explanation is given.

In rare instances when someone pushes for a confrontation, continue to smile, question, and move in. If need be, stand right next to the individual. If you must, break eye contact by walking behind the difficult participant. If the person responds by rising from the chair and turning around to face you (never in my experience, but theoretically possible), again break eye contact by turning away and walking back to the front of the room. This way you are using both your power as leader and the increased personal space that power gives you to intimidate the obstreperous individual. Of course, it is a technique to use only on someone who is trying to intimidate or confront you. One final word of caution, however. This is a culturally biased response. People of different cultures will respond differently to this kind of pressure. If you train the foreign born, don't use the technique of closing in unless you know the likely response in that culture.

As soon as you see the challenger back down — that is, start to explain and cooperate — stop moving in. Continue to smile and ask questions. When you can feel the tension ebb, move back away toward the front of the room to lessen confrontation. If the person presses, move in again. When the individual (and others in the room) begin to relax, back away, and remove the pressure.

Silent Members

There are at least two reasons for participants to remain silent: either they are shy and are afraid to speak, or are resistors who aren't going to openly disrupt the class. The first type you should encourage to participate so they will share with others and learn more. The second type may be fighting what you're teaching, influencing others behind your back. They can hurt you by undermining not only your authority but also what you've taught. Your problem is that you'll never know which type the silent ones are unless you ask. It's part of your job as leader.

Modus Operandi

As just discussed, a leader must be assertive. This is not a matter of choice. People expect leaders to be decisive and authoritative. How would you respond to an indecisive, nonassertive surgeon or dentist? Would you fly with an airline pilot who was unsure about which way to go? We want to feel we are in good hands.

On two occasions I was conducting seminars when a fire broke out, once in the room below and once in the room next door. On both occasions I had trained firefighters in the seminars, though I didn't know it until later. In both situations, the classes looked to me to decide what to do and how to do it. Afterwards, the firefighters told me that they would have spoken up had I made a mistake or ignored the alarms. Although they were in a position to know what to do, even they expected their leader to show the way.

As a trainer you must behave assertively:

1. Be decisive. Don't stew over which way to go, just do it.
2. Never apologize. When you are wrong, simply correct yourself and move on (as television news reporters do). People don't need or want excuses. This doesn't mean, however, that you should be rude. Common courtesy is expected. When you step on someone's toe, apologize. When you leave out part of a lesson, either ignore it or fit it in elsewhere, for example, when you review that section.
3. Avoid confrontation. The Socratic Method (described fully in Chapter 3) and the "question reflex" (discussed next in this chapter) allow you to hold firm to a point without creating extremes on the issue. Don't allow participants to become your enemies, yet be prepared to show why what you teach is true.
4. Move in and solve problems as soon as they become apparent. Most problems only get bigger the longer they last.

Question and Answer Skills

Asking questions can be a means of establishing authority, fulfilling leadership functions, and ensuring effective learning. In fact, asking questions is probably the most subtle power you have for controlling people. The person who asks questions controls the conversation.

Often we become so engrossed in our own thoughts and desires that we spend our conversation time thinking of what we want to say rather than listening to the other person. Yet if we could discipline our minds to ask questions instead, we could lead any conversation to wherever we wanted it because the other person would still be wrapped up in thinking what he or she wanted to say next. This is particularly true in training. By probing with questions, you challenge learners to think for themselves. If their answers are wrong, you can ask them why or probe further. When learners discover an answer for themselves, they really have learned it because it is their answer. If you have to tell them, it is your answer and will be theirs only if you have built a solid conceptual bridge for them to cross.

One of the rights you have as a trainer is to ask questions and expect answers. This is why question-asking is such a powerful tool. It challenges and avoids confrontation at the same time.

Types of Questions

There are six types of questions you can use in training: closed-ended, open-ended, overhead, direct, relay, and return.[2]

Closed-Ended Questions

Closed-ended questions are by far the most common in our society. A closed-ended question demands a specific, often detailed, answer. Typical questions are: "What is your name?" "What is the next step in this procedure?" "Can you name three relevant facts?" "Where can this information be used?" Sometimes the answer can be just a yes or no, but always a specific answer is demanded.

Most of us feel interrogated if asked a series of closed-ended questions. We resent being probed at and pried into, so we are reluctant to answer. Yet when I ask trainees at all levels of authority and in all types of businesses to write a series of questions they normally ask their customers, subordinates, co-workers, or bosses, 70 percent of their questions are consistently closed-ended. Most people are locked into closed-ended thinking.

Perhaps the closed-ended question is so prevalent because our system of education presents subjects in closed-ended, usually chronological arrangements. Or perhaps it is because our mass media always ask for and supply simple, direct, immediate, closed-ended solutions to problems. Maybe it is our political structures, which forever put closed-ended Band-Aids on open-ended problems. Whatever the reasons, we are firmly entrenched in closed-ended thinking patterns. At the end of this discussion of question types are some tips to help you break the closed-ended question habit.

The principal uses for closed-ended questions are to:

1. Review previously covered material.
2. Force a group or individual to come up with a specific solution to a problem (as in math).
3. Test for learning, understanding, or knowledge; for evaluation.
4. Control by interrogation; for example, to pin a self-proclaimed authority down to specifics.
5. Get back to the point when a discussion has gone astray.
6. Organize a disorganized thinker.
7. Encourage a shy participant to respond when he or she knows the answer.

Open-Ended Questions

The direct opposite of a closed-ended question is an open-ended one. This type encourages discussion, and allows a variety of responses. It is, therefore, a more low-pressure question. It still demands an answer but with much less pushiness. People don't feel interrogated because they can talk freely and say what they please. Open-ended questions are low-keyed and, when asked warmly and with interest, are an invitation to talk. Of course they demand listening skills of the trainer. Later on, there are tips on how to enhance your open-ended question skills.

The principal uses of open-ended questions are to:

1. Foster discussion.
2. Draw out opinions and feelings rather than only facts.
3. Create an open climate in which trainees don't have to be right.
4. Begin and encourage the debriefing of a self-proclaimed authority.
5. Provide a strong but nonthreatening response to challenges.
6. Find out what trainees know.

Good questioning technique is a blend of these two question types. As a rule, use closed-ended questions to speed up, narrow down, and zero in on a topic under discussion. Use open-ended questions to explore, evaluate, widen, and slow down a discussion.

Overhead Questions

An overhead question can be either open- or closed-ended. It is a question asked of the group at large and anyone can answer. The value of overhead questions is that they put pressure on everyone to think of an answer. The questions engage the group and get each member involved mentally, if not vocally.

Use overhead questions to:

1. Open a discussion.
2. Maintain a discussion.
3. Introduce a new topic or segment.
4. Open up the floor and give each participant an opportunity to comment.
5. Draw several comments or opinions on a given topic.

Direct Questions

The opposite of an overhead question is a direct question. This is simply the same open- or closed-ended question with a name tacked onto it, either at the beginning or the end. It is called "direct" because you designate the answerer. The drawback is that it takes everyone else off the hook. They can all say, "Thank goodness I don't have to answer that!" Such a drawback is countered by asking a number of direct questions of several different people until everyone realizes that sooner or later you're going to get to him or her. Then each person will think and talk freely.

The advantage of direct questions is that they provide flexibility. If you ask an overhead question that no one answers, you can tag a name on it and easily turn it into a direct question. What you must *never* do is answer a question you have asked, yourself. To do so signals to the group that they can stop thinking for the rest of the course. If you tag a name onto an overhead question and that person can't answer it, you can direct it to others until someone ventures an answer and the discussion is begun.

Use direct questions to:

1. Open a discussion.
2. Call on an individual for an answer you know he or she has.
3. Involve a silent participant.
4. Avoid an over-talkative or over-responsive participant who answers every overhead question.
5. Provide recognition or status to an inner-group leader or knowledgeable participant.
6. Bring a talker or drifter back into the discussion.

The direct question is more assertive than the overhead. Use both as needed, but adjust the balance to suit the group you are instructing. A more resistant group may require more direct questions at first; a more cooperative group may open up right away with overhead questions. Become comfortable with both formats, and use either as you need it.

Relay Questions

Relay questions are like the child's game of hot potato. They are a tool for when you do not want to answer a question that is asked of you. Simply relay it to someone else by saying, "_____, what do you think?" Or "Who can answer _____'s question?" This lets you off the hook, but don't use it to cover up if you don't know the answer. Doing that will eventually trip you up and, in any event, it undermines your authority.

Relay questions allow you to spread responsibility for answers across the entire group and give you an added opportunity to focus the learning. People expect their teachers to know the answers, but they come to rely on that to the point of not thinking for themselves and beginning to treat the trainer as an easy resource. Relaying questions is an important educational tool because it lets you step away and forces the group to think and use its own resources.

Use a relay format to:

1. Get others involved in the discussion.
2. Solicit opinions other than your own.
3. Engage a knowledgeable participant.
4. Draw in a talker or drifter.
5. Avoid committing yourself to an answer.

Return Questions

Return questions are those you re-ask of people who have asked them. They are a gentle reproof to tell those people you feel they are capable of answering them themselves and that they should rethink their questions. Of course the return question loses gentility if you return it harshly. Then it becomes disciplinary, perceived as unfair by the rest of the group. Always return a question without rancor, either warmly or, at the very least, neutrally.

Use a return question to:

1. Encourage the questioner to think for himself or herself.
2. Avoid giving your own opinion when you feel it's important to withold it.
3. Call the bluff of someone who is challenging you.
4. Allow someone who really only wants a platform to have one.

In this last instance, there are people who know the answers to their questions and who ask them anyway, merely to open the subject so that they may expound upon it. When you answer such a question, you put these people in control to lead the discussion wherever they want. If you return the question to them, you maintain control, they still have their say, but you can end the matter much more easily.

A balance of question types should be your goal. When originating a discussion, draw information and opinion from the group. To gain a balance of participants, use overhead, direct, and relay questions. To control the kind of information you get, use open-ended questions to ask why and get examples, then use closed-ended questions to pin down the specifics.

Developing Your Questioning Abilities

As has been pointed out, your ability to ask questions is your principal tool for maintaining leadership of the group and controlling your training seminars. Every trainer should become skilled, indeed be an expert, in this crucial area. Here are two techniques that will help you increase your expertise at asking questions.

Break the Closed-Ended Habit

The goal should be to become ambidextrous, so to speak, with different question types. Most of us are locked into the closed-ended format. These questions are easier for us to think of. By becoming just as skilled at forming open-ended questions you will free yourself of that bias and comfortably choose whichever question form suits your objectives in any situation.

Bring a tape recorder to your next training session. Insert a one-hour tape and have a colleague turn it on (or do it yourself) as you begin a discussion. Record until the tape runs out. Then listen to the tape and write down every question you asked. Underline the closed-ended ones. For every closed-ended question, figure out a way to ask the same thing in an open-ended format. Write down the new question. Repeat these steps until asking open-ended questions is second nature.

Remember, there is nothing inherently better about an open-ended question. This exercise merely brings your skill in forming open-ended questions on a par with your "more natural" habit of making closed-ended questions.

Play the Question Game

The question game is not particularly fun. It is a skills practice game that is not in any way unpleasant, but enjoyment is incidental to the purpose of the game. Here's how to play:

Whenever you are with someone — anyone at all — try to see how long you can keep the person talking without your saying anything except questions. If you have to answer a question yourself, or respond with anything other than a question, your time has run out. You have to start over again. Play the game every chance you get. It is particularly effective (and challenging) with hotel desk clerks, waiters and waitresses, cab drivers, and people who sit next to you on an airplane. Use your advanced active listening skills (discussed earlier in this chapter) to encourage them to speak.

What you'll learn from this game is what I call the "question reflex."

Improving Your Question-Asking Skills

1. Record one of your training sessions for at least one hour.
2. Play back the recording and write down every question you asked.
3. Underline every closed-ended question.
4. Rephrase every closed-ended question in an open-ended format.
5. Repeat as necessary.
6. Play the question game at every opportunity.

You become so adept at asking questions that whenever anything happens, your first reaction is to ask a question. If you are challenged, instead of rising to that challenge, you will deflate it with a question. When a trainee errs, instead of becoming impatient, you'll respond with a question. When others defeat your efforts at making a change, instead of an angry outburst, you'll ask a question. This technique gives you power. Remember, the person who asks questions controls the conversation. The question game reinforces the question reflex, which in turn gives you leverage — and, therefore, control and leadership — in every situation.

You can practice the question game with anyone. They won't mind; in fact, they will appreciate it. A college professor I know is the finest question-asker I've encountered. His name is Neil, and Neil plays this game all the time. I've asked many of his students and colleagues why they like to talk to Neil. The answer is always the same, "Because he is such a great conversationalist!"

Giving Good Answers

We've been discussing how to ask questions, but do you know how to answer them? If you create a climate for the open exchange of ideas, you will be asked questions almost as often as you ask them yourself. Here are five steps to follow in responding to a question:

1. Listen. Use your active listening techniques to understand both what is *said* and what is *meant.*
2. Acknowledge the question. Show that you understand what has been asked. Use your active listening skills here, too.
3. Ask for clarification, but *Only* if you need it.
4. Answer the question. Be brief and to the point.
5. Verify that the question poser is satisfied. Check with the person to agree that you've addressed the point to his or her satisfaction.

In following these steps be careful not to disparage in any way the person who has asked the question. Also, don't try to answer a question you can't. Say you can't, but that you will get the answer and have it by a specific time. Then do so!

It is also important that you don't change the subject or wander far afield to answer the question. If you must explain other material first, tell the questioner what you are doing and then relate that material back to your answer. Lastly, don't treat two questions as one. Answer each separately, otherwise you might confuse rather than clarify.

When listening to and acknowledging the question, as well as asking for clarification if necessary, there are several possible responses you can use. For example, you can give a neutral response while encouraging feedback such as, "I see" or "That's interesting." This response is used to great effect by psychoanalysts. It conveys your interest, yet keeps the questioner talking. Sometimes when you do this the person will answer his or her own question.

Another possible response is to probe, or gather more information. Challenge the questioner's thinking by making him or her explore other facets of the question. Usually this response involves asking *who, what, when, why,* and *where* questions. In effect you are answering the question by asking another question that causes the person to look more closely at the original question.

A third response is to restate the question. A part of active listening technique, this is the simplest and surest way to indicate that you are listening and have understood the question. While restating the question, you can reflect on how the questioner feels. It requires you to use the advanced active listening technique to help the person clarify his or her thinking attitudes. Lastly, you can summarize the question. This is the final step in active listening. It is not necessarily either restating or reflecting on the question but rather is a consideration of, or perspective on, what was said.

Once you have listened to and clarified the question, you can move on to answering it and verifying that you have addressed it sufficiently. With practice you can develop a very smooth and professional manner of asking and responding to questions.

Nonverbal Behavior

Up until now we've been discussing various aspects of the trainer's role that involve verbal communication. But a trainer communicates in other ways as well. Now we take a look at nonverbal communication.

Projecting a Positive Image

1. Move briskly. Choreograph your opening moves, if need be. Enter the room from the rear and stride to the front.
2. Stand firm and erect. Don't hide behind lecterns or tables.
3. Smile — and mean it.
4. Maintain eye contact with the group.
5. Greet the trainees in an enthusiastic tone of voice — demand the same in response.
6. Give the group a task to perform right away.
7. Walk around the room — take possession of your space.
8. Establish credibility at the beginning.
9. Demonstrate identification with group early on.

There are various kinds of nonverbal behavior. For our purposes, we will define nonverbal behavior loosely to include kinesic, proxemic, vocal, and cultural behaviors, as well as habits of thought and expression. Each exerts a different degree of control and creates a different impression. Most important, each makes a strong contribution to fulfilling your leadership role. The four basic types of nonverbal behavior are:

1. Body language, or kinesics
2. The use of vertical and horizontal space, or proxemics
3. Vocal tone and implications of key words
4. Dress; you are what you wear

Kinesics

The first, and still most detailed, work on the meanings of gestures, body positions, facial expressions, and so forth was done by social scientist Ray L. Birdwhistell, who gave these behaviors the name *kinesics*. His studies have pointed out that we convey a great deal of unspoken information to each other by the way we stand, move, smile, and so on. Birdwhistell has been trying, with little success, to formulate a complete language of gestures and their meanings.[3]

Psychiatrist Paul Watzlawick has theorized that all communication consists of two different types of messages: the content of what we are saying and the relationship we want to have with those to whom we are speaking.[4] Watzlawick believes the latter to be the more important one. In fact, if the relationship is not mutually agreed upon, no content will be exchanged. Another way of saying this is that until both parties accept their respective roles in a conversation, neither pays attention to what is being said. Instead, each jockeys for position in a relationship struggle.

This is why it is so important for the trainer to respond to any leadership challenge immediately and assertively. As long as the relationship of learners and trainers is unsettled—as it is when you are challenged—no learning will take place.

Building on this concept, psychologist Albert Mehrabian has observed that there are three basic relationship messages we look for when speaking with another person.[5] We instantly measure the person for (1) the degree of general involvement (that is, what emotional state the person is in; is he or she enthusiastic? depressed? neutral? sad?), (2) the person's degree of liking or disliking of us, and (3) the degree of dominance or submissiveness the person feels toward us.

These messages are read in the tone of voice, the rate of speech, animation in the face, expression in the eyes and mouth, body posture, and general physical animation. Mehrabian's point is that we learn to read these messages in early childhood, and continue to do so, unaware that we are responding on this level. Within the first 60 seconds of your training session, your trainees, without realizing, will measure you and respond in accordance with the kinesic messages you give them. Don't throw those 60 seconds away. Accept your role as leader, and the group will relax, and be ready to learn, because it will feel it is in good hands.

The nonverbal messages you give should all be high. Figure 4-1 shows involvement on a scale of from one to ten. You should be on the up end of the scale—enthusiastic, but not manic. Figure 4-2 illustrates the degree of liking you should project. Again, you should be on the upper end of the scale—liking, but not loving. People learn better when they feel an instructor cares about them. Lastly, Figure 4-3 gives the range for dominance over the training group. This time you should be even higher up on the scale. People must feel that you are in control—that you are a leader they can trust—not bossy, but firm and assertive.

comatose   1 2 3 4 5 [6 7] 8 9 10   hysterical

Figure 4-1.   Degree of involvement.

hatred   1 2 3 4 5 [6 7] 8 9 10   adoration

Figure 4-2.   Degree of liking.

submissive   1 2 3 4 5 6 [7 8] 9 10   authoritarian

Figure 4-3.   Degree of dominance.

As just noted, your group of trainees can size you up in the first 60 seconds. Here are some ways to control the initial relationship messages they receive:

1. Move briskly. If need be, plan a series of movements; for example, plan to enter the room from the rear and walk to the front. Move to a chalkboard or flip chart and back, and so on.
2. Stand firm and erect in front of the lectern or table. Don't hide behind furniture or objects.
3. Smile — and mean it. Be warm and friendly. Remember that negative first impressions that go against you can become sources of resistance.
4. Maintain eye contact with members of the group.
5. Greet the class with an enthusiastic note in your voice. The way you say "good morning" can make a difference. I make certain I say it loud and strong and insist on a similar response.
6. Gain a commitment from them. This is why I insist on a response to my greeting. It gives a strong message of dominance, involvement, and desire for involvement from them.
7. Assign a task such as filling out name tags, organizing their workbooks, changing the seating arrangement, breaking into discussion groups, and so forth. This not only sends a message that you are in command, but if you are nervous, it takes attention off you and allows you to read their nonverbal behavior for the three Mehrabian relationship messages.
8. Walk around the room, either while they work or as you introduce the course. Take possession of the room.
9. Establish your authority and knowledge of the material (more about this later).

In addition to the initial impression, you can use Mehrabian's relationship messages for several other circumstances. When you deal with a challenger, your smile, your move closer, and your request for an explanation send positive messages. It is hard to resist someone who appears to like you and is enthusiastic about your challenge, and yet who moves assertively closer and closer toward you. Likewise, when you seek to involve silent members you are saying you care. When you handle questions well, you are re-affirming your relationship messages. When you go out of your way to protect a student's rights in the class, you are also filling your leadership role with positive messages. This is why you must be courteous but never apologize for errors.

Proxemics

Derived from the same root as *proximity*, proxemics is the study of our use of space. It covers everything from positioning offices in a building to choosing the best place to sit on a crowded beach. Elements of proxemics include room arrangements, but that is covered in Chapter 10. At this point, we limit the application to a trainer's personal use of space.

In our culture, as in most others, leadership assumes and is awarded more space. According to anthropologist Edward T. Hall, we create invisible boundaries that come into play in varying circumstances.[6] North Americans regard proximities of up to about 1 1/2 feet as intimate. In normal circumstances, we allow only those we care about to be so close. On public transportation or in other crowded situations, of course, we break down this barrier but often feel intense discomfort at doing so. This is an acquired characteristic; children do not show this trait because they have not yet learned the rules.

In contrast, the space from 1 1/2 to 4 feet from us we regard as casual personal space. This is our normal interaction space, and people will sit or stand to talk to each other about this distance from one another. A space of 2 1/2 feet is the normal distance for conversation, but any position within the casual space is still regarded as comfortable. When these rules aren't followed, we become uncomfortable, as we would in a crowded restaurant where tables are too close together.

The distance that concerns us most as trainers is the next one: areas of 4 to 12 feet. This is formal social distance, and it is the distance we sit across the desk from another person. Most important, it is the distance in the formal training seminar that we maintain between ourselves and our nearest trainees. If you move closer, you create discomfort. It is interpreted as either an invitation to greater intimacy or an authoritative encroachment on a trainee's personal space. This is also why moving in toward a challenger is assertive behavior and why moving very close to one is a powerful exertion of authority.

Edward Hall's fourth distance is what he calls public distance, which is any area over 12 feet. With large groups, a trainer uses this distance as well, in much the same way as with formal social distance.

Coupled with this sense of space distinctions is a culturally-defined sense of territory. (Incidentally, I use the word *cultural* with considerable emphasis. These rules all vary from culture to culture. All cultures have unwritten, unspoken rules of behavior but the boundaries and responses to violations vary considerably. If you train non-North Americans, discover the limits of and rules for their space barriers.) In our North American culture, we stake out territories and then set up barriers within and around them. This is why trainees usually return to the same seat day after day and feel uncomfortable if someone else takes it. In setting up our own space, we leave others what we perceive as fair space for them. The front of the room usually fills up last. If the participants perceive the training as a public event to which they are not yet committed, they may distance themselves by sitting more than 12 feet from the instructor. If they perceive it as a formal, businesslike activity, some will sit closer but no nearer than 4 feet. No one normally sits closer than 4 feet from the trainer because training is not regarded as casual social intercourse or intimate communication.

In our culture, leaders are always given more space. Use your space. If you wish to give an impression of strong leadership, walk around the room. Take it all. At the very least, use all of the space in front of you. Fill the space as the group allows, but take more if you need it. Most people are unaware of space rules, so you can use these rules to control without creating friction. Don't hide behind lecterns, desks, or tables. These items are symbols of power but they are passive and far less effective than your personal use of space.

Vertical space is important, too. In our society height lends authority. Judges sit on raised benches, traditional stages are raised above eye level, top floors are usually reserved for senior executives. No one is allowed to sit until the king or queen sits. Many seminar rooms have formal platforms at one end. Therefore, you stand while they sit. If they are standing, you can sit, and so on.

As already mentioned, moving forward while standing is a very authoritative action. In contrast, moving backward or sitting on the same plane decreases your authority. If you want to draw a shy participant into the discussion, back away while asking a question.

One final word on the use of space. As said before, space is a powerful element because most trainees are completely unaware of how you use it. But use space with care. If you are large or tall and have a strong voice, you may never need to use space to control the group. But if you are short, are younger than your trainees, or are a female in a male-dominated group, you will find space a great help in maintaining your credibility and authority.

Vocal Tone and Implications

Throughout this chapter I have used the word *control* in reference to your trainees. Has my use of that word bothered you? Does it make me sound paranoid? Would it have been better if I'd used the word *influence* instead? Would you feel the same way if I'd used *manipulate*?

If you are like most managers and trainers I have worked with, you'll probably say *control* is okay though a bit strong, *influence* is certainly acceptable, but *manipulate* is offensive. Yet whichever word I choose, the techniques of leadership in no way change. It is only your perception of those techniques that differs, and that perception is shaped largely by the implied meanings behind the words I choose to describe the techniques.

All words have implications, even prepositions. One of the most powerful forms of control over a group is a knowledge of the implications words have. In a recent planning session, a client was concerned that trainees might perceive the proposed training program as punitive and resent being singled out. I suggested two concurrent remedies.

- The training should be advertised in-house as part of an ongoing program to change the customer service image of the entire organization. This seminar would be for one segment of the company population—for example, clerical workers—while other seminars would be for other workers and management.
- The purpose of the training should be stated as a service that management was giving trainees to help them make their jobs easier for them.

Indeed, both of these statements were true. The fact that management was dissatisfied with the performance of these workers and wanted it improved was also true but immaterial. By describing the training as a small part of a larger policy and by showing how it would benefit them, the management would nullify resistance. No one felt singled out. The training was perceived as a positive rather than a punitive event, and the trainees came to the sessions prepared to learn.

Understand that this is not a recommendation for lying or using underhanded tactics. You are choosing words to shape the perceptions of those who hear them. It is to your advantage (and the trainees' advantage) to select words that create positive perceptions. But do this carefully and honestly. People recognize euphemisms. Words with positive implications help you avoid resistance that might come from misinformation and incorrect interpretations. They can help motivate learners, and be an important tool in creating a positive learning environment.

The figures of speech you use also have implications. Dr. Beverly Hyman performed a fascinating study in 1980 that investigated what metaphors people use and how these metaphors control their thinking.[7] She asked a number of teachers and trainers to talk about their jobs and to describe their goals and work. She recorded the conversations, then reviewed the recordings and wrote down all the nouns, adverbs, adjectives, and verbs. She wanted to see if there were any consistent patterns. There were, and they were very clear. Slightly more than half the conversations were filled with words and phrases like *held in, controlled, discipline, teach a lesson, hands are tied, shut up, marking time, show them,* and so on. They used words quite suitable for describing life in a prison rather than a school. Fortunately, the other group—almost half the teachers surveyed —used words and phrases like *take them, travel to, open up to, visit, view,* and other travel terms.

As the meanings behind the words illustrate, one group subconsciously saw itself as prisoners, the other as travelers. Which would you rather have teaching you? More to the point, which way would you have your trainees perceive you? When you record yourself, listen to the metaphors you use. If you find it hard to discover them, tape a lesson and write down all of the verbs, adverbs, nouns, and adjectives you use and look for patterns. If they are in any way negative, change them.

Finally, words set the tone for your training sessions. Occasionally I have been accused of using $2 words. I'm glad. That's the tone I've chosen. It is challenging to my trainees rather than boring. I've had trainers who make everything so elementary that I felt as if I were in first grade. In choosing an appropriate level of language, consider the following:

1. The educational level of your trainees.
2. Any technical vocabulary involved with the subject.
3. The sex of the trainees (especially important if it is different from yours).
4. The objectives of the training program.
5. Your personal objectives in the program.
6. The linguistic norms of the region and of the trainees.
7. The group's attitude toward profanity (mild or gross).
8. The group's attitude toward sexist language.

Dress

Another important nonverbal factor that helps set the tone for your training session is the way you dress. Remember, first impressions are strong determiners of how a group will respond. How you look creates a strong first impression. This is not a book about dress; there are many excellent ones, including John T. Molloy's *Dress for Success.* There are, however, some considerations that impact on trainers especially.

Always dress to suit the group you are training. An $800 suit looks out of place among bank tellers or field workers. On the other hand, an $89 polyester special will create a strong negative impression among senior managers. Dress well for the group but not flashy. Estimate the cost for clothing in that group and wear something in its middle range.

Be conservative. Estimate the degree of stylishness in the group and wear clothes that tend toward the quieter end. This choice gains you credibility. If you need more authority, wear a dark blue or a dark pin-striped three-piece suit (men need to make sure the vest covers the belt line, all day long). If you want credibility without extra power, wear a gray or light pinstriped two- or three-piece suit. If you want a warm reception and have no need for power, wear a brown or dark green suit. These color and style considerations currently apply to women as well as to men.

Your shoes must be comfortable, yet dressy. Avoid suede and other soft looks (such as sneakers) unless you are training in a casual environment or have trainees who expect that. High heels are very uncomfortable to wear all day.

Wear clothes that fit well. Your trainees will be looking at you for a number of hours. Don't distract them with bagginess or bulges. Also, be sure everything you wear looks neat and well cared for. If you appear sloppy (with wrinkled shirts or blouses, undone or missing buttons, worn-down heels, and so on), you lose respect.

Suits are best; slacks, or skirts for women, and a blazer are second best. Dresses or slacks for women are not as good as skirts or suits with skirts. The jacket button should always be fastened at the beginning of each session. This applies for men but is particularly effective for women, too. It is also proper over a vest.

Jewelry distracts, so keep it to a minimum. This is particularly true for long necklaces or earrings. Clear all pockets of jingling change, distracting toys (for example, a pocket knife, lighter, or watch) and eliminate unsightly bulges.

Hair hides the face. Women should pin hair away from their face for training. Men should either shave off beards or mustaches or trim them back so they don't hide part of the face.

Lastly, have someone check you just before beginning class for any open zippers, showing slips, dandruff on your shoulder, and so on.

Styles do change. Those women who broke into the boardrooms in the 1970s and 1980s are reported to be easing the strictures of feminine executive fashion. Perhaps the rules I've listed will eventually ease for all women, but for the present, high fashion has not filtered down to the training room. Conservatism is still the rule.

Establishing Your Credibility

There is one final aspect of personal training skills yet to be explored. As emphasized before, trainees will evaluate you within the first 60 seconds of your first session. If they are unsure, they'll hold off judgment for a while but those first moments will remain crucial in their ultimate decision. Leadership skills can convey a strong, most necessary message, but there are two other messages they will be looking for. Have you been where they've been? Do you know what you're talking about?

The first of these questions is referred to as identification. Can they identify with you? Are you one of them? The second is credibility. Are you knowledgeable? Can they trust you to be right? You will always be on trial in these two areas. If you can establish your credibility early, your leadership will be unquestioned and you will set the stage for learning.

You must get the relationship issue settled right off the bat. Use what they already know and what they want to know (see Chapter 2) as a starting point for your preparation stage (see Chapter 3, for details). As an alternative, begin with a case history or a critical incident from their experience. Ask them for their input, and base your course on that. I know a trainer whose courses consist solely of working through the problems that were brought out at the beginning of the seminar.

Build mental bridges for them from the known to the unknown. By starting where they are you gain credibility. Also, if you've been where they are, say so. Illustrate with examples from your experience. Cite authorities or give examples from other companies and projects. Show them you know your stuff. Be careful not to show off or be smug. Just state facts.

Learn and use the jargon of their field. But don't fake it. If you don't know, ask what their name is for something or how something has been done before. Answer questions promptly; don't evade them. If you can't answer, say so and get back to them with the answer as soon as possible.

Be tolerant, not picky. Once you've taught them something you can correct their performance, but until then, don't criticize. They are not ready to be corrected yet. Lastly, don't apologize, be condescending, or ridicule others. Be straightforward, honest, and open with your trainees.

Summary

This chapter was about you, the trainer. It is frequently not what is taught but who taught it that makes learning difficult or easy. You are the main message, and this chapter showed how you can become an effective and productive trainer.

We began by outlining the need for trainers to take a strong leadership stance, then went on to look at the roles of leadership and how you can fulfill them. We looked in detail at the purpose of asking questions and provided methods for improving your skill in this crucial area. We discussed how to give good answers to questions and reviewed ways of improving listening skills.

Nonverbal communication is also an important aspect of training programs. We examined ways of controlling your impact upon the group through the use of kinesics, proxemics, semantics, and dress. Finally, we concluded with procedures for establishing your credibility with the group.

PART II

Planning and Preparing for Training

Introduction to Part II

THIS part of the book is about the planning and preparation that take place outside the classroom. In these seven chapters we look at the day-to-day training tasks that lead eventually to actual instruction. All too frequently trainers are appointed because of their ability to perform a task well. It is assumed that they will be able to teach others how to perform that task, too. But training is a different job with its own skills to be mastered. Equally as common, new trainers are hired for their platform skills, and it is assumed that they will be capable of fully performing all the other tasks that comprise the job of training. If you find yourself in either situation, or are managing those who do, Part II will provide you with the means to discover and develop those other necessary skills of training.

In Chapter 5, we look at needs analysis. Changes can be planned for only when you know what needs to be changed. Needs analysis establishes a baseline. The discussion of needs analysis, however, is intentionally practical and based on rule-of-thumb procedures. For all practical purposes, the steps outlined in Chapter 5 are ample and far less intimidating than more formal procedures.

Chapter 6 deals in much the same practical manner with what are often regarded as arcane procedures for evaluating the changes brought about by training. Once again in keeping with the guideline of "less is more," I've simplified rather than formalized the evaluation process. In its practical approach, Chapter 6 provides everyday measurements of progress and helps you measure the effectiveness of your training efforts. In short, Chapter 6 is not about statistics, it is about evaluation.

Chapters 7 and 8 take you through the vital steps of gaining expertise in a subject and planning how to communicate that expertise, by shaping your material into a coherent training program. Again, the approach is to simplify and demystify. The tools are practical and applicable to all training situations, useful to both the novice and the expert.

Writing a training program requires an overwhelming amount of work. Consequently, a large service industry has sprung up to address this problem, with off-the-shelf packages, outside consultants, and professional generic seminar organizations. Chapter 9 helps you decide when, where, and which of these services to use.

An important part of any training effort is the physical environment in which learning is to take place. Chapter 10 provides guidelines on the environmental aspects to be considered and outlines several steps to take to ensure a positive training environment, both on and off site.

Chapter 11 is the longest in the book. It is a detailed examination of visual and electronic aids in training, including how to use each type of aid, rentals versus purchase, budgeting, availability, and so forth. It is, in fact, all you need to know about audiovisual aids. In addition, there are tips on creating your own aids, especially in regard to video equipment and computer-assisted training programs.

Parts I and II embody the skills and background knowledge a trainer needs to function fully and effectively. In Part III, we will go one step farther to management concerns.

CHAPTER 5

Preparing
a Needs Analysis

NEEDS analysis is an examination of the existing need for training within an organization. It is a gathering of data that enables you to make an informed estimate of the changes desired or demanded by that organization. Needs analysis performs two distinct functions: (1) It establishes what the present practices are, and (2) it projects what the desired results should be. To conduct a needs analysis you gather data of present performance, then compare the data to the desired performance standards projected by management or mandated by external forces such as market conditions. Your needs analysis should provide you with the overall management goals that your training will be designed to fulfill.

Needs analysis is a vital step toward establishing a training program but unfortunately it is a step that is frequently overemphasized. I know of at least one company that hired a consulting firm to perform a needs analysis. The consultants took so long that the company began its training program without them. When the needs analysis finally came in, it was irrelevant to the by-then-flourishing training department. Needs analysis is an aid to training but not a substitute for it.

The problem arises because often needs analysis is easier to do. In effect, all that a needs analysis entails is gathering data. It can be as detailed or as general as desired. Those who like numbers and need them for making decisions tend to gather data to an infinite degree. Seldom is such a detailed study necessary.

Ancillary Uses of Needs Analysis

A needs analysis fills other roles. Training is usually on the wrong side of the ledger: as a cost factor that seldom makes a profit. Consequently, trainers frequently encounter the attitude, especially from the accounting department, that their work is a frill. "It's nice to train employees, but it's not really what we're in business to do." When there are financial restraints, training is among the first cutbacks. A needs analysis helps develop a solid data base on which to build the justification for your training program. You must always be prepared to show how money spent on training will benefit the entire organization. Whenever possible, you must show how training either saves more or earns more money than it costs. Needs analysis is the starting point for such a defense.

The third function of a needs analysis is to define your starting point so you can measure progress from it. By knowing the *status quo* you can train for change and then evaluate the results. You can measure your own progress as well as the impact your training has on the organization.

Finally, needs analysis establishes a data base for future training. Generally, training lies in the "soft" area of management. Management, from the senior staff down to shop foremen (and women), is concerned with numbers and hard data. Hunches, theories, and communication skills are all very well, but traditionally the end result must be higher profits and more efficient production: more orders shipped, more cars unloaded, more letters answered, and so forth. Training is perceived as soft, a "like-to-have it" not a "got-to-have it" situation. Needs analysis creates a numerical justification for training. It is particularly important where the training need isn't obvious.

Anticipating Training Needs: Becoming Pro-Active, Not Re-Active

Most training in America is re-active. That is, management discovers a need for training and either creates a training function to respond to that need or, if such a department already exists, informs the head of training that a new program should be developed. This should be a perfectly acceptable approach. But in reality few senior managers have the time or foresight to predict training needs. They see the need when it is nearly too late to do an effective job. Much training is a quick-fix Band-Aid slapped on with little notice and no time for careful preanalysis. Management wants results — now! So one day is given to perform two or three days' worth of training, and one or two weeks set to research, analyze, write, and test the new program. The trainer is forced to try to catch up, to perform more in less time, to be harried into reacting on short notice to sudden demands.

A far better stance for the trainer is that of a pro-active consultant. The classic re-active situation always puts time pressure on the trainer, who is continually catching up. The pro-active stance allows the trainer to anticipate training needs and prepare a response ahead of time. Such a view lets a trainer anticipate peak demand rather than hustle to catch up. Needs analysis is the tool for this anticipatory approach.

Sources of Information for Needs Analysis

As explained earlier, needs analysis is a gathering of data. The following outlines the steps to take in collecting that information:

1. Monitor your standard sources of information to learn about needs before they become obvious.
2. Identify the types of problems you find in each area and determine which are training-related.
3. Gather data to establish present levels of performance.
4. Examine the feasibility of training as a solution to the problems.
5. Determine the size and scope of the program.
6. Justify the cost of the program.

Now let's examine each of these steps more closely. There are five available sources you can consult for information about the current practices in your organization and about its future direction.

Management

A re-active training approach is totally and exclusively responsive to management as its source of information. Although a pro-active stance is recommended, let's begin with a set of guidelines for gathering information in the re-active phase.

Re-Active Management Questions

Ask your management contacts the following questions:

1. Who will receive the training?
2. What is the nature of the population to be trained?
3. What problems have created the need for training?
4. What specific results would management like the training to achieve?
5. What is the time frame for training?
6. What is the budget for training (if appropriate)?
7. What level of response does management anticipate?

Begin by establishing for whom the training will be designed. Remember, *who* is more important than *what*. What is the nature of the population to be trained? This includes both the number of people to be trained and a description of them — for example, their average age, sex, level of education, experience, and location (if facilities are scattered).

Next find out what problem(s) occasioned the request for training. In other words, you need to know management's assessment of current performance. If management has called on you to solve the problem, they ought to have the situation fairly well defined. Try also to uncover the results they would like. Again, it helps you (and them) if those requesting the training have given it some thought.

How much time are they giving you? Will they give you enough time with their people, or will you have to limit the depth of your training because of time constraints? Another important point is cost, though it may not be appropriate to all situations. Can they afford the training? Cost is a factor when there are divisional or departmental charge-back systems.

Lastly, what kind of a response do they anticipate? If, for instance, they want every member of their staff to have the same basic orientation, you won't have to worry about trainees' transfer of learning to their jobs. If, on the other hand, they expect a full change from each participant, you (and they) will have to accommodate a considerably more detailed lesson structure and allow more time for instruction and followup.

Most of the time such an informal analysis is adequate. You define both the *status quo* and the desired results. In addition, you gather data on the population to be trained. Unless someone in the hierarchy demands more data to justify the training, you can build a very effective course on the information gained from these questions.

Often writers of training manuals or teachers of trainers stress the need for a detailed, statistical needs analysis. In my experience this is usually unnecessary. Those who teach needs analysis or who are needs analysts surround their work with a mystique. The often overly complex language of law or medicine fulfills the same function. If people knew how simple it can be to incorporate or to write a will, or if they knew the inexpensive ingredients in some of their prescriptions, they would be loathe to pay the high fees of many doctors, lawyers, and pharmacists. Understand that I am not attacking these professions, nor am I implying that all practitioners charge exorbitant fees for simple services. But promoting a mystique, a specialness about what one does, is usually in the self-interest of those who do so. Needs analysis doesn't have to be complex. In fact, it should be as simple and practical as possible. Most trainers do not have time or money to waste gathering data merely for the sake of having it.

Finally, I am also not suggesting that detailed data is never necessary. Certainly in evaluation procedures and at budget time it is vital to document your training performance. But Occam's razor should apply. The most effective procedure is the simplest and least time-consuming one.

Pro-Active Management Questions

To take a pro-active stance you will need to find ways of anticipating management's training needs. When senior management rushes to you and says the company urgently needs *xyz* training in the next two months, you will be able to respond quickly and efficiently. You'll be prepared. Here are some ways to anticipate management's training needs:

1. Make friends with people in the purchasing department and ask them for information on orders or requests for new equipment that might mandate training.
2. Establish contacts with the real estate department, if your company has one. New plant sites will probably require training for new personnel.
3. If you work for a publicly held company read the annual report. Pay particular attention to forecasts, acquisitions, or expansion plans and watch for other new directions.
4. Ask people in public relations to send you copies of speeches made by the president of the company or other key executives. Monitor the speeches for predictions of where executives see the company going. If your firm doesn't have a public relations section, talk to the boss's secretary.
5. Most senior executives have regular assessment meetings to take stock of the company and where it is headed. Such meetings usually include ideas for attaining planned goals, and often they are the point at which planning decisions are made. Ask to sit in on

such meetings. You are, in effect, monitoring senior management's needs. If you are not allowed, find someone who does attend and ask that person to pass on potential training information to you. Failing this, try to get a copy of the minutes from a secretary, an executive, a supervisor of the typing pool, or a clerk in the copy or mail room where the minutes are duplicated. There are no better sources of information on future training needs than these meetings.

It is usually best if you make and maintain these contacts informally so the process remains free of red tape or multiple-approval levels. However, such contacts should in no way be clandestine or underhanded. Follow whatever policy is operative in your organization. Try informally if you can; if that fails, go through regular channels.

Customers or End-Users

Remember that pro-active analysis spots problems that will lend themselves to a training solution, thus anticipating a demand for training. Usually a company has some form of customer feedback. It may be a customer service or complaint department, market research, receptionists, shipping and expediting, and so on. In fact, any area or department that regularly interfaces with the company's customers or end-users is a way to gauge customer response to your company. Here's what you should look for.

Number and Pattern of Complaints

If you can, document both the weekly or monthly number of complaints and what articles, services, or employees are involved. Any distinct pattern with sufficient numbers is a ready-made rationale for re-training.

Service Records

Too-frequent service calls imply both inferior quality and inadequate service. If your company services hardware of any kind, look for patterns in the frequency of service, both in the items serviced and among the departments or service people themselves. Re-training might be an effective solution.

Customer Service

One of the techniques covered later in this chapter comes from Tom Peters' phrase "Management by Walking Around," or MBWA. There are few better sources of information for needs analyses than simply walking around observing how things are done. Look at how customers react to company personnel. Are there problems? Can you document a sufficient number of cases to justify a training thrust?

Government

Most managers are aware of the impact a change in government regulations has on company operations. Yet such a change seldom comes as a surprise. The government debates it, the media report it, the issues are discussed. But time after time organizations scurry to create last-minute procedures to comply with new regulations.

Here's a case in point. Deregulation of banking was a long time in coming. It was debated in Congress and in state legislatures for many months. Yet when it finally happened, the banks had not anticipated the change. Many bank training departments were unprepared for the considerable re-training that was necessary. Everyone knew deregulation was coming, they all could have prepared for it and developed new programs, but most failed to monitor the change. Don't be caught napping. Monitor government's behavior whenever it impacts on your organization.

In particular, follow the State-of-the-Union and your State-of-the-State addresses. Follow any court cases or lawsuits that might affect your operation. Lastly, read up on congressional hearings that relate to your industry.

Workers

Frequently the workplace can tell you when some form of training or re-training may be in order. Here are areas that can be monitored:

Absenteeism and Turnover Rates

These are costly problems when they occur. There are many possible causes of such behavior completely outside the control of training, but frequently training or re-training becomes a part of the solution.

Union Bargaining Positions

Even if your organization is nonunion, sooner or later it will have to offer some benefits to stay nonunion or to attract workers from union shops. The Quality of Work Life benefits are a case in point. The QWL movement became a strong issue for unions in the late 1970s, before management became interested in Quality Circles. Union pressures and contractual QWL benefits smoothed the way for Quality Circle-type improvements in working conditions and quality control. QWL is still an active force in working America. By monitoring union demands, trainers can anticipate areas for developing future training.

Outside Seminars

Monitor how many requests are made for or what the actual attendance is at outside professional seminars or college courses. You may be able to offer these as part of your training program. For example, if there is considerable demand for a course in business writing, perhaps the training department can create such a course in-house. If certain courses are taken regularly to qualify for key positions — say, a supervisory course for newly appointed supervisors — the training department may have an opportunity to take a pro-active stance.

Exit Interviews

If your company conducts interviews with departing employees, ask to review them with the personnel interviewer. Look for patterns of discontent that can be addressed by training.

Employee Surveys

You can arrange your own surveys in accordance with guidelines outlined later in this chapter, or you can piggyback on other sources such as an in-house publication or an employee suggestion box.

Technology

If your department does not currently offer new managers training in word processing or computer applications, you will have to provide it sooner or later. Be prepared. Monitor technological changes that affect the workplace. For example, electronic mail and interactive video telephones are becoming current. As these changes become widespread, prepare to offer seminars to help your company smoothly incorporate the changes.

In many organizations work-at-home programs are being tried. If they catch on, they will be enhanced immensely by on-site training that allows the company to maintain control over home-workers through procedural standardization and technical dependence.

Summing Up

Nearly all training thrusts arise from one or more of these five monitoring areas. Perhaps you cannot keep track of them all or just one or two are applicable to your situation. Fine. Pick the two you think are most likely to reveal the future of your organization and track them. The purpose is to give you a means for taking a leadership role in planning the training for your company. Even when the training has already been mandated by management, you can tie your program into a demonstrated need to create a strong and efficient pro-active stance to help justify the program.

These five information sources are really only problem finders. Before you can gather data to define the *status quo*, you must decide the extent to which the problem you've discovered is correctable by training. This takes us to the next step toward a needs analysis: identifying the problems.

Types of Problems

Not every problem you uncover is a training problem. If you take on the job of training to correct a problem that is not a training problem, you guarantee an automatic failure. Training is not a panacea. It can only accomplish changes of a certain kind; other problems demand other solutions.

In your investigations, there are four kinds of problems that possibly can turn up.

Systemic Problems

Many of the railway systems in America have been in trouble for years, while in other countries many are flourishing. Our rail system was once a source of great wealth, one of the building blocks of the nation. What happened? There are many theories, but all can be summed up as systemic. Our system of government, new methods of transportation, and so on all worked to diminish the importance and therefore the use of the railways. All the training in the world could not redress such a problem. A systemic problem has to do with the way the system—whatever it may be, in whatever instance—works. Training was unable to stave off the recession of the early eighties. Today, small merchants in New York City are forced to close their well-established businesses when their 20-year leases expire and unregulated landlords raise rents by 800 percent. No training in the world could solve such problems. The change must be in the system itself. There are many such systemic problems. If you turn up one in your monitoring, leave it alone. Training cannot solve it.

Organizational Problems

I once had a client who, despite having built his business into a multimillion dollar concern, insisted that every decision be made by him. Procedural decisions in Europe and Australia had to wait until his New York office could track him down. The operation was grossly inefficient and created many problems, but none was even approachable through training. The problem lay in the chain of command and in my client's failure to delegate some decision-making authority.

In another organization, a major customer service operation was completely stalled because middle management stopped and held all actions on customer complaints. It was a policy decision made at a low level of management but it stymied all attempts by customer service personnel to resolve complaints. Although re-training those managers might help, as long as the policy remained in effect the problem would also remain. This is another example of an organizational problem. Unless organizational bottlenecks are removed, steer clear of the problem because training won't correct it.

Motivational Problems

Quite often training departments are called upon to motivate employees. They can succeed, but if the employees return to poor working conditions, organizational problems, dull and uninspiring jobs, long and frequent unpaid overtime, and other such situations, their morale will worsen regardless of training. Motivation is *not* a function of training. Supervisory people can be taught techniques for motivating and working with others, but unless the system backs up such efforts with rewards and changes circumstances that are de-motivational, the training is wasted. Training is and should be an integral part of any motivational thrust, but it cannot alone create motivation.

Skills Problems

Skills problems are the province of training. In my seminars I am often asked the difference between training and education. There is a difference. Training is responsible for achieving results, and these results always take the form of a change in trainee skill levels. Education is much broader and more conceptual. It is not responsible for results; it is up to the student to pass or fail, to use the material or not. Training can educate, but it still must produce concrete results and must, therefore, teach measurable skills.

Skills problems can be addressed by training. When a problem crops up, before launching a full needs analysis ask yourself, "Is this a training problem?" If not, end your analysis there. If so, go ahead to the next step — gathering data to define the present levels of performance.

Gathering Data

Without further information it is not always clear exactly what kind of problem you've uncovered. If it is a skills problem, then you need to gather data to establish the present level of performance — your baseline against which you'll measure progress. But even if it is too early to tell if it's a skills problem, gathering data is still your follow-up step once a problem is discovered. Of course, if it's obviously not a skills problem, there is no point in pursuing it. If you are in doubt, however, or if it is clearly training related, you need to define the *status quo* — in other words, the need for training.

There are six formats for gathering information, depending on the depth and detail you need. Most of us don't have the time to be as thorough as we'd like. Choose the method that produces adequate results for you and that is feasible for your organization. If you have the time and want more scientific evidence, use a second method to verify the findings from the first. Remember, the simpler, the better; but remember also that

---

Guidelines for Gathering Data

1. What information do I want?
   (a) What is happening?
   (b) What skills are involved?
   (c) What problems are created?
   (d) What is the dollar cost of the problems?
   (e) What is the political climate surrounding these problems?
2. What use will the data have?
   (a) Is it a basis for developing a training program?
   (b) Will you use it to justify that program to management?
   (c) Will it cover you politically?
   (d) Will it convince those who are part of the problem?
   (e) Will it motivate the eventual trainees?
3. Which method or combination of methods will most easily and accurately supply the information needed?

---

you are after *real* data, and the results of your training will depend on the accuracy of your findings.

Ask yourself, "What is the information I want?" In other words, what is happening? What skills are involved? What problems are created? What is the impact, in dollars, of these problems? What is the political or organizational structure surrounding these problems?

Next, determine what you are going to use the data for. Is it as a basis for developing a program? Will you use it to justify that program to management or as a means to cover yourself politically? Perhaps you'll use it as a means of convincing those who are part of the problem that something must be done. Will you use the data to motivate your trainees? Choose which method or combination of methods will most easily and accurately supply the information you need. The standard data-gathering methods are arranged here in order of difficulty, from easiest to most difficult:

Field observations
Surveys
Interviews
Record checks
Task analyses
Assessment sessions

Let's look at each one in turn.

Field Observations

Going out and looking at the problem is one of the simplest and best ways of establishing the performance baseline. I heartily recommend all trainers do it on a regular basis whether or not they are conducting a needs analysis. If you've trained people, walk around and see how they are doing. It is one of the best ways to monitor your own effectiveness.

To perform field observations specifically for a needs analysis, consider the following.

- If you are likely to need it, get permission from whoever is in charge of the people you want to observe. This usually means you will have to explain why you want to observe the people and you will have to persuade that individual to approve. To bypass such a person, however, could make you an enemy who could undermine any future training you might give to those subordinates.
- Prepare a reasonable, persuasive rationale for your observations.

I've had success when I outline my ignorance of current procedures and emphasize that, as a trainer, I'd like to learn how the department operates so I don't teach useless or wrong ways. This approach is usually persuasive because it is nonthreatening. At the same time you are being persuasive, you must open up the possibility of training to change the department in such a way that they won't feel stabbed in the back. Diplomacy is a must. An enemy can only hurt you, but a friend can be relied on. In effect, you need to balance your humility in wanting to learn with the frank knowledge that changes might result.

- Know what it is you are looking for. Have your objectives clearly framed. You should be looking to discover what is happening — what the process is. You should also investigate what skills are involved and what the apparent problems are (if any). Analyze what the dollar impact of those problems is. Lastly, find out about the political climate and organizational structure involved. Be as casual and unobtrusive as possible. Try not to make a big thing of it. Simply walk around and observe, ask a few questions, but always keep your activity informal.

Surveys

Send out a written survey. Despite much socio-scientific literature to the contrary, you can design and interpret an effective employee survey without outside help. You don't need a technical document that plumbs many subtleties at once. You don't need to validate your findings with statistical safeguards. You're not conducting a scientific study. Apart from the data it generates, no one will ever see your survey except your colleagues and those who respond to it. If you are concerned about absolute accuracy, the data can be changed or verified through observations and interviews. Otherwise, make it easy on yourself. If you know what you want, ask for it — simply and directly.

In a survey you are asking employees to evaluate some aspect of their work. The best tool for doing so is the semantic differential, which makes a statement (for example, "morale on the assembly line is excellent") and then asks the respondents to mark their opinions on a scale of, say, 1 to 5. In this instance, 1 means they agree fully, 2 means they think it's probably right, 3 indicates maybe or maybe not, 4 is probably not, and 5 is definitely not. Variations would have responses as excellent, good, fair, poor, and terrible or by frequency of occurrence: always, often, sometimes, seldom, never. The five categories aren't a magic quantity. You can devise two (agree, disagree) or six or seven, even eight gradations for response.

Be careful though, because the more complex the question, the harder it is to answer and so the less likely it will be answered.

Because they ask for judgments, surveys are excellent for measuring attitudes. They are less viable when you are investigating procedures but a little thought can still produce results. Surveys are least effective if you want to gather specific skills information.

Decide how you will distribute the survey. They could be given to employees as they leave from work, mailed to their homes, included with their paychecks, inserted in the in-house publication, or placed in the cafeteria to be picked up at will. Including the survey with the paycheck carries authority, so it may get a higher response but that response is less likely to be critical and honest. Distributing them to employees as they leave work gets a response that is usually balanced. Mailing them to the home will most likely give you the most honest results but also sometimes gets a low response. Surveys inserted in in-house publications or left in convenient places tend to produce honest responses but have the lowest return rate.

Consider the following when you prepare your survey:

1. Key the survey to the educational and work levels of the group.
2. If you have a previous survey that was successful, use that format.
3. Keep the survey short. Twenty questions is too many; ten is better.
4. Write questions that are easy to answer. You'll get a larger response and it will be easier to interpret the data.
5. Make your questions short and, if possible, friendly.
6. Narrow down each question to a single idea.
7. Keep it anonymous. Don't phrase questions so that the answers reveal who responded.
8. Make sure the form is easy to read and respond to as well as easy to return.
9. Ask someone reliable to check the survey for errors or potential misunderstandings.

When you compile the results, don't force the data. If you draw too many conclusions, you could end up training to solve the wrong problems. If there are job descriptions, company goals, or personal objectives involved, measure your results against them. Then publicize your survey. Try to tie it in with some major company thrust or activity. Let management know what it is, why it is, and what should happen because of the results. Let everyone know the general results (overall response, percentage breakdowns for each answer, and so on). Use the in-house publication to call attention to it and to thank the respondents.

Interviews

There are two problems with interviews: They are very time-consuming, and much of what is discussed may be irrelevant. The first problem can be solved by limiting your interviews to checking the accuracy of data you've collected in other ways. Simply select individuals at random from the group you've observed or surveyed. Alternatively, interview only management or supervisory personnel to clarify the data you've gathered. This approach has the added benefit of establishing connections with these managers or supervisors. It also introduces the risk that they will distort or falsify to cover poor performance. If that is a problem, combine the interviews for a valid cross section.

The second problem, too much irrelevant data, can be avoided by carefully planning your interviews. The interview generates the fullest and most complete data. It is an integral part of both task analysis and assessment. It can be an important part of field observation and, as just seen, it also can be an effective check on survey data. If you plan your interviews, they can give you very effective results with a minimum investment of time.

Here are some steps for planning and using the interview format for needs analysis data gathering:

1. *Select key people.* Unless you want first impressions, new employees probably won't give you meaningful data. When interviewing supervisors, select those who will tell you what you need to know.

2. *Keep your interviews short.* Not only don't employees have time to spare, but the longer the interview is, the more time it will take you to sort the data.

3. *Establish your goals before you set up the interviews.* Know what you want to accomplish in each case. Don't think it, write it down. Keep that goal in mind as you interview so you stay on the topic and the interview is short.

4. *Know to whom you are talking.* Do your homework and find out where they stand in the political and organizational network.

5. *Plan the questions and the sequence you are going to use.* Then use them. Remember, you need to know what is happening (how they do what they do), what skills are involved, what problems there are, what these problems cost, what the political and organizational structure is surrounding these tasks, and what their attitudes are toward the work and the problems. If there are delicate or emotional issues, you may have to think through your choice of words and phrases. Use open-ended questions and practice active listening. (See Chapter 4.)

6. *Keep the interview brief.* Ten minutes should be all you need un-

less you're using only one key individual for all your data. Even then, don't waste time.

7. *Clear the results with the interviewees.* Let them know what you're doing with the data and give them a chance to approve or suggest changes in your proposal to change their procedures.

Record Checks

Several types of records can be checked to investigate the problem phase of a needs analysis. These records can also be used to establish the present level of performance. Here are some of the records that produce useful data:

Absenteeism records	Reports of safety-related accidents
Complaint records	
Customer service call records	Sales call reports
Employee evaluations	Scrap and reject figures
Exit interviews	Shipping figures
Infirmary reports	Training evaluations
Inspection reports and figures	Turnover figures
Production figures	Workmen's compensation claims
Quality control figures	

Remember, the purpose of a needs analysis is not to establish blame or even to solve problems, but merely to gather data that provide a picture of what skills can be changed to improve the situation.

Task Analyses

A task analysis serves two functions: It can be a diagnostic tool in needs analysis and a prescriptive or regulating guide in preparing training programs. When used for a needs analysis, it becomes a detailed observation of what exactly *is* being done. In connection with the training program, it is a detailed description of what *should* be done. The prescriptive use — the formal task analysis — must be perfect because it is the model for performance. We cover it in Chapter 7.

The diagnostic use, however, need not be as detailed. You are simply documenting how the job is presently being carried out. For the most part, this entails making close observations and writing them down. When detailed technical skills are involved, say, in a lathe operation, you must study each move minutely and interview the operator on what is being done and why. The study then sets the baseline of performance.

In conducting informal task analyses, here are a few guidelines:

1. Get permission of both supervisors and the people you will be observing.
2. Make several observations of the same people. The first time they may feel self-conscious or perhaps obliged to perform the task "better" than they normally would.
3. Assure the people that your purpose is not punitive and that only good can come from helping you. Make them feel special, that the job of being observed is an honored one.
4. Since standards will be set later, remember that what you are recording is strictly what is being done, not what should be done or what you or others would like to be done.
5. Once you have recorded the activities, review them step by step with the person you observed to be certain you have captured the actual performance.
6. If you can (and it is appropriate), videotape the operation, with permission. You can study it in slow motion and the tape will stand as inarguable documentation. Do make a written, step-by-step analysis of the videotape, which will be much more useful in writing your program.

Your results should resemble a computer program in its step-by-step detailing of procedures. A task analysis is exactly that — a detailed record of how a task is performed.

Assessment Sessions

Some occupations have regular assessment requirements, usually mandatory performance tests that key employees take to maintain their standing. For example, airline pilots must undergo simulator tests every six months. In a similar way, but without the pressure of being tested, volunteer fire departments compete with each other to maintain their skills. Rodeos originated in the West for much the same reason. They are both for fun and for an assessment of skills. Assessment sessions of many types can be excellent opportunities for trainers to evaluate performance levels. If your company has such activities, use them.

A more widely used form of assessment is the personal interviews that supervisors or managers use to evaluate an employee's performance. Different companies use different names and formats for such interviews, but they all are, in effect, assessment sessions usually recorded in the employee's personnel file. Gather data from these sessions by interviewing the supervisors or managers. If you have access, look over the personnel reports. This can be a touchy area because the employees being examined don't usually know you are doing so. If you have qualms about it or your company is not comfortable with it, don't use this approach.

Determining the Level of Performance

Most of the time, the information gathered will reveal the level of current performance. This is certainly so for task analyses and assessment sessions. In surveys or interviews, however, the level of performance isn't always apparent. In these cases, you will have to follow up with an informal task analysis to establish the performance baseline. It need be no more detailed than necessary to (1) indicate what functions need training, and (2) convince management that the training is necessary.

If you are taking a pro-active stance and are anticipating a need for training in a task that isn't being done now — for example, word processing skills for secretaries before the company actually has acquired the full hardware — you must go outside your company to establish performance parameters. This can be done by networking with trainers in other organizations, shopping for vendors or service agencies that already have courses to train in the area of concern, and comparing your proposed requirements to existing practices in similar or related tasks.

Examining Feasibility

Once you have discovered a problem and have probed to find its exact nature and cause, you must ask once again, "Is this a training problem?" If not, there is no point in proceeding further. If so, go ahead. Your next step is to evaluate the political climate in the organization.

Rarely do we achieve what we want without opposition. Others have their own agendas and goals, which are seldom completely parallel to ours. This means that some managers are almost sure to oppose your pro-active training thrust. Before spending time and effort working out the details of what you propose, look into the political feasibility of your plans.

One of the cardinal rules of office politics is, "never call a meeting unless you know the outcome in advance." This means that you must know what your sources of resistance will be. If they would succeed in blocking you, don't go on. Hold your data in readiness for changes in climate or personnel or wait until the problem itself changes. When the time is ripe, proceed. But always assess your likelihood of succeeding before you put a lot of work into the project. Here are some tips to help you evaluate the political climate:

1. Find out who has opposed training proposals in the past and who has supported them.
2. In each previous case, ask those who supported training in the past why they did, and why they feel others objected.
3. Decide what you can do for those who are likely to oppose you. If you don't know, ask them. Take the position that you want to provide the best possible service and need to know what you can do for them. This is a negotiation like any other (see Chapter 14). Be prepared to make concessions and trade-offs.
4. Use the organizational network. Bring as much pressure as possible on your opponents to help them move in your direction. If they remain adamant, examine all their arguments or points of opposition and create strong rebuttals.
5. When you propose your training program, include your rebuttals to every opposition (see Chapter 13).

One final question must be asked when examining feasibility. Are there any other solutions to the problem? Ask this of yourself and of those you are winning over to your side. It will position you as a reasonable person. You won't appear to be building an empire for yourself if you ask others for their solutions. Also, you will find out if there really *are* other solutions. You will broaden the responsibility for correcting the problem so that the solution doesn't rest entirely on you. Lastly, you allow those who oppose you to solve the problem their way. This step alone may turn an enemy into an ally.

In effect, asking others for solutions makes you a team player, which is an excellent stance for a service function on the wrong side of the ledger.

Determining the Size of the Training Thrust

If the political air is relatively clear, it's time to shift from gathering data to projecting a response to that data. You must decide on the scope, length, format, location, cost, frequency, and population that will be involved.

Scope. Ask yourself what the program will cover. How much information needs to be taught? What is the management goal of such new training? What will the training accomplish for the company?

Length. How much time will you need to effect the change you want? What are the costs of having workers or managers away from their jobs for considerable time, for example, 10 hours, 30 hours, 80 hours, and so on?

Format. Does this subject lend itself to a participant format? For example, three hours per morning for six mornings, one day per week for six consecutive weeks. Is the work force already comfortable with one particular format? Have other formats worked for this organization in the past? For other organizations?

Location. Where is it best to hold this training? See Chapter 10 for more information on this. What are the cost factors involved in different locations?

Cost. What are the outright costs of creating this training package? What are the costs of buying an off-the-shelf package? See Chapter 9 for more on this. Which of these alternatives best meets your need? What is the cost of new visual aids or equipment?

Frequency. How often will the training program be offered? What are the cost amortization figures for each of several different possible frequencies?

Population. Who will be trained? What will be the cost per person of the training?

When you have answered these questions and have decided which way best brings about the needed change that earlier research uncovered, then move to the final phase of your needs analysis: justifying the expense to the company.

Justifying the Cost

At all levels management is concerned with the bottom line — what it's going to cost. The formula for determining cost is really very simple. Total the costs for the program as you'd like to do it, then as you may have to do it, and finally, with at least one of the alternatives you've examined (buying an off-the-shelf program, calling in a consultant, and so on). If you are preparing the program yourself, include the cost of your time. Also include any preparation costs (duplicating, typing, supplies). Tally the results, presented in two ways: (1) the total cost to the company, and (2) the cost per person to the company.

Now figure what the results of improved performance will be in terms of dollars and cents. If you give the accounting people the data, they usually will work it out for you, but avoid the end of the fiscal year and the week before payday; choose the first two weeks of a slow month instead.

Steps to Justify Cost

1. Create a dollar amount per instance (item, customer, day, and so on).
2. Use data from an outside source (industrial averages, D & B reports, surveys) to place a value on intangible losses.
3. Relate the cost per instance to the average loss figure.
4. Relate each loss to one aspect of your proposed training program (increased safety, reduced errors, better negotiation skills, and so on).
5. Multiply total loss figure times the number of people your training program would involve.
6. Compare the improved results with the cost of training.

If you would rather do it yourself, remember that you can put a dollar value on almost anything, but it carries more weight when it can be documented directly. I had a client whose company slashed its safety training budget by $800,000 during an economic downturn. After monitoring the safety-related downtime and the time lost because of accidents during the following 12 months, the training department was able to show that the cut in safety training cost the company $7.5 million in the first year alone. Needless to say, management quickly restored the training budget.

Admittedly, the task is easier when there is a direct dollar relationship, such as to scrap rates on an assembly line. But even something as hard to pin down as the attitude of those who answer the telephone can be given a dollar value. For example, you could figure the average dollar value of a customer, and then cite the results of a 1960 retail chain store survey, which indicated that 68 percent of the customers who switched to other stores did so because of the attitude of a single employee. If you estimated the number of customers your organization lost in a given period, took 68 percent of them, and multiplied that figure by the dollars in business from each customer, you would have a dollars-lost figure that related to employee attitude. Multiply that figure times the number of employees you'd train, and you have a rather convincing argument.

To assign a dollar value to such intangibles, therefore, estimate a dollar amount per instance (per item, per customer, per day or whatever), then devise or use another source (a survey, industrial averages, Dun & Bradstreet reports, and so on) to demonstrate the value of a loss to the company. Relate the average cost per instance to the average loss based on the statistics. Apply each loss to one performance aspect of your training (safety procedures, reduced errors, training in negotiation skills, and so on), and multiply that figure times the number of people you expect to train.

An alternative method is to cite a single massive instance in which the company lost out because employees lacked training. For example, suppose a company won a $10 million contract but lost money on it because of poor budgeting. You could easily justify offering managers with bidding authority a course in budgeting.

Summary

In this chapter we discussed the various stages of compiling a needs analysis. We examined the primary and auxiliary uses for the needs analysis, and made a distinction between the pro-active and re-active approaches to meeting needs for training. It was pointed out that the needs analysis is a data-gathering operation which ultimately provides you with the basis for determining the size and scope of a proposed training program, as well as helping you justify the cost of that program.

CHAPTER 6

Evaluating Your Effectiveness

TRAINING is the business of bringing about change. To know whether you have achieved any change, you must be able to evaluate the effects of your instruction. You've defined your objectives and determined what the change should be. You've assessed the present status and have a program for changing it to meet those objectives. Now you need a means of measuring the success you've achieved. This last step is that of evaluation.

The process of evaluation, however, doesn't take place only at the completion of training. Evaluation is an important ongoing function for the trainer. It is also a vital function for the trainees. If you remember, one of Thorndyke's principles of learning is the Law of Effect: nothing succeeds like success. Trainees must get constant feedback to develop the motivation to continue. Constant evaluation not only lets you know where you are, but it also does the same for your trainees. For convenience, the evaluation function has been divided into several operations, but there is considerable overlap and much mixing of technique. It is likely that you will be using several methods at the same time.

Short-Term Evaluations

A short-term evaluation is the type we are most familiar with. This is the typical test used in schools and it usually consists of some challenging task set by the instructor and performed by the student. How well the student performs the task is the measure of his or her success at learning it (and, incidentally, the instructor's success at teaching it).

Many people dread exams because the results were associated with passing or failing. Such tests were the basis for vital judgments affecting their future. When used this way, it isn't surprising that exams are almost punitive to some of us. You will have to reposition the purpose and function of exams, showing your trainees how tests let them know how they are doing. Let exams be a service to them, a diagnostic to point out their strengths and weaknesses. The fact that you can also use them to evaluate yourself is really immaterial. Tests exist solely for them, to provide important feedback. We'll talk about how to structure those tests later in this chapter.

There are, however, several other types of short-term evaluations. We'll take a look at these, then discuss how to create and use these evaluative tools.

Alternative Types of Evaluation

Socratic Questioning

In Chapter 3, we established the power and teaching value of asking questions. But one of the other major benefits of asking questions is that it lets you monitor the state of mind of the learners and assess the degree of learning taking place. To develop your questioning technique, see Chapter 4.

Eye Contact

Also in Chapter 4, we mentioned the importance of eye contact as positive nonverbal communication between instructor and learner. As with most communication, eye contact is a two-way exchange. Contact is initiated and maintained by the instructor, but the learner sends back a message as well. What your trainees' eyes. Eyes that stare or glare at you are challenging you or disagree with what you say. Eyes that frown are expressing challenge and doubt. Eyes that are glassy and expressionless have had enough. It's time to change the subject. Eyes that shine are challenged and interested, while eyes that droop are sleepy. Ask ques-

---

Interpreting via Eye Contact

Glare or stare = challenge or disagreement
Frown = doubt or deep thought
Glassy or blank = had enough
Shining eyes = challenged and interested
Droopy or sleepy = tuned out or bored
Blinking or wandering = nervousness or hiding something

---

tions or change the topic. Eyes that blink rapidly or wander about are nervous; the person may be holding something back.

Spot Quizzes and Reviews

By reviewing a topic using a question format, in either a written or oral quiz, you can take the pulse of the group and find out how well they understand the material. Formal testing and how to structure questions for tests are discussed later in this chapter.

Project Sessions

Assigning work to be done in class allows you to circulate and check their understanding as they work. In a project session you are looking for how well the trainees can use what you've taught them. You also have the opportunity later on to respond in writing to their projects, expressing your evaluation of them. I usually follow up by discussing the project with the group, using several of their efforts as examples.

Case Histories

The case history is a more involved, practical project. It challenges the learners to use what they've learned, while it allows you to see how well they are doing. Case histories are discussed further in Chapter 8.

Practice Sessions

Hands-on practice serves to lock in learning. It also provides you with an excellent opportunity for evaluation and correction.

Assessment Sessions

Assessments usually take place at the end of a program. Where mechanical training has been involved, it might be a trouble-shooting session

Methods for Short-Term Evaluations

1. Socratic questioning
2. Eye contact and observations
3. Spot quizzes and reviews
4. Project sessions
5. Case histories
6. Practice sessions
7. Examinations
8. Formal and informal assessment sessions
9. On-the-job training

in which equipment has been intentionally maladjusted. Trainees are evaluated on their speed and accuracy in correcting the situation.

On-the-Job Training

Seventy-five percent of all training in America is done on the job. Feedback and evaluation are immediate, practical, inarguable, and effective. The only trouble with OJT is that the trainer is not usually the one who does the evaluation. This does not preclude the trainer from using OJT for self-evaluation, however. After all, achieving objectives is the trainer's responsibility. If trainees perform well, it lets them know they've learned well, but it also lets the trainer know he or she has taught well. (See Chapter 8 for further coverage.)

Creating and Using Short-Term Evaluation Tools

Let's look more closely at the evaluative tools just cited. Asking questions and using eye contact have been covered in Chapters 3 and 6, so let's begin with quizzes and reviews.

Oral Reviews and Spot Quizzes

Oral reviews are a series of well-framed questions. You want to get the trainees talking about what they've just learned. Don't recite what you've covered — ask them to. I like to ask my classes to highlight what they remember from the previous session. This forces them to review the material and allows me to expand upon key areas, correct misunderstandings, and include material that was inadvertently missed.

Structure the review questions around your objectives. This creates strong redundant patterns. Also, never answer your own questions because that allows the class to stop thinking, and it defeats the purpose of the review.

Don't review large blocks of work at once. Break them down into segments and review each shortly after you finish it. You can always test overall knowledge later. Likewise, keep your reviews short. If you find, however, that the group doesn't know the material, you may have to cover it again by prompting Socratically. Look at it as an effective redundant loop. Lastly, be consistent. Review regularly, and don't miss a chance to review. Reviews not only provide feedback and evaluation of what they have learned but give the trainees a perspective on what they will be learning.

Written quizzes are similar to oral reviews, but remember that the level of understanding you are testing is simple recall. The quiz should (1) see what the trainees have grasped, and (2) provide a redundant loop to help lock in learning. Questions should be straightforward, not tricky.

Keep the quiz short. Ten questions are more than enough. Fill-in-the-blank questions or questions calling for one- or two-word answers usually work best. Avoid true-false, multiple-choice, and essay questions; save them for full exams.

Since the real value of a quiz is to let the learners see how they're doing, have them self-score the quiz. Do ask, however, to look over those with more than a couple of wrong answers. You may be able to correct a problem before it escalates.

Alternate quizzes with oral reviews, but be sure to cover each segment of your course with one or the other. In addition, consider using a pretest–posttest format to measure growth and mastery. Administer a quiz at the beginning of the class; most will do poorly. Upon completion of training, give them the identical test; their responses will show a marked improvement.

Project Sessions

As mentioned earlier, project sessions are in-class assignments. For them to work, make the tasks real. There are several ways to do this, but my favorite is to ask participants to bring a critical incident to the training seminar. (A critical incident is an event they recently experienced that was crucial to or had a significant effect on the performance of their job.) If the group is with you for several days, collect the incidents and choose the most germane. Assign them to be worked on the following day, then discuss them.

Other methods for developing project sessions are to take a real-life situation with which you are familiar or the worst situation you can imagine and present it to the group. A third way is to simply provide routine

Developing and Evaluating Project Sessions

1. Make them real.
   (a) Critical incident
   (b) Worst-case scenario
   (c) Actual case
   (d) Routine problem
2. Fit the project to the group and the content of the course.
3. Have correct answers ready, based on the material taught.
4. Make the difficulty level realistic for the time allowed. Allow seminar time for at least part of the project. Be available to help and explain.
5. Alternate assignments between individual and group projects.
6. Give each project a written evaluation, with both positive and negative feedback.
7. Set clear objectives for critiquing and remain consistent.
8. Take up the project with the whole group. Give them feedback.

problems they would handle every day. But whatever project you use, make your sessions fit the group. If they are not training in crisis management, don't give them a crisis to manage. If they are learning routines, give them routines to perform. Have correct answers ready if there is a chance there may be some doubt about the outcome. Use the material you've taught to verify their answers. (This repetition also locks in learning.)

Assign a project that can be completed in the time you allow. The projects should be challenging (nothing is more boring than an easy project), but not unreasonably so. Allow seminar time for at least part of the project to be completed. Homework is good, but practice time at the learning site (with the trainer available) is better.

Projects can be either individual or group; in fact, give them both. An individual project ensures that everyone participates and gets a chance for feedback and evaluation. A group project builds teamwork, and reflects the more realistic working environment. Group activities set up the personal interactions that all of us must cope with every day.

Evaluate each project, usually done most easily at home. Give each individual attention and indicate that you have seen the work by making marginal notes, corrections, responses. Give both positive and negative feedback. If you allow only the negative, you will discourage the learners. If you give only the positive, they will not correct bad habits.

Remember also that you are not grading! Make no comparisons. You are providing feedback on how each trainee or group has done. Set in your mind the specific things you will look for, and remain consistent. Usually these things relate to your objectives, which will help you target your criticism. Don't hesitate to correct the work if it appears they don't understand, but be wary of doing it for them. If you feel they should be able to respond, challenge them with your critique. Make them rethink their work and correct the errors. After all, they will be expected to do that in their job.

Discuss the projects with the whole group. Explain what you were looking for and show examples of those who did it correctly (use different people each time if possible). Select one or two that weren't up to par and ask the group to explain how they could have been done better (again, not always the same people).

Case Histories

A case history is an enlarged project session. Rather than addressing an isolated incident, it encompasses many separate events in realistic complexity. It is usually structured around a single large problem or event that must be solved by using techniques covered in your training.

Case histories can bring the subject alive for your group. They are a way of approaching real-life problems. In writing a case history for the group, remember to define the basic situation (company, division, and so forth) and then describe the problem and the events that led up to it. Also mention any complications, barriers, political drawbacks, or missing data. Provide all necessary and relevant data, then ask specific questions which will help the group solve the case.

Make the case history real. Use the same sources and approaches as for project sessions, but develop a rich context for them. People love stories. The more realistic texture you can provide, the more you'll motivate and involve the group.

The cases should be realistically complex; they need to be challenging. Therefore, save them until trainees have mastered enough material to solve them, or use the case histories as a topic around which to structure each step or phase of your lesson. Have answers to most of the questions but leave some unanswered as would be the case in real life. Use the group's answers whenever possible as correct or acceptable ones.

Case histories can be assigned to individuals or to groups. If given to individuals, they can challenge and motivate learners who are ahead of the others. They can also be used to involve shy participants who wouldn't get much input in group work. On the other hand, it is more work for you to evaluate. If you are not prepared to give them individual attention, don't assign cases to individuals. When groups handle a case history, the work simulates the real world in that it forces the members of the group to cooperate. It also builds team spirit in class and encourages sharing of knowledge—the most experienced help the least experienced. Group work also encourages division of labor, as more complex tasks are divided up. Lastly, the group activity can be evaluated in more detail because you'll have fewer case histories to review.

Practice Sessions

As with the project sessions, make these hands-on practices as real as possible. Again, material should come from real-life situations. In the case of technical training, use the actual equipment that would be in the field. If that's not feasible, use as close to the real thing as possible. The purpose here is to simulate reality. Use real forms, real computer programs, real job templates, and so on.

However, when they are not available, alternatives to actual situations include computer-generated data (which involves either writing or buying a program—see Chapters 9 and 11); buying or building a working model of the equipment; acquiring a similar piece of equipment; using old equipment that approximates the operation; working with real equipment that is not on line (after hours, back-up equipment, equipment being serviced, and so on).

But regardless of what you have to work on, create clearly defined, structured tasks that involve the skills you have taught. Make sure each objective is covered, but nothing more. Be certain your trainees know what it is they are to solve or do. If possible, have checkpoints at which everyone can stop and evaluate the work in progress. These checkpoints give you more control and give the trainees an early chance to correct errors. Lastly, have a correct method or model to refer to.

Whereas hands-on practice is most appropriate in situations involving equipment or procedures, role-playing is a good way to practice interaction skills. If there is reluctance to participate in role-playing, assign teams, with each team responsible for one role. Have the teams prepare a strategy for their side and select who will play the role. This takes each player off the hook. Individuals can blame the team's strategy, if need be. Also, using teams allows the "hams" to go first and break the ice, but it keeps them under control too, because they don't want to let the team down.

Team role-playing allows everyone to participate. If you don't have enough time for everyone to role-play, the team approach lets you begin it in an organized way, yet stop when you need to without cutting anyone off. If you have time, it ensures that everyone role-plays without your having to force them. Lastly, the team activity builds the competition that makes the team a group.

As an alternative to the team approach, you can encourage greater realism by breaking the class into groups of three. Each one then takes a turn playing a role while the third critiques the other two. This frees you to wander and critique other trios.

If understanding is lacking, interrupt the role-play and have participants switch roles. If the situations aren't public and your trainees are self-conscious, consider videotaping the role-play in private. Then allow the group to view and critique the tape. If possible, videotape all role-plays in any event to let participants see themselves in action. See Chapter 11 for how to use video.

Always schedule time to discuss and analyze the performances. The evaluations are as important as the sessions themselves. Also, structure your evaluations. Don't critique off the top of your head, but, rather, set objectives for yourself and the trainees, then cover all bases. Avoid information overload. If an individual is very poor, pick the most readily correctable problem, forget the rest of the performance, and concentrate on bringing that one skill up to par. Once you succeed, work on each of the other problems in turn. Lastly, praise in equal measure, but praise only what is truly good. False praise de-motivates almost as fast as too much criticism.

Examinations

Exams test for "book" learning. They cannot really test practical experience. In fact, because most colleges rely very heavily on exams as a means of evaluation, a common criticism of recent college graduates is that they have good academic, but no hands-on, background. In a business environment, case histories and projects, assessment sessions, and, of course, on-the-job-training are much better means of evaluating actual performance.

What exams can tell you is the extent to which the trainees have learned and can recall what they have been taught; used for this purpose, exams are effective measuring tools. Where content, vocabulary, formats, formulas, and the like need to be mastered, the exam is a vital evaluation mechanism for both trainer and trainee.

The Effectiveness of Tests

It is important to consider two defining factors about exams: reliability and validity.

Reliability means that the test you've created gets consistent results over a period of time, with similar groups of trainees. It means the results are probably quite accurate. The more times a good test is given, the more reliable it becomes because each administration increases the data base

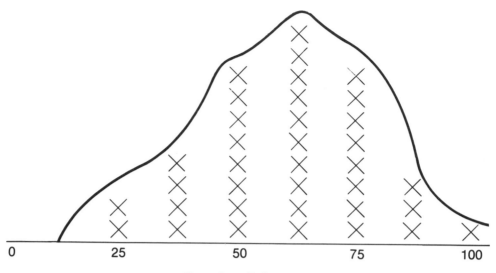

Figure 6-1. Trainee test results.

against which an individual's or group's performance is measured. Reliability is a statistical function.

To test for reliability, record all of the raw (actual) scores for each group of trainees who take the examination. Figure 6-1 is a graph showing the scores on a scale from 1 to 100. Each "x" represents a trainee's score. That is, for each trainee who scores a 99 on the test, make an x above 99 on the graph. For each score of 98, place an x above 98, and so on. Stack each x for a particular score on top of the previous x. When the tops of columns of x's are connected, you have what statisticians call a standard bell, or distribution, curve. In any large population, a small percentage of the people will score very high, a slightly larger percentage will score quite high, still more will score high; most will score in the middle range; and fewer will score below average, still fewer well below average, even fewer yet will be poor; a small percentage (about equal to the group that scored highest) will score very poorly.

Remember you are not being graded yourself. No one will see these results but you. You need only use a rule-of-thumb measurement to keep on track and establish consistency. It is possible, even desirable if you are a statistician, to make a detailed analysis incorporating a standard deviation and correction for possible errors and with means, norms, and so forth. But it is not necessary. I have informally tracked hundreds of exams over the years and found them as reliable as those tested by sophisticated analyses. If you like statistics and work for a boss who thrives on them, compile the information. If you don't, and your boss cares only that the results be accurate, you will find my simple system more than adequate.

Record the results each time you give the test. Once you have a dozen or so instances, chart them on a master bell curve. Each time you give the exam, compare the results with your master curve. The same test should get approximately the same spread of scores, forming the same basic curve. If so, you have a sufficiently reliable test.

If you fail to get consistent results, either adjust your teaching or change the exam. A single aberrant score for an otherwise reliable test indicates either an exceptional group or a change in content emphasis. To fine-tune a test that scores outside the normal range you expect, make the questions more difficult if you want to lower the scores and easier if you want to raise them.

Reliability refers to whether you can depend on test results to accurately reflect performance. *Validity,* on the other hand, indicates whether people have learned the material you have taught. For example, standard Intelligence Quotient tests are among the most reliable ever devised. Thousands upon thousands of people have scored in classic distribution curves, and each score is ranked in relation to other scores. However, no one has yet proved that an IQ test is a valid indication of intelligence. There is only marginal proof that a high IQ score indicates a tendency to earn high grades in white middle-class American schools. This is why the U.S. Equal Employment Opportunity Commission has long regarded them with suspicion, and requires prospective employees to be tested directly and legitimately for the job for which they are applying.

Validity establishes what is being tested. The process of validating a test can be complex and time consuming or relatively easy. All you really need is what is called "surface validity," meaning that the questions you ask are directly related to the material you have taught.

To establish formal validity for a test, make each question relate to one of your written objectives. If you have assigned a manual, write the questions to relate to specific statements in that manual. As a help, if teaching from a particularly detailed manual, I include at the end of each question the page number where the answer can be found. This facilitates self-correction.

Be prepared to accept discussion from trainees (in fact, you might want to solicit it) on how fair or difficult your test was. Another approach is to run the test by several area experts or other trainers for their feedback.

Maintaining both reliability and validity records will provide you with (1) hard data on the effectiveness of your training, and (2) documented evidence of your fairness in evaluating trainees, should a dispute or E.E.O. lawsuit arise.

Types of Questions

Most of us are so familiar with *multiple-choice questions* that we turn automatically to this format. It is effective for evaluating straight recall of facts and for testing recognition of principles but otherwise this question type is rather limited. If you do use it, offer at least four choices. If you wish to test the ability to discriminate among alternatives, make several choices correct but only one perfect. Use "all of the above" and "none of the above" sparingly. They encourage guessing.

The multiple-choice format allows humor. Lighten the pressure from time to time by making one choice absurd. This can be particularly effective if the humor comes from some event or situation shared by the group. Try to vary the format with other types of questions, too. Use only 20 multiple-choice questions in a set (several sets are possible in a longer test). This gives a built-in break.

If you give regular exams and worry about having different questions for different groups, write and store about 100 questions in a computer and then program it to select at random and print the quantity of questions you need. This is a great time saver.

Fill-in-the-blank questions serve much the same purpose as multiple-choice but are not as easy to guess right. Include enough information in the sentences so they can be understood. Few questions are more frustrating than ambiguous fill-in-the-blank questions.

Never use *true–false questions*. These are temptingly easy to write, but psychologically they reinforce the false statements as strongly as the true ones. Frequently, trainees come away remembering the negative statement rather than the true one.

Matching questions are excellent for evaluating recall and discriminating between choices. *Labeling diagrams* are perfect for subjects in which trainees must recall the names of parts.

Tests also include *short and long essays*. If you are evaluating judgment — that is, a trainee's ability to use the material taught — then the essay question is hands-on problem solving. It forces thought and involves the test-taker far more than any other question format. The essay question is the type from which the Harvard Business School developed the concept of case histories. Short essays (a sentence or two) draw specific responses; long essays probe thinking processes. Also, the essay format exposes those who don't understand and need extra help.

When making essay questions, keep your objectives in mind. Be sure the question asks for a specific response, since this makes it easier to evaluate and is more valid than generalizations. Mini-case histories work nicely, too.

Assessment Sessions

If your training programs are used to assess employee performance, for legal reasons you must keep accurate testing records. Convert performance to numbers, and chart both reliability and validity, as we described earlier. Informal assessment sessions, however, can also be effective forms of evaluation. Here are some common types:

1. *In-basket exercise.* Each participant is given an envelop of materials that are imagined to be from his or her in-basket that morning. Each participant must deal witn all of the items during a limited time. Some tasks are hard, some impossible, some frivolous — even fun. You then evaluate them in terms of creativity, use of time, correct procedures followed, and so on.

2. *Presentations.* These are particularly effective for training sales representatives, platform speakers, or anyone who regularly makes presentations. Videotape the talks if possible, so trainees can see themselves; few critiques are as powerful as your own when you see yourself as others see you. In addition, give the participants time to prepare. Provide specific instructions for what you want them to do. Evaluate immediately, and praise as well as critique their presentation.

3. *Role-playing.* As mentioned earlier, role-playing is excellent for improving communication. Role-playing as a practice session has already been discussed. For an assessment session, make sure that the assignment demands participants use the material you've taught. If the role-play wanders off the subject, interrupt it and make the participants replay it, then discuss the difference. If you are comfortable doing so, you can role-play with them, but don't be too hard with them.

On-the-Job Training

As we suggested earlier, follow up your training with visits to the workplace to see how what you have taught is being used. Watch your trainees at work and talk to their supervisors. See whether the material you've taught is holding on.

After the formal training session, when a newly trained employee meets his or her supervisor, the supervisor often says, "Forget all that stuff you learned in training. Here's how you're gonna do the job. . . ." The training is wasted. If you find yourself in such a predicament, remember that you are a service function, not a judicial system. It doesn't matter if your way is "right," since your job is to see that the training is consistent with the OJT follow-up.

Change your course to match the supervisor's procedures. Talk with the supervisor and get his or her input. Explain your position as one of serving and nail down what should be taught. If the supervisor is a maverick, try to persuade him or her to go with your way. See if the other supervisors can bring the maverick in line. Failing that, teach both ways so trainees won't be confused.

Of course, if the supervisor wants to do it one way and your manager wants it done another way, you have an organizational problem, not a training problem. You'll need strong management support to retrain or bring the supervisor in line. Bring the supervisor to the training and let him or her coach your trainees in class. This will help you gain respect and cooperation. You can also retrain the supervisor to the standard way. Supervisors will be more cooperative if they decide which way will become the company standard.

In any event, provide some training classes for the supervisors. Show them how to evaluate the trainees and coach them on the job. This will standardize the approach for you, for the supervisors, for the trainees, and for the company.

Self-Evaluation

So far, we've talked about the evaluation of trainees. You, too, need to know how you are doing. Bring a tape recorder to your classes and record an hour here and there at random. Do it several times, then listen to the tapes and ask yourself if *you* could learn from that trainer. If so, why? If not, why not? Then do the same with a video camera. The trainees won't mind, and the experience is invaluable.

Invite someone whose judgment you respect to observe and critique you. Give that person a list of attributes to evaluate.

Ask your trainees to fill out evaluation forms during or at the completion of their training. Follow their advice. You can't please all of them, so don't try but look for patterns in negative comments and change in response to them. Enjoy the positive comments, but seriously weigh the negative ones. Ask questions like, "Was the material too theoretical? Just right? Too practical or too elementary?" "What did you feel you learned?" Have them rate you or the seminar on a scale of from 1 to 5, where 5 is excellent or just use categories of excellent, very good, good, fair, and poor.

When you want to change your own pattern of teaching, set goals for yourself with set time limits. Don't be locked into certain methods. Try different things and see how the group responds. Go with a good response. If you have to break a bad habit, like saying "okay" at the end of each thought, try these:

1. Create a mnemonic device to remind yourself you are breaking a habit. It can be putting something unusual in your pocket (my

favorite is a pegboard hook), wearing a watch upside down, tieing a string on your finger, putting a sign in the back of the room. Use anything that will remind you not to do the habit.

2. Invent a new behavior to replace the old one.
3. Every time you notice your mnemonic device, immediately stop the old habit for 5 minutes and do the new habit. Increase to 10 minutes, then 20, then 45 minutes and so on.
4. If all else fails, ask your trainees to help. Explain that you are trying to break a bad habit and show them what it is. Ask them to make a loud noise whenever you do it. I have used this with great success to break several bad habits. (I ask them to give me a Bronx cheer.)

Evaluating Affective Learning

So far the discussion has focused on evaluating cognitive learning. It is relatively easy to tell when people improve their performance of a job. It is more difficult to ascertain whether you have influenced someone's attitude. The key, again, is finding a variable that changes with attitude change. By monitoring this variable you can gauge the change in attitude as well. Here are some variables that indicate attitude change:

Facial Expressions

The face is so obvious we tend to forget how much it is a barometer of attitude. A smiling, alert, animated face has an "up" attitude. A stiff or drooping face indicates the reverse. Maintaining eye contact, using the Socratic method, and moving closer to the group cause changes in facial expressions that reveal true attitude. Monitor these to determine immediate moods.

Instructor Evaluations

Receiving an "excellent" rating on evaluations not only means that your training skills are good but that the group has a positive attitude toward both you and the material. The two are directly related. Exciting material makes the instructor look good, and a good instructor can make even poor material exciting. Of course, if you receive a "poor" rating, you can assume the trainees have learned little and feel "down" about the session. Ask questions such as "Did you achieve your personal objectives in coming here?" "What do you feel you've learned?" You can garner feedback that reveals the trainees' attitudes.

Word of Mouth and Formal Surveys

It is possible to gauge how employees feel about a subject, a type of work, an impending or recent change, their training, and other trainees by tapping the company grapevine. Find someone who always knows what's going on. You won't get hard data, but you'll find out how well you've achieved your affective training objectives.

As mentioned earlier, the in-house magazine or newsletter is a good place to run a survey. Surveys are usually anonymous so that they invite honest answers. If you are not perceived in a hostile light you might circulate among workers and ask for their responses to key attitude questions. This technique was used in the famous Mayo–Hawthorne studies,[1] which discovered that people work harder and better when they know others are watching them. Dr. Mayo and his team interviewed employees and asked them to tell how they felt. If you want to use a survey read the discussion of surveys and interviews in Chapter 5.

Participation

If you have been doing motivational training, monitor the figures on voluntary participation in such things as blood drives, the United Way, toy collections for needy children, and so on. In a similar vein, watch for employee activity in company-sponsored events such as Little League or the annual picnic. Participation in such activities usually reflects positive attitude.

Confrontations

Look at the company records on confrontations. A reduction in the number or types of arguments in the workplace reflects shifts in attitude.

Absenteeism and Turnover Rates

High absenteeism is related to employee attitude, as are turnover rates. Employees who stay with the company usually like something about it.

Safety-Related Accidents

The number of accidents tends to decrease with increasingly positive attitudes toward safety, safety training, and the company as a whole.

Scrap (Reject) and Error Rates

Happy workers make fewer errors. People who care about quality take the time to do a job right. On the other hand, excessive errors and wasted materials point to poor work attitudes.

Long-Term Evaluations

People grow and change constantly. Many things in our daily lives impact on our behavior. In the work environment, training is only one cause of change. Consequently, long-term evaluations are difficult to compile. How can we know: (1) that any changes which have taken place are a result of our training, and (2) whether other powerful influences have counteracted our training somewhere along the line?

The task is complicated further by a gradually diminishing population. True, we may train more people but over the years each group grows smaller as people retire, move, or change jobs.

Yet long-term evaluations are needed. If you are happily training hundreds of employees yet have no idea whether they perform to the standards they've been taught — or even if they use the skills you've given them — you are failing in your mandate. Remember, the purpose of training is to bring about change. If you don't measure the change that has taken place, you can't know if you are performing the task. There are, fortunately, several ways of overcoming the previously mentioned difficulties.

1. *Set key variables.* Plant a method or a word in the midst of your program — some particularly clear example or acronym. Years later, as you talk to those you've trained, listen for those key terms, techniques, or descriptions. They may have forgotten how they learned them, but you'll know. Of course, this technique assumes that you'll keep in touch with at least some of those you trained.
2. *Take posttraining surveys.* Let your trainees know that at some future date they will be asked to respond to a survey. Send out a simple survey no sooner than three to six weeks after training, asking which skills they are using and which have benefited them. Have them describe an instance in which they feel their new skills helped them do a better job. Ask for comments on the validity of the training now that they have had a chance to put it into practice. If you explain while they are still in training that the future survey

---

Methods for Long-Term Evaluations

1. Set key variables to follow.
2. Send posttraining surveys.
3. Offer segmented training over months or years.
4. Prepare a follow-up needs assessment.
5. Check data on performance impacted by training — scrap, sales, and so on.
6. Convert data to percentages whenever possible.

---

       is an aid to *your* performance rather than an evaluation of theirs and that you need their feedback, you should get a reasonable response after training when you send the survey out. Do the survey a year after the training, if you can.

3. *Hold follow-up sessions.* Structure your training in well-spaced intervals. If you get the same group every six months or even once a year, evaluate how well they have used what they were taught last time. Use pretests and posttests as well as assessment sessions, projects, case histories, and role-playing. I've had particular success with this technique in sales training. Often in unsupervised work such as sales, the trainees enjoy the session but fail to put into practice much of what they are taught. One or two of them do, however, and their sales performance soars. At follow-up sessions, I use those who've succeeded as examples to motivate the others.

4. *Perform a needs analysis.* One year after training, collect data in the normal way (see Chapter 4), then compare that data to your earlier results.

5. *Monitor company records.* If your training impacts directly on measurable data like scrap rates, sales, customer complaints, and so on, track these data over the years and see what the accumulated information reveals.

    A useful tip for long-term evaluations is converting your data to percentages. As the population shrinks, fewer and fewer trainees can respond. Straight data would erroneously imply a decline in training effectiveness. By converting the results to percentages, you can report such facts as 98 percent of those responding to a recent survey felt that training significantly impacted on their work — even though only six or seven former trainees were left to respond.

Summary

Evaluation is the feedback that keeps training programs on track. It is how you can measure the changes you are bringing about. Evaluations are also vital for trainees to see how they are progressing. Evaluation engages the Law of Effect by forming the base against which performance can be measured.

There are two forms of evaluation: short-term and long-term. There are also two areas in which to evaluate: cognitive and affective learning. Of these, the short-term impact of cognitive training is the easiest to evaluate, using traditional tools such as exams, quizzes, questions, or projects. Affective learning is harder to evaluate because it is more subjective. However, by observing mood and effort, you often have enough information for a short-term evaluation.

By far the most difficult are long-term evaluations of affective learning. Measuring long-term cognitive skills is only marginally less troublesome. For either, the essential tasks are (1) to monitor key variables, (2) to remain in touch with those you've trained, and (3) to convert all long-term data to percentages so as to counter the problem of a shrinking population.

Finally, remember that the purpose of evaluation is not just to see how well you've done, though that is important, but to diagnose those areas in which you can do better. We don't evaluate just to prove we did something but, rather, to improve how we do it in the future.

CHAPTER 7

Researching
the Subject Matter

THIS chapter could have been called "How to Become an Expert in any Field." Of course you won't really become an expert in complex fields, since that would take years of study, but you can easily gain enough expertise to train others in most subjects. Let me explain.

One of the principal errors new trainers make is to confuse content with method. As a trainer, you are an expert in method. Content, while obviously important, is subordinate to method. It is not what you teach, but how you teach it that makes you an expert. I realized this years ago when, as a high school English teacher, I was approached by students to help them with their math. I didn't know the math, having been very poor in the subject myself, but I was able to teach them a great deal by using the Socratic method, challenging them to deduce for themselves the principles behind the formulas. Their grades improved, and I learned math from them. When I taught college, the same pattern reconfirmed my discovery. I was able to teach subjects I knew little about because I could recognize a learning difficulty and devise a method that would help the learner around it and stimulate him or her to become excited about it.

Recently I was driving with my ten-year-old daughter and one of her friends. The friend asked what I did for a living and I answered, "I teach teachers to teach."

"To teach what?" she said.

"To teach whatever it is that they teach," I replied.

"Yes, but what?" she insisted, puzzled.

"To teach better," I said.

"To teach *what* better?" She was becoming angry, thinking I was playing a game with her.

"Just how to teach better," I said gently. She had simply never considered teaching as a thing in itself—a science or art, a discrete activity. Yet this entire book is about the art, science, and activity of teaching. It is said that a good salesperson can sell anything; a good teacher can teach anything.

Understand, I do not hold this view out of arrogance. I am not making a boast that I can teach anything better than the experts or without expertise. I am not saying that I can become an expert in the sense of being vastly knowledgeable about a subject in a short period of time. I *am* saying that any of us can gain sufficient understanding in most subject areas to be able to apply sound teaching methods to motivate learners and help them to master those subjects.

There is no charlatanism, no hype here, just good, solid, analytic, methodical, problem-solving techniques. We are expert teachers who can use subject experts to train others. This chapter is about how to do so.

Let us say you train customer service personnel for a manufacturing company. Business has been off lately, and senior management asks if some form of training would help. You offer to perform a needs analysis, and they agree. Your needs analysis uncovers the fact that there is no one in the company who knows about marketing. Products have been sold off the shelf in the same way since the company was founded 150 years ago. No one knows a different way.

You recommend that the senior staff be trained in creative marketing. Management likes the idea and says, "How soon can you teach a course like that?"

"Well, I really don't know anything about marketing either," you say, having been a school teacher before you moved into training.

"We certainly can't wait for everybody to learn it on their own, and I don't have the budget to bring in an outside expert. Take whatever resources you need and put together a course in three weeks," says management.

How do you begin? You look for information on the subject. There are two basic sources of information on any subject: printed matter and people.

Information from Printed Sources

You can obtain a great deal of information by reading what others have said on your particular topic. Begin your search by going to your local public library, nearby college library, or perhaps a private library in your area. Also check general and business bookstores as well as college bookstores. These sources should have two or three books or articles on whatever subject interests you. To become reasonably well informed on the topic, read three books and at least three articles. Cross-check topics in each, then tentatively decide which topics are most applicable and what methods you'd use to best teach them.

Public Libraries

Know what information you need before you go looking for it. For instance, if you ask for books on marketing, a librarian will have too many to refer you to. Narrow down your topic to, say, creative marketing techniques in your industry. Also, don't wander the aisles aimlessly. Ask the reference librarian for assistance, because he or she knows the library from top to bottom. If there is an appropriate book, the librarian will locate it for you. Ask for exactly what you want, and chances are it will be there.

The *Subject Guide to Books in Print* is a useful set of volumes available in all libraries. It lists every book in print, arranged by subject. Find your topic in the guide and you'll have a list of current books that you can borrow from the library or have a bookstore order.

The *Business Periodicals Index* is another set of volumes found in all libraries. It lists articles that have appeared in the most important business journals and magazines. Arranged by subject, the listings give title, author, name of the periodical or magazine, volume number, and date of issue. The index also categorizes book reviews, which might prove useful.

College Libraries

Colleges and universities that offer business courses, especially at the graduate level, usually have excellent libraries with good selections of current and classic business books. Even if your topic is not related to business (advanced physics, for instance), college libraries are often better resources for specialized information. You may have to be a student to use the library, however, but simply enroll in an evening class and you'll receive an ID card. (You may be able to hire a graduate student to do your research for you; check with the college librarian or appropriate graduate department.)

Private Libraries

Many professional organizations, even some private companies, have excellent libraries which can be a good source of information, particularly for technical subjects. Most public libraries have a copy of the *Directory of Special Libraries and Information Centers;* check it for names, addresses, and phone numbers for nearly all of the private libraries in the United States. An alternative route is to contact the appropriate professional association. In the case of training, you could call the local chapter or national office of the American Society for Training and Development. In the marketing area, you would try marketing associations, which are listed in the *Encyclopedia of Associations* or the *National Trade and Professional Associations of the United States.*

Bookstores

Most large independent bookstores have a section devoted to business books. The bookstore chains, like Waldenbooks, usually don't stock many business books, but specialized business bookstores have a very wide selection of current titles. If a book is in print but the store doesn't have it, ask them to order it for you.

College bookstores are excellent resources because their books are always arranged by subject and are usually very current and first rate. Furthermore, the books are sometimes discounted, and you rarely need to prove you are a student. To return to our example of marketing, you would find a first-year text to be the fastest way to learn about the field. You could then follow-up with specialized books on creative marketing.

Direct Mail Promotions — Catalogues

Every day your company receives literature promoting seminars, books, and audio- and videocassettes on topics of interest to people in the field. These brochures contain lists of topics that experts see as relevant to the field. Essentially, they give you outlines and summaries that you can use to research a training session.

Information from Experts in the Field

The second major source of information is people. Interviews with experts can make you knowledgeable very quickly. Television reporters and talk show hosts seem very well informed, even when the topic is new to them. Read up on the subject first, then talk to the expert to discuss finer points.

Experts are all around you, but look especially among in-house people at your company and at nearby colleges and universities, those involved in service or professional associations, the regional chamber of commerce, and a local speakers bureau or Toastmaster's club. Direct mail catalogues are also a useful source of names.

In-House

By far the most accessible and credible source is the expert who works for your company. To find such an expert, go to personnel and review your needs with them. Check their files for résumés to uncover work experience, education, hobbies, and so on. Also go to the department in question and ask the supervisor for the name of the best worker, sales rep, clerk, machine operator, secretary, researcher, scientist, or whomever.

Colleges and Universities

Go to the chairperson of the appropriate department and explain your purpose. Most professors are more than happy to help local businesses. Make your visit official, and you should be received warmly.

Professional Organizations

The professional organizations know who their stars are. The stars have written books on the subject and are leading speakers in their field. Several associations, like the American Society for Training and Development, publish directories of their members, and some organizations rate their speakers, courses, and off-the-shelf packages. A phone call to one of these groups can get you advice, a proposal, or a schedule of when and where one of its experts will be giving public seminars. The American Management Association, for example, regularly offers public seminars on many business topics. You can be sure nearly every speaker or seminar leader is terrific. However, some organizations and associations maintain a rating service for their members to evaluate speakers, courses, and off-the-shelf packages. For a reasonable fee and a few days or hours of time, you get immersion in the subject with an expert. There are few better ways of learning something.

Chambers of Commerce

These are organizations that service the community and promote local business. They often compile lists of member experts or consultants, and can be very helpful.

Speakers Bureaus and Toastmaster's Clubs

These clubs are starting places for people building their consulting businesses. The Yellow Pages of your phone book will list a nearby bureau or chapter. Ask if it has speakers in the subject area you are researching. There may be a small fee, but you will have an expert who's more than willing to help.

Direct Mail Promotions — Catalogues

We've already discussed how brochures and catalogues that come in the mail can give you information on a subject. Most of these brochures also describe the background and expertise of the speaker or author. These people are reachable at the addresses or phone numbers given in the brochures, but remember that they make a living selling their time. Don't expect free advice.

Interviewing the Experts

You will have to polish your interviewing skills, either to obtain information from experts or, later on, to identify the tasks involved in particular job skills. In Chapter 5, interviewing skills were discussed in relation to needs analysis. The same techniques can be used to draw information from your experts.

1. Know what you want to accomplish. Plan the interview to be thorough and efficient. Plan your questions to meet your objectives.
2. Know to whom you are talking. Experts will relax and be more open with you if you can establish credibility right away.
3. Use active listening. Probe for full information and ask questions to clarify information. Ask, don't tell. You are there to learn, even if you disagree.
4. Keep the interview short. Key people are usually busy, and they don't have much time to spare. Furthermore, the closer you stick to the point, the easier it will be to analyze your results. Set a time limit and stick to it, unless your expert wants to run over.

If you are using the interview to identify the tasks involved in a particular job, structure your questions so you obtain a title and complete job description, full delineation of constituent jobs for which the individual is responsible, and a complete list of the tasks involved with each constituent job. Clear your conclusions with the expert. Let the person know you will come back to verify the information, so he or she can give you that extra time.

Preparing a Task Analysis

To make yourself a subject expert, prepare a task analysis. Locating information or a subject expert is the first step in preparing a task analysis. Let's look at the other steps; first, here's a checklist, then the steps are discussed in detail.

1. Locate information or an expert on the subject.
2. Define a preliminary task list — how is the job done?
3. Observe an expert performing the job.
4. Refine the task list.
5. Check the refined task list with the expert.
6. Verify the task analysis with management — is it the procedure they want?
7. Validate the list with others performing the task.
8. Develop specific criteria for training others to perform the task.
9. Refine the list after each training session.

Locate Your Information or Expert

The sources of information have been mentioned, but remember not to become bogged down with this phase. The nearest, most accessible, and easiest-to-work-with expert is the best one. If yours is a leader in the field, so much the better. But someone closest to home is usually easiest to get to, talk to, and work with. Keep it simple; this should be an easy step, not a complex one.

Define a Preliminary Task List

Start with a job description, usually a single paragraph to describe what a job entails. People actually on the job are best for this, since a written source is often too generic. Once you have the job description, define the separate jobs it involves. For instance, if you are to train sales-people, you will need to break that job into its component parts: market analysis, prospecting, proposal writing, presentations to clients, initiating appointments, closing sales, and doing paper work. Each of these is a function most salespeople must perform. By breaking each into a subject area for separate analysis you facilitate the process of learning. Then break down these job parts still further into specific tasks. In our example, prospecting might consist of telephone skills, setting objectives, probing skills, territory management, and ways of working with secretaries who screen callers. At this point you will have enough data to know what your course needs to cover.

Observe an Expert Performing the Job

Most people who are very good at something find it hard to describe precisely what they do. They seem to just have a knack — an instinct or talent that guides them. Putting your finger on that element can be difficult. It is often impossible for those with the talent to tell you what it is that works for them. You need to observe very closely how they perform their tasks. Videotaping can prove useful in allowing you to study the expert's performance. You are looking for the components of each task. For example, you might have to list the ways a salesperson talks to secretaries and receptionists. What are the smallest units of performance you can observe? These are the steps to mastery. Perhaps one of them needs to be broken down still further to yet another sublevel of activity. Ask yourself with each step or skill, "Can anything else happen at this point?" If not, you've reached the essential task. If more can happen, break it down to still-smaller tasks.

Refine the Task List

The best way to put it all together is by creating a flowchart. Figure 7-1 is an example of such a flowchart. With the flowchart you have laid out at least four distinct layers of work: the job description for that particular function, the constituent jobs within that function, the specific tasks involved in each constituent job, and the steps (and substeps) necessary to complete each task.

Check the Refined Task List with the Expert

Ask your expert to go over the steps with you in order to verify the information. This is an iterative task. It is not only a check but also a

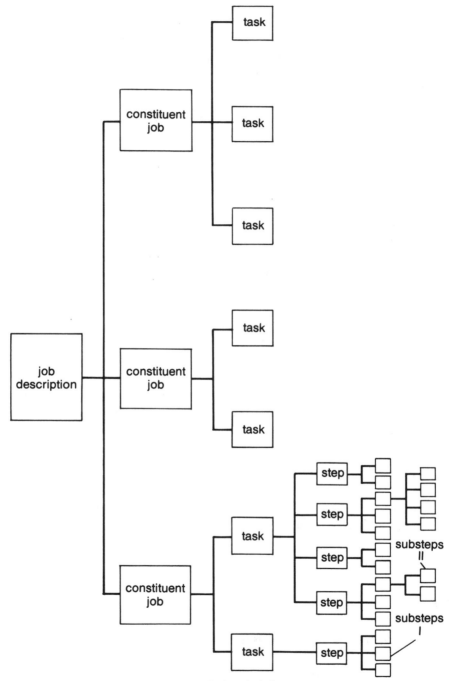

Figure 7-1.   Task analysis flowchart.

negotiation. Use the videotape, if you have one, to clarify perceptions and validate your observations.

Verify the Task Analysis with Management

If you have full autonomy, this step is unnecessary. On the other hand, if you have been given this assignment by someone higher up, now is the time to get that person's okay. Make sure that management fully understands the discrepancies between present and ideal performance of the task. Show how your training program will correct the situation. If possible, get approval in writing.

Validate the List with Others

Give the list a dry run with other experts. Find out how close your observations come to the defined performance level. Check the analysis with the supervisors to be sure it is accurate and meets the demands of those for whom you'll be training.

Develop Specific Criteria for Training

Break the steps into training sequences. Group similar sequences and arrange the material to make it easy to learn. Remember, it seldom *has* to be chronological; there may be better ways.

At this point you should also establish your standards of performance. Must the trainees match the performance of the expert? What margins are you allowing for individual differences? How will you measure their ability? Under what special conditions will each task be performed, and how will this affect your training?

Specific Criteria for Training

1. Which tasks or steps are similar and can be grouped together?
2. Which steps can the trainees already perform?
3. How can these tasks be broken into learning sequences?
4. What is the sequence easiest to learn?
5. At what level of mastery should I aim?
6. What margins should I allow for individual differences?
7. How will I measure trainee performance?
8. What special conditions must be met before I can assume they have mastered the subject?

Refine the List After Each Training Session

This is how you validate your course. Use the task analysis to fine-tune the course, then use the course to fine-tune the task analysis. When your trainees are learning each step without difficulty, you can feel you've completed the task analysis. Even then, check back about once a year to make sure you are still on track.

When you don't have an expert to guide you in compiling the task analysis, written information becomes your only source and your ability to verify steps is seriously impaired. In such cases you have to depend even more on management review, on checks by supervisors, and on refining the analysis during and after each session.

It is obvious that there is a great deal of work involved in creating a formal task analysis. Remember, the purpose of training is to bring about a change in performance. Your needs analysis should be only as formal as you need it to be. When you compare the *status quo* with the first three levels of the task analysis, you are likely to find similarities, even identical behaviors. In such instances, you don't have to analyze those steps. Do a formal analysis only on those tasks that must be changed. Of course, if the purpose of your task analysis is to create a detailed job analysis for company records, you can't skip any steps. In addition, the nature of the trainee group also dictates the detail of the analysis. A group of experienced systems engineers might not need the detail that a group of new employees might. Such considerations depend upon the group, the degree of change desired, the standards set with supervisors, the demands of management, and the subject to be studied.

Be careful. While spending grueling hours perfecting a task analysis may sometimes be unnecessary, taking shortcuts may mean detailed re-evaluations later. And those usually are more grueling.

Justifying the Task Analysis

Why should you perform a task analysis? What benefits do you gain? Here are some of the benefits of a task analysis.

Training Content

A task analysis describes what a job is. Consequently it specifies what needs to be taught. It sets the content for your training program.

Performance Requirements

One of the essentials of training is some form of evaluation. Task analysis provides measurable, goal-oriented performance objectives. You can determine how well or how poorly your trainees are learning because the task analysis defines performance standards.

Trainee Objectives

A formal task analysis provides trainees with criteria by which they can gauge their own performance. Remember, one of the principles of learning (see Chapter 2) is that people learn better when they have a perspective on what they will be learning. Also, they are motivated by seeing how far they've come. The task analysis gives them this learning aid.

Training Evaluation

Task analyses are a crucial way trainers can demonstrate their effectiveness to management. If those who you train can perform their tasks to the set standard, you will have trained them well. Of course this can come about without a task analysis, but the analysis gives you a written standard. This is particularly important when you must justify a budget, an expansion, or your own survival in the organization.

Standardization

As we've seen, on-the-job training can lead to problems of standardization. The training department teaches one way, supervisors demand a different way. Sometimes both agree initially but over time the concept shifts until both are at odds again. Task analysis can be the standard against which all performance can be measured.

Basic Performance Data

Any improvement in employee performance is likely to go unnoticed without basic performance data. Those who excel at their jobs will show up clearly when measured against company standards based on observed data.

Planning Aid

During budget crunches, many large organizations look to eliminate duplication of effort. Frequently these duplications become apparent through task analyses. Task analysis also resolves misunderstandings about what various jobs actually entail by defining the limits of each.

Summary

In this short chapter we have concentrated on the preparation phase of a training program. The need for such preparation and how much time you spend are determined by the degree of expertise you feel you need to have to plan and deliver a training program. We looked at ways to become sufficiently expert in any field, either through research or by working with an expert. Lastly, we covered the steps for performing a task analysis, as well as considered the benefits that such an analysis can bring.

CHAPTER 8

Writing the Training Program

IN Chapter 3, we looked at how to structure effective lesson plans. Now we look at the overall training program. Many of the same principles apply, but the perspective must expand beyond a single lesson to encompass a series of lessons. The series must show the relationship of one lesson to another and to the program as a whole. I usually look at the program as a necklace where each planned lesson is a bead. It is a useful metaphor.

Remember that you are creating an environment to make learning easy and attractive. Environments are more a result of structure than of content. Put differently, it is what you do with the material that enhances learning, not the material itself. At this point you have already set the content of your program. You've completed your needs analysis (Chapter 5) and your task analysis (Chapter 7). You are now sufficiently expert in the subject to consider how you should best present it.

To have a fully written program, you should have for each course: (1) a detailed 13-step proposal, as outlined in this chapter; (2) lesson plans for each sequence, as outlined in Chapter 3; (3) a detailed trainer's manual, as described later in this chapter; and (4) a trainee's manual (workbook), also described in this chapter. In the same file, you also ought to have all visuals and support materials (discussed further in Chapters 9 and 11); any needs or task analyses done earlier; any publicity or advertising; plus all evaluation materials (or summaries of them) and their results.

Writing the Program

When asked to prepare a training program, many beginners start by writing the manual or workbook. If you do that, you create several problems. You lock in the content too early. Your course can't reflect the needs of the trainees because it has been planned without them. Frequently, the course later shapes itself to the trainees' and the company's needs and is completely different from the workbook you have written, so you need to write a new, more meaningful book.

Many more problems can occur, but all can be prevented by following 13 logical steps. When you finally get to writing the manual, you will know your audience, your needs, your structure, your content, and your methods.

A training program embodies what is to be taught, to whom, and why. In it you need to address the 13 elements that follow:

1. A budget
2. Supervisory and management support
3. A tie-in to a larger company effort
4. A system for advertising the program
5. A rationale expressing the company's need for the program
6. A set of management goals
7. A plan for recruiting participants
8. A demographic statement outlining the population the program addresses
9. Training objectives
10. A decision regarding who will deliver the program
11. A set of evaluation tools
12. A step-by-step agenda that outlines when each element will be covered and how much time is allowed for it
13. Training manuals and handouts

Now let's consider each of these elements in detail.

Budget

If you do not yet have a budget for your course, you may be putting in a lot of work for nothing. Know how much money you can spend before you plan the course. On the other hand, you may have to do some preliminary work to acquire a budget for the program. In any event, you need to know what costs will be accrued. Budgeting procedures are covered in Chapter 12.

Supervisory and Management Support

If you have been following the procedures in this book up to this point, you will have already gained support from managers and supervisors during your needs analysis and evaluation work. If you are starting at this point, however, make sure you get that support now. To proceed without managerial or supervisory support is a waste of time. See Chapters 13 and 14 for ways to build that support.

A Tie-in to a Larger Company Effort

One of the surest ways to sink a new training program is to promote it in competition with a major management project. By the same token, if you tie your training into a company-wide thrust that has already galvanized the staff, you'll guarantee its success. During your needs analysis find out what key management people consider important or what the major thrust of the company will be, then align your training program with it.

A System for Advertising the Program

Unless you already have a system in place for getting out the word on training, don't proceed any further until you've built a public relations network. We discuss ways of publicizing your training opportunities in Chapters 1 and 13. Let's list them briefly:

1. Use in-house publications as much as possible to call attention to upcoming programs as well as report on successes.
2. Develop a word-of-mouth program with graduate trainees.
3. Send memos to all appropriate managers extolling the virtues of your training programs.
4. Post flyers and handbills on company bulletin boards and in cafeterias.
5. Ask for time at key meetings to plug your training programs.

A Rationale for the Program

Use the results of your needs analysis to explain why the company needs the training program. This is a vital element if you are preparing the program as a proposal, but it is important even if you have approval and a budget in place. The rationale summarizes the findings of your needs analysis and expresses them in management's terms, outlines the desired results, and lays out a format for achieving them. Two or three pages of justified rationale should always head the document that defines and outlines the program.

Management Goals

With the rationale your training program will be on target. Frequently, training programs are given simply because someone feels they should be or because they've always been given. I've been hired on several occasions to hold in-house seminars merely so "the employees will feel better . . . feel management is doing something for them." Such reasons are fragile justification for training programs. Instead, spell out exactly what management will gain from the training program. Remember, these are not training objectives; they come later. For the difference between training objectives and management goals, see Chapter 2.

Recruitment Plan

An important part of any program is the method of selecting candidates for the training. You must consider the qualifications trainees will need for the program, and who will select the participants. Also consider which areas or divisions of the company the training will address and which will be excluded. Should there be a minimum or maximum number of participants? How do you arrive at these figures? What happens when these numbers are exceeded or not met?

Trainee Population

Using your needs analysis, the answers to the questions just asked about recruitment and the management goals, describe the training group. Remember that who you train is far more important than what you are training. Describe the trainee population you will reach, covering such areas as:

1. Age.
2. Sex.
3. Years of experience.
4. Years with company.
5. Specific jobs or tasks.
6. Levels of aspiration.

7. Performance levels.
8. Common problems.
9. Elements from your recruitment plan, if needed.

Make your description of the trainees real. It will shape the environment you create for learning. Obviously, all the items I've listed are not always applicable, and you may need to consider other specific questions for your application. The end result is a profile of your trainees. The more detailed it is, the more helpful it will be when you structure your lessons (see Chapter 3).

Include also in this section a brief mention of the overall size of the group (that is, all entry-level employees, 10,000 clerical workers, and so on) and the anticipated length of the program (that is, how long you think it will take to train such a group). Decide and say how long each session should be and what patterns the sessions should follow (for example, Monday mornings, 8–12 noon for three months or three consecutive weekends from Friday 7 P.M. to Sunday 6 P.M. or one week 9–5 in the spring followed by one week 9–5 in the fall of the same year, and so on). The pattern and hours you choose will depend upon:

1. Your training population.
2. Your objectives.
3. Management's goals.
4. Your budget.
5. Your available time and resources.
6. Management support for the program.

Training Objectives

Using your needs analysis and task analyses, write your specific training objectives. We've covered these objectives in Chapter 3; here you are pulling together all the thinking you've done and all the material you've collected to set down exactly what this group of trainees will achieve so as to fulfill management's goals and bring about the changes mandated by the needs analysis. All of this, of course, should be accomplished within the usual constraints of time, budget, and facilities.

Program Delivery

Once you know exactly what must be covered (your objectives), give some thought to who the best person is to conduct the training. You may want to do it yourself, in which case proceed with the remaining steps and the rest of this part of the book. On the other hand, you might want to use an outside public seminar organization like the American Management Association or a private consultant. You might also want to consider commercial off-the-shelf training packages. Choosing among the alternatives is covered in Chapter 9; however, you will need to justify that choice in your program. The reasons you might choose another source to present the program could be cost, expertise, flexibility, suitability, and applicability to the trainee population as well as the corporate needs, the outside source's availability, and ownership for repeat uses.

Evaluation Tools

Specify the means of evaluation before you write the program. This helps you ensure that what you test will be what you taught. We tend to think "teach first, then test," but by deciding on and writing the tests, projects, case histories, and role-playing assignments first, you know that you will be teaching to pass the tests — that is, the short-term mastery of skills.

All this material does not necessarily belong in the description of your programs, however. Keep a file on each program, and put the evaluation material there. In your program write-up, spell out the elements of the course, and include a paragraph describing the evaluation tools you will use. Write another paragraph specifying the long-term evaluation plans, too. But *do* create these materials before you write the program agenda. They will keep you on track and make the program easier to assemble.

Program Agenda

This is the agenda that will be the heart of your program. There are several important aspects to drawing up such an agenda.

Overall Structure

Begin by dividing up your total time into separate blocks. For instance, you may have decided after your needs analysis that the trainees need 12 hours of instruction to master the skills to a level at which they can work independently. You have also decided which are the most flexible or available time frames — say, two 6-hour days. Now further divide these into smaller blocks of time: two mornings and two afternoons. Break each block into yet-smaller units, such as the morning session before break, morning session after break, afternoon session before break, afternoon session after break. Depending on your needs, or common practices in the organization, or the needs of the trainees or nature of the subject, you may want different chunks of time — say, one-hour periods (as are

---

Six Steps in Writing an Agenda

1. Divide your training time into smaller blocks of time.
2. Using needs analysis, task analysis, and training objectives, select the learning pattern (funnel, spool, or whatever).
3. Match each unit of time with one or more objectives, then select appropriate substructures (problem solution and the like) for each unit (module).
4. Select the best methods for each module.
5. Fine-tune the program by checking for variety and proper timing.
6. Write a lesson plan for each module.

---

common in high school). Use whatever elements are relevant to your situation to set up the basic time chunks for instruction.

Content Learning Pattern

Using the needs analysis (see Chapter 5), set your training objectives. Using the task analysis (Chapter 7), break the content into individual topics that correspond with the steps in the analysis. Then match the steps with your training objectives. If you have more tasks than objectives, either eliminate those tasks not relevant to your objectives or cluster related tasks so that each cluster supports a training objective. Once you know the trainees to be taught and the material to be covered, as well as the objectives to be met, you can decide on the overall pattern for your course: funnel, inverted funnel, tunnel, or spool (see Chapter 3). Arrange your topics to follow that pattern.

Module Substructures

Once you have your overall pattern, match each unit of time with an objective or series of objectives. The content of the program will now be broken down into separate time slots—modules—in a logical sequence of steps. Decide which substructure (Chapter 3) is most engaging for each module (problem solution, cause and effect, and so on). At this point, your program should look something like what is shown in Figure 8-1. (See also Figure 8-4 later in this chapter.)

Methodology

Decide which method (discussed later in this chapter) is most appropriate for your trainees, your objectives, and the substructures you've

		Objective		Task	
Day 1					
	9:00 A.M.	1.	Objective	1.	Substructure
Pre-break		2.	Objective	2.	Substructure
	10:30 A.M.	3.	Objective	3.	Substructure

Break

	10:45 A.M.	1.	Objective	1.	Substructure
Postbreak		2.	Objective	2.	Substructure
	12:00 noon	3.	Objective	3.	Substructure

Lunch

	1:00 P.M.	1.	Objective	1.	Substructure
Pre-break		2.	Objective	2.	Substructure
	2:30 P.M.	3.	Objective	3.	Substructure

Break

	2:45 P.M.	1.	Objective	1.	Substructure
Postbreak		2.	Objective	2.	Substructure
	5:00 P.M.	3.	Objective	3.	Substructure

Figure 8-1.   Sample training module.

chosen. You are already engaged in structuring each lesson plan at this point; however, consider the overall pattern of the program as well.

Fine-Tuning

Now fine-tune your program by considering some of the other factors that influence learning. For example, most participants are best able to respond to lectures in the morning. Schedule passive activities (if you need them at all) before lunch. In addition, lunch makes people sleepy, so schedule a project or stimulating activity to follow closely after lunch. Most trainees fade after 4 P.M. Either end the session at 4, or schedule your most stimulating or challenging work for this last hour of the day.

The average adult attention span isn't longer than 20 to 30 minutes. Keep *all* presentations shorter than 30 minutes. Remember also that even great techniques grow dull if they are used constantly. Vary your methods. In the presentation, practice, and evaluation stages use variety in your techniques. Adjust your material, if necessary, to accommodate these changes — it will be worth it. Vary your audiovisual aids as well (see Chapter 11).

Make the final adjustments to your program. Figure 8-2 shows the fine-tuning that was done on Figure 8-1.

Writing the Plan

You are now ready to write the lesson plan for each module. Use the four-step method (Chapter 3). Log in each substructure by time unit. I find it useful to use blank sheets of standard planning paper with time frames marked off in ten- or fifteen-minute intervals.

Figure 8-3 shows part of the final program plan begun in Figure 8-1.

Manuals and Handouts

Once you have completed the preparation steps and you've chosen an appropriate blend of teaching methods, you can finally write the training manual. Later in the chapter I discuss formats for two basic sorts of manuals: the trainer's and the trainee's. The trainer's manual is a detailed, step-by-step outline of what you will do, when you will do it, what responses you can anticipate or work for, and what tools you need. It is your reference for the course. In contrast, the trainee's manual is a workbook containing exercises and other activities, background materials, supporting charts and graphs, and room for notes. When you write these manuals, begin with the trainer's version because that will help define and structure the trainee's manual as well.

One of the saddest experiences is to start a new training job and find all the office shelves empty. Often the former trainer took everything or never had any materials in the first place. Almost as bad is finding reams of disorganized notes and random inserts. A professional program prevents these situations. In the file for each program should be at least the following: (1) a multipage document detailing the items in Figure 8-1, (2) a trainer's manual, and (3) a trainee's workbook or manual. In addition, it is helpful for future reference if there are needs analyses, task analyses, visual aids such as overhead projections or slides, classroom handouts, and evaluation materials. A good reference file facilitates the training of new instructors and the re-evaluation of older program materials. It is also a source of information when you want to refresh yourself on a course not

Day 1		Objective	Task	Method
Pre-break	9:00 A.M.	1. Objective	1. Substructure	Method 1
		2. Objective	2. Substructure	Method 2
	10:30 A.M.	3. Objective	3. Substructure	Method 2 : key activity
	Break			
Postbreak	10:45 A.M.	1. Objective	1. Substructure	Method 4
		2. Objective	2. Substructure	Method 6
	12:00 noon	3. Objective	3. Substructure	Method 3 : key activity
	Lunch			
Pre-break	1:00 P.M.	1. Objective	1. Substructure	Method 2
		2. Objective	2. Substructure	Method 5
	2:30 P.M.	3. Objective	3. Substructure	Method 4 : key activity
	Break			
Postbreak	2:45 P.M.	1. Objective	1. Substructure	Method 1
		2. Objective	2. Substructure	Method 6
	5:00 P.M.	3. Objective	3. Substructure	Method 5 : peak activity

Figure 8-2. Sample training module after fine-tuning.

Objective	Task	Method
Day 1 9:00 A.M.		
1. Define need to change self.	a. Handle erratic callers. b. Handle irate callers. c. Handle confused callers.	a. Individual project and Socratic discussion
2. Define professional.	a. Describe four characteristics of a professional.	a. Socratic lecture
3. Create a log.	a. List all calls. b. Type all calls.	a. Socratic definitions
4. Diagnose problems from log.	a. Weigh each one.	a. Lecture b. Socratic discussion c. Project
5. Prioritize problems.	a. Compare each. b. Adjust each.	a. Group project
6. Write script for each.	a. Brainstorm. b. Write script. c. Refine.	a. Lecture b. Group project c. Socratic discussion
10:00 A.M.		
Break		

Figure 8-3. Final version of program plan, in funnel pattern.

often offered. And if you move on to another position, that file of past programs will help your replacement. Don't take it with you. You owe the company the materials you developed on their time. By all means, take a copy but leave the information there, too.

Determining the Methods of Training

The section earlier on preparing the agenda made reference to one of your most important considerations—methodology. Let's look at some of your options. (More information on uses of the methods discussed here will be found in Chapters 6 and 11.)

Lectures

Often the best way to convey information is to lecture. The lecture method can save time and is to the point. It is probably the most frequently used teaching method and the most familiar to your trainees, but it can create problems as well as benefits.

Effective lectures are short. Know the group. If you have college graduates, you can lecture for 30 minutes, but no longer. If your trainees are high school graduates, don't go over 15 or 20 minutes. If you train high school dropouts, keep your lectures under 10 minutes.

Making the most of your available time takes careful planning. Here are some tips:

1. Select among your substructure formats (Chapter 3) and create problem/solutions, cause-and-effect relationships, or other ways to illustrate your points quickly.
2. Make one or, at most, two points in a lecture. Remember, "less is more."
3. Make your point directly and clearly. Don't wander around the point—come to it head-on. Avoid extraneous material.
4. Follow the lecture immediately with a practical application of the concept. Create Socratic interaction.
5. Ask questions of the group to keep their attention focused on the topic.

Record the lectures or ask others to sit in. Check yourself to be sure you are saying what you want to say in as simple a way as possible, in the least amount of time.

Training Method Options

1. Lectures
2. Written materials and handouts
3. Demonstrations
4. Panel discussions
5. Class discussions
6. Team teaching
7. Role-playing
8. Case histories
9. On-the-job training
10. Project sessions
11. In-basket exercises
12. Games
13. Programmed instruction
14. Computer-aided instruction

Using Handouts and Other Written Materials

Supplementary materials are a speedy and efficient way to communicate factual information. They enhance your oral explanations by providing carefully worded examples and illustrations. They are also a means for bringing in outside sources such as quotes and charts. When done in checklist form, they are notes of lessons and lists of steps trainees can study. Here are some tips for using written materials:

1. If you pass out materials in class, give trainees time to read them. Don't talk until they've finished.
2. Discuss the material or relate it immediately to the topic at hand.
3. Hand the materials out before explaining them—or explain after—but never explain while you distribute them. People aren't listening. They're too busy examining the handout.

If you are writing the materials yourself, remember that "less is more." Make them simple and direct. Use handouts only to make a point or get across information that you can't explain better another way. Be sparing in your use of supplementary written materials. If you assign the material as homework, it becomes a redundant loop (see Chapter 3). Be sure, however, to discuss it the following day or trainees will learn that they don't have to do such assignments.

Demonstrations

A demonstration is an opportunity for you to convert a concept into a practical application. The biggest problem, however, is that not everyone sees exactly the same thing. This is particularly true when you show a group how to handle a piece of equipment. Those close to you see everything while those in the back see next to nothing. Using videotapes has helped to a large extent because the camera shows actions at close range, so every participant sees everything the camera sees.

Here are some tips for using demonstrations to instruct:

1. Streamline the demonstration. Showing involved and intricate tasks will overwhelm the trainees with too much detail.
2. Structure the demonstration around key points or steps. Create such keys by setting precise objectives. Unless you are asked a question, ignore areas not part of your key objectives.
3. Let the demonstration show the basic processes or principles. If you must teach skills by demonstration, break the skills down into small steps that show the process and the principles involved.
4. Practice ahead of time. Demonstrations that don't work usually are detrimental. If something goes wrong, use the old sales dodge, "I'm glad that happened because it allows me to show you what to do if it happens to you." Of course, be sure *you* know what to do.

Build redundancy into your lesson by referring to the demonstration later on. Ask questions about it, and use the demonstration to start discussions. Also, don't expect the demonstration to train for you. You must engage their minds in the activity. The demonstration can't have its full impact until they get their hands on equipment or perform the skills. Lock in the process with practice, as early as possible after the demonstration.

Panel Discussions

A panel is, in effect, a debate in front of an audience. Each person presents a point of view, then argues it with other members of the panel or answers questions from the audience. Panels are useful for examining ideas and for sharing experiences. You can explore the different sides of important issues and can engage the group in controversy, but you can't really teach skills. For example, I use panels most often to discuss Equal Employment Opportunity issues, but the panel always needs to be followed or preceded by E.E.O. content, regulations, and guidelines. There must also be hands-on practice for trainees to apply those concepts debated by the panel.

Panels are particularly effective for capitalizing on available expertise. Use the knowledgeable trainees in your group or people from other areas of the company (or outside of it, but that gets expensive) to address the class. They engage the group, vary the presentation, and open up controversial or ambiguous issues to discussion. Panels can also be used to culminate activities, such as when you have groups present their work projects to the entire class.

To make panel discussions work, follow these tips:

1. Focus on your objectives. Know exactly what you want to accomplish and keep those objectives in mind. Don't let the discussion degenerate into a free-for-all.
2. Draw up specific guidelines for what is to be presented. If you bring in experts, make your purpose clear. This not only keeps your objectives in focus but also lets you maintain leadership.
3. Be the moderator. Lead the discussion. If you use a panel as a culmination, let the members present their materials, then moderate the questions or discussion from the group. This allows you to control and direct the discussion.
4. Prepare good questions in advance in case no one in the audience has any. These questions will get the discussion going and relieve tension among the panel members. As an alternative, plant key questions with knowledgeable trainees to enhance the group's image and to prime the audience for greater participation.
5. Set time limits and stick to them. Attention spans are short, so don't exhaust the panelist trainees before you've had a chance to pull the ideas together and draw out the essentials from them.
6. If you use outside experts, prepare both accurate introductions and concluding thanks for their presentations.

Class Discussions

Discussions can serve many purposes. By using the Socratic method you can pose overhead questions (see Chapter 4) to the class and thus start discussions, which you moderate and control. This approach seems (and often, indeed, is) spontaneous. People get involved and voice their views. The discussion lets you quickly and pleasantly cover subjects they know, creating strong motivation for learning new subjects. It also allows you to discover what they know and how they feel. New material (theory or practical information) can be interjected by you as part of the discussion so that it can be used as a teaching tool.

If you begin discussions with an overhead question, here are some tips:

1. Unless the discussions happen spontaneously, practice your Socratic skills ahead of time.
2. Don't dominate the discussion. Loosen the reins to open up the group and pull back only to summarize and draw out key points.
3. Maintain order at all times. Protect the rights of all participants and be prepared to deal with challengers to your authority (see Chapter 4).
4. End the discussion when it has gone on as long as time allows or when it threatens to take time away from other areas of your course. Also, end it if the discussion begins to wander off the topic or the arguments degenerate into factionalism.

Another way to start discussion is to break the trainees into groups of four or more and assign a topic to each group. The groups discuss their topics, then share the results of their discussions with the rest of the class. At this point, of course, you can also add your input. This is an excellent method when you have a series of points to cover about which they are likely to have opinions. I often use this approach to show how theoretical principles relate to their everyday experiences.

If you assign groups to initiate discussions, here are some tips:

1. Have your objectives in mind and specify what you want each group to discuss.
2. Wander about the room while the groups discuss their topics. This underlines your authority and allows you to learn more about them. It also makes you available for questions.
3. When the groups present the results of their discussions, pull those results together by adding to or correcting their impressions. Draw out the basic principles you want them to remember.

Team Teaching

Team teaching can be an effective approach or an expensive frill. The concept is simple. More than one instructor trains the group at one time. The advantage of team teaching is that there is a stimulating variety of voices, training styles, and personalities. As with most joint efforts, there can be a synergy that stimulates instructors to perform more effectively. Trainees gain several perspectives on the material, which in turn promotes deeper insights.

The problems most frequently encountered in team teaching are variety and synergy not taking place. Sometimes the instructors do not have clearly defined roles, and much time is wasted dividing up tasks or repeating work. Also instructors may openly disagree with one another, causing confusion among the trainees. Consequently, the trainees gain nothing but the instructor costs are doubled.

To avoid these problems, select instructors carefully for their contrasting styles and personalities which galvanize one another. Also, balance the teaching load. Divide content by area of specialty, and to create variety, divide structure by skill level. For example, one instructor could give the lectures and lead the discussions while a second carried out demonstrations and coached group projects. A third could lead role-playing exercises and manage case history projects. Together they could participate in a panel discussion.

Have all instructors reach an agreement on any controversial topics before beginning to teach. Devise a system for airing disagreements outside the training class. For example, allow each instructor one or two preemptory challenges. If he or she feels strongly on an issue, that instructor may claim a preemptory privilege, which forbids other instructors from arguing or even discussing the point. If the number of such preemptory bids is limited (only once in a given week, for example), and is distributed equally, you'll keep peace in the training room and reserve disagreements for planning sessions.

Team teaching can be effective as on-the-job training for instructors. Experienced people can observe and coach the less experienced. Everyone has a chance to work with the best trainers, too. In short, team teaching can be a fabulous method, but, as with anything in training, it requires careful planning around precise objectives.

Role-Playing

We discussed role-playing as an evaluation tool in Chapter 6. It is also a hands-on teaching method that allows trainees to practice what they've learned. Role-playing can be used very effectively in the preparation stage, too (see Chapter 3). Allow participants to show how they would normally handle a situation, then use this performance as a reference point from which to teach principles and techniques. In fact, you can even use role-playing in the presentation stage by coaching the players much as in master classes in music, where the maestro interrupts and fine-tunes the performances of the learners, using their errors as a springboard for instruction. But vary the role-playing format occasionally. Even an exciting practice like role-playing gets dull if it is always the same.

In using role-playing, here are some tips:

1. Carefully set up your characters to prove your point. Provide two characters who are going to clash in exactly the way you want. For example, use one player to force another either to use the skills

you've taught or to illustrate what happens when those skills aren't used. Don't write a script (unless you are teaching rote responses), but provide detailed background on characters' habits, attitudes, goals, personalities, and mood, as well as business restrictions that motivate or restrain them.

2. Use role-playing to illustrate one key problem. Don't try for more than one topic or you'll diffuse the impact and distract the learners with too much information.

3. Take the time to introduce the situation. Give them enough background to understand what's at stake. Then assign the roles.

4. Both the role-plays and the discussions can tend to get off the topic. To prevent this, make sure participants understand your instructions. For example, tell them, "The customer service representative must: (1) use the customer's name three times; (2) organize, clarify, and confirm the nature of the customer's problem; (3) empathize with the customer; and (4) offer to do something for the customer." Have each of the observers use an observation sheet to look for key behavior and to respond to key aspects of the performance.

5. If the role-play gets off the topic, stop the performance and ask, "What are the problems here? Why isn't the conversation moving in the right direction?"

6. After the performance always discuss what happened. This is when learning takes place. Ask questions of each player, and have the group advise the players. Encourage discussion. Challenge them with alternatives — "What would have happened if . . . ?"

Case Histories

As described in Chapter 6, case histories can be a means of evaluation. There are two other ways to use a case history: (1) as the practice stage of a lesson or series of lessons and (2) as the structure for the skills you teach.

The practice use is perhaps the most common. A case history challenges people to apply what they have learned to solve a real problem. It is used in military training, in the sport of orienteering, for management simulation training, and throughout the academic world as a final step to a graduate degree — in fact, it appears in most situations in which showing performance is the final step of training. The latter use is common in teaching situations in which assembly or disassembly of parts is mandated. For example, it is found in auto mechanic courses, aeronautical construction courses, computer training, medical school cadaver labs, law school mock trials, and biology lab classes. Use case histories either or both ways. Their value is in challenging the learner in real situations.

Here are some tips for using case histories:

1. Let your objectives govern the level of difficulty.
2. A case can be used to practice and evaluate one skill or twenty. Therefore it can be used as a single practice step, as a progressive series of steps, or as a final test of all that has been learned.
3. Have a correct solution, but leave some areas open. In the real world, there are usually several effective approaches to solving problems.

On-the-Job Training

Details of on-the-job training are discussed in Chapter 6. To review briefly, on-the-job training is a classic and still popular method. It was the basis for the medieval guilds, and every civilization has used it to pass on information. Every primitive community perpetuates itself by it. Today, 75 percent of all training in America is conducted on the job.

The principal problems of OJT are: (1) standardization, and (2) control. Each supervisor in the field has idiosyncrasies and individual approaches to the job. Each will do it his or her own way, often completely differently from others handling the same work. To be effective, on-the-job training must be standardized. Likewise, if you have a mandate to train, yet field supervisors actually do most of the training, you must set standards and maintain supervision over that training.

To establish OJT methods, talk to those involved in the training. Get their input to design the course of instruction that meets *their* demands. When their demands conflict with your objectives, negotiate to set agreeable standards. Agree first on the objectives, then use these to set the performance standards.

Next, draw up an outline of the program and check it with the field supervisors and with management. (The written program will add authority to your training.) Include in your program the need for and intention to supervise the supervisors. An excellent way to do this is to organize your training in stages so that *you* train the trainees first. They then go for a period of on-the-job training, followed by a return to you for additional training before their final on-the-job session. Such an approach gives you much more control and monitoring ability.

If you find serious variances from the standard, meet with the supervisors involved and negotiate a solution as quickly as possible. This, too, gives you an added degree of control.

Project Sessions

In Chapters 2, 3, and 4 we discussed how learning must come from the learner, how the trainee must connect the known with the new. Project sessions are, perhaps, the most effective way to bring these two educational principles together. They ask the learner to use new skills. But because they offer hands-on experience, they also draw on the learner's established abilities and help build both skill and knowledge bridges to new learning.

To create effective project sessions, follow these tips:

1. Make the project a task they will have to perform on the job. If this isn't possible, develop one that is as close to the real situation as possible.
2. Set up the project for them to practice as many new skills or processes as possible. If necessary, include skills or processes you haven't taught yet, but only if they are closely related to those you have taught. In other words, the project can challenge them to do more than practice what you've taught if such steps are a logical outgrowth of what they have already learned.
3. Make the project challenging, but not impossible. Projects that are too easy are boring; ones that are too difficult are disheartening and de-motivating.
4. Allow time for work on the project during your seminar, if only for initial planning.

Project sessions are excellent vehicles for group activity. They can be effective as individual assignments as well, so alternate the two for best results.

Be prepared to give considerable feedback. It is direct evaluation and correction when needed that provides the core of your instruction. Pick key principles or skills and concentrate on those.

In-Basket Exercises

As mentioned in Chapter 6 in-basket exercises are excellent for evaluation. They also can be used as an instructional format in much the same way that a case history would be used. Additionally, they are practice exercises. The in-basket exercise is a typical set of tasks likely to be faced on the job. It can encompass anything trainees might reasonably face.

The value of the in-basket exercise is that it is completely flexible, realistic, and challenging. Use it as a pretest or posttest, or as an assessment session. You can scale it to the work and skills levels of any group, and because the content is so flexible, you can use it several times with the same group without risking boredom. Finally, it is fun. The in-basket exercise is rather like a scavenger hunt; participants enjoy the sense of competition that grows among those struggling to solve the same problems.

To use an in-basket exercise, follow these tips:

1. In-basket exercises don't need to be paperwork tasks. The most common example of its use is in sports training. Batting practice, pattern running (football), tennis practice, trapshooting, and the like all follow this basic idea: Trainees (players) handle whatever is tossed their way. Be creative if you train in areas other than desk work.
2. Gather as many exercises from real situations as you can. If necessary, get ideas and solutions from several people who handle these tasks frequently.
3. Use several tasks (at least five and no more than 15 to 20), based on what you've taught or want to teach, the skills level of the group, your training objectives, and the time available.
4. Set a realistic time limit for completion. The time limit adds challenge and lends a sense of completion.
5. Prepare detailed, step-by-step instructions, both written and oral, and state the goals (objectives) they should achieve.
6. After the exercise evaluate the performance. Use a discussion of the exercise to crystallize the learning experience.

Games

People love to play games, yet games can be fabulous teaching tools, too. The problem is that games can be so much fun that trainees forget to learn. Games can also get stale. Most are fun only for the first or second time; after that, they de-motivate learners.

Use games to test for recall, recognition, and skills; challenge participants under pressure to use the material taught; and introduce topics or areas for discussions. Games can encourage behavior that increases a trainee's depth of understanding or sensitivity to problems. They also provide a common experience upon which future lessons can be based. Lastly, you can develop essential principles from the interaction of the game, which can then be redefined in terms of the tasks you are teaching.

To use games, follow these tips:

1. Be creative. You can buy books on training games, but it's often more fun to invent your own. Or adapt popular television game shows and table games.
2. Relate the games to your training objectives. If the games don't address your objectives, don't use them.
3. Schedule your games at the end of the day, when they need a lift. Or let the game mark a change of pace. Games are best for starting seminars off on a challenging note, or for ending a hard day (but do allow time for full de-briefing).
4. Don't overdo it. One game in a day is enough; never use more than two. When you play too many games, their impact lessens. Participants have a wonderful time and love your training, but either don't remember or confuse what they have been taught.
5. De-brief the players at the end of the game, so as to make your points clear. Let the trainees have fun, but always pull the experience together so they realize the principles involved.

Programmed Instruction

Programmed instruction is a series of written questions, with the answer to each immediately verifiable by the learner. Most frequently, programmed instruction is available as a commercial package on a generic topic such as Handling Customer Service Responses. You can write a programmed learning series for your own needs as well (see Chapter 11).

Programmed instruction doesn't require an instructor. It is a self-study program best used in situations where individuals are too remote to gather in classes or too varied in training needs for a single course to help them. It is also useful in bringing individuals up to the level of the rest of the group or in challenging faster learners. Programmed instruction can be assigned to an individual who, after completing it, can move on to other topics. It can also be used in classroom situations but is mechanical and de-motivating — not as effective as a Socratic session and discussion asking the same questions.

The main drawback of programmed instruction is that it is dull. There is little inherent motivation, and the minimal interaction involved (answering questions, checking answers, moving on) is extremely repetitive. In the late 1950s, when the concept was introduced in conjunction with "teaching machines," it was lauded as the teaching method of the 21st century. But programmed instruction failed to catch on except among educators. Unless the learner is already highly motivated, he or she will never overcome the tedium of the format.

Programmed instruction should be used only with great care. It is effective to a degree, but only with close supervision. Here are some tips for using programmed instruction:

1. Carefully evaluate the trade-off between convenience and demotivation. If need be, work in motivational rewards for completion of the program.
2. Remember, less is more. Assign small units or sections of units. Off-the-shelf packages almost always attempt too much in each unit. Break them down to more learnable components.
3. Have frequent personal, oral evaluation sessions. Use informal questions or role-playing to keep the learning personal and the learner motivated.
4. Whenever possible assign group discussions of the material so the learning is social and interactive. We learn best by talking, teaching, and doing.

Computer-Aided Instruction

Academics are very excited about CAI (Computer-Aided Instruction).* CAI is programmed instruction in a computer format. However, it still is beset with nearly all of the problems that weaken any programmed instruction approach. Insofar as working with a computer is in itself motivational, CAI is only marginally more motivational than standard programmed instruction. Basically it is still a nonsocial, repetitive, and intrinsically unrewarding activity. It can be made somewhat richer by tailoring it to offer a wider range of possible answers (see Chapter 11). But learning still occurs exclusively through repetition and trial and error.

This will not always be the case. Future developments really *are* exciting but they remain for all practical purposes *in the future* for now. For example, with a greater understanding and perfection of artificial intelligence, we will be able to create almost fully interactive computers. People will be able to discuss what they are learning from the computer in much the same way as the characters in the movie *2001* interacted with *HAL.* When we reach this stage, the CAI will use the Socratic method and become a meaningful surrogate teacher. However, we are not there yet, and there is a strong movement among some computer scientists that believes we will never reach such levels (for example, Joseph Weizenbaum of M.I.T. and his followers).[1]

There is an alternative. Within the next few years, hardware manu-

---

* Many industrial trainers prefer to call it CAT, for computer-assisted training, or CBT, for computer-based training. For our purposes we will refer to it as CAI, computer-aided instruction.

facturers will shift to laser disks for storage and software. The laser disk stores so much more data than either floppy or hard disks, and stores it so securely (for example, laser disks are not affected by power shortages or surges) that this shift is inescapable. Laser disks were first used in the video industry, but are being applied to computer technology for fully interactive video programming. In the future, programs could be written to demonstrate learner error realistically by following through with live or animated action based on learner commands. Learning by trial and error would become much more meaningful. In addition, through animation or live action, the learner's responses could actually control activity. It becomes a form of hands-on learning rather than passive testing. Because of the interactive action format, learning would become much more of a game, finally self-motivating. After all, we've all seen people become very adept at video games. Laser technology makes it possible to program learning into a video-game format.

This technology is already here. The only factors slowing its advance are the current high cost of production and the rate at which computer manufacturers will redesign their hardware. The future for training is perhaps not as promising as the technology would lead us to think, however. Few companies are willing now to purchase enough personal computers for training unless used for teaching computer operators. Additionally, the software packages for such training will be expensive and generic, which is a major drawback (see Chapter 9). Finally, such software has yet to be written.

For the future, computer-aided instruction looks exciting, even potentially quite effective. Certainly it will improve. But learning is still largely an oral experience, and it is unlikely that even artificially intelligent, sophisticated, Socratically programmed computers will satisfy the need for human interaction in the learning process. Face-to-face training is — and appears destined to be — the most effective means of bringing about change through learning.

If you now use or are considering using CAI, here are some tips:

1. It is most effective when specific. Consider writing your own programs (see Chapter 11). Even if you are not computer literate, this is a viable route.
2. Be wary of generic programs. Unless they teach exactly what you want and teach it well, they are unlikely to be worth what they cost. Be a careful consumer here (see Chapter 9).
3. Assign specific, short units and vary assignments with other types of work (projects, case histories, and so on) to prevent learner burnout (which happens quickly with any form of programmed

instruction). CAI is best when integrated into an overall lesson sequence.

4. Schedule frequent sessions to discuss what has been learned. In cases where learners are remote, consider conference telephone calls, but live is best.

The Trainer's Manual

The final step in developing a training program is to write a trainer's manual and a trainee's workbook. There are several possible formats for trainer's manuals but perhaps the simplest was developed by Beverly Hyman,[2] for the AMA's Training the Trainer course. The left-hand column of each page shows the units of time. Next to each time is an entry stating what the trainer will do at that point. To the right of each entry is a description of the trainee's activity. Finally, on the far right is a notation of visual or other aids to be used during that segment. See Figure 8-4. In our example, "OH proj #1" is an overhead projection of the questions each participant would ask his or her neighbor. It would remain on the screen as long as the trainer felt it was needed. The agenda would be listed on a flip chart.

This description of events would continue, step by step in timed sequences, until the course was completely outlined. The manual then becomes a record of the course. It would brief anyone with knowledge of the subject on how to teach the course. This document should stay on the shelf if you leave. It is your legacy for those who come after you, because it has several strong features:

- *Standardization.* No matter who teaches it, the course is basically the same.
- *Consistency.* No matter how often you or others give the course, it remains essentially the same.
- *Quality control.* By detailing the procedures and events you set a standard for regular evaluation of both your own training and that of others who teach the course.
- *Documentation.* When questioned by management or challenged by an unhappy employee, you have documentation of the content and methodology of your course, as well as the normal response patterns of the participants.

The trainer's manual is not the same as the lesson plan, although the manual contains the four steps of the lesson plan. In the manual, you simply outline the steps as you use them. For example, in the preparation

Time	Trainer Activity	Trainee Activity	Audiovisual
9:00	Introduce self and group by having each participant introduce his or her neighbor.	Each person interviews the person on his or her right for 5 minutes. Each asks: (1) who the other is, (2) what he or she does, (3) the reason for being there, (4) other pertinent or pleasant information. Upon instruction from trainer, trainees take turns introducing their neighbors, starting from the trainer's right, front of the room.	OH Proj #1
9:20	Review agenda for the day and spell out ground rules (breaks, smoking, and so on).	Refer to handout.	Flip chart
9:30	Ask group to list two behaviors that customers perform that upset them.	Each participant lists two.	
9:35	Divide class into groups of five and instruct each group to share problems and select the two toughest ones.	Groups share and discuss problems.	
9:45	Ask each group for its problems and lead discussion of possible solutions for each one.	Groups provide problems, and individuals offer solutions.	

Figure 8-4. Model of trainer's manual.

step, list what the trainer and trainees will be doing. If your preparation step is Socratic questions, list your questions under "Trainer Activity" and the anticipated responses under "Trainee Activity." If, instead, you are using a game, say so. Tell what the trainer does to explain the game (but you need not give all the descriptive material or rules; these belong in the trainee's manual) and what the trainees are expected to do.

In the presentation step, list the activities of both trainer and trainees (taking notes, answering questions, discussion, and so on) and also list any visual aids you may be using. You also might want to list page references for similar material in the trainee's workbook. This helps coordinate your lesson with the trainee's workbook.

For the practice step, detail the activity of the trainees and describe what the trainer will say to introduce and monitor the practice.

Finally, in the evaluation step (which may be combined with the practice step), state what the evaluation is. Describe how the trainer will introduce it, but relegate the actual evaluation to the trainee's workbook, especially if it is a test, performance, or similar exercise. If, however, the trainer is expected to evaluate a project at home, say so under the "Trainer Activity" column.

What is *not* needed in the trainer's manual is a list of objectives, management goals, needs or task analyses, philosophical discussions (though you might want to briefly describe your approach to the subject both as an orientation for other trainers and as a disclaimer for yourself), cost factors, budgets, learning pattern, and so on. What you *must* include are a timed agenda, application of the four-step method for each topic, the teaching methods you will be using, necessary visual aids and other equipment, patterns of redundancy (through reviews, aids, tests, and the like), means for evaluation, what-to-do descriptions of the trainer's performance, and anticipated reactions and behaviors of the trainees.

The format shown in Figure 8-4 is too detailed for a trainer to teach from, however. I work from a simple topical agenda, supplemented by notes when needed (lists of points, examples, acronyms, and the like). But I use the manual to brief myself and as a foundation for my topical agenda.

The Trainee's Workbook

As the last part of writing a program, you'll need to put together the handouts and other materials for the trainees. Think of it as a workbook, not a textbook. The trainee's workbook should contain an agenda (not timed) for the course, plus space for work on exercises and for notes; instructions for all planned activities and projects, plus tools for such activities (facts, figures, tables, descriptions, letters, and the like); charts, graphs, and other data used in the course; case histories and role-playing situations; and any descriptive or background material not fully covered in the training sessions.

The workbook may optionally contain the objectives for each lesson, descriptive or textbook essays on the subject, supplementary materials (for example, magazine article reprints), a bibliography for further reading, biographies of any guest speakers, speaker evaluation sheets, and title pages, company logo, and so forth.

Summary

Writing a training program can be a prodigious task. We reviewed the 13 elements of a training program, including establishing budgets and support networks within the company as well as developing a rationale for your program in terms of solving management's problems. We also explored the need to know the potential training group, how you'll reach them, and how they will be selected. The chapter further explained when, based on your findings and your rationale, you should set specific training objectives. It also showed how to describe to management how best to meet those objectives; how to decide whether to write the program yourself, hire a consultant, or buy a generic package; and how to determine whether or not you did meet your objectives.

We also considered the six steps in writing an agenda, including decisions on structure, methods, lesson plans, and so forth. To help you, we covered the most popular teaching methods, from Socratic lectures to computer-aided instruction. Finally, with all elements in place, we explored the actual writing of the program. As noted, a training program has two manuals. We described the purpose and content of the trainer's manual, with its lists of what to do, where to do it, which aids and tools to use, and what to expect from the trainees. The characteristics of the trainee's manual were described as complete with the necessary agenda, assignments, charts and graphs, case histories, work space, and so forth.

CHAPTER 9

Alternatives to Writing Programs

AS we saw in the last chapter, it takes considerable time and effort to write a training program. In the end, however, you have a specific training course that can bring about dynamic changes in your organization. The program has been tailored to meet the needs you have identified. For your purposes, there is probably no finer program available anywhere. There are alternatives to this lengthy process, however, and they are the subject of this chapter.

Because of time constraints, many trainers look for outside sources when they need a new program. Outside sources are quick, frequently cost-effective, and often quite successful at meeting both demands and expectations. Their drawback is their inability to be specific. They are, by nature, generic programs. To be successful in the marketplace, they must aim at the majority's needs, with a general content and structure that appeals to widely diverse groups. As a rule, assume that the more general such programs are, the less useful they will be for you. To some extent they can be adapted to your needs, but almost never can they be as effective as a program you have built to solve a problem in your organization. With this limitation in mind, let's look at some of these alternatives.

Off-the-Shelf Programs

An off-the-shelf program is a complete package, ready for your trainees. These programs are mass produced like books, hence the name "off-the-shelf." They can take several forms:

Textbooks of all kinds and on any subject
Textbooks with study questions at the end of each chapter
Study questions and/or tests arranged by topic, available in limited subjects (math, health care, psychology, and so on)
Self-study programs that combine explanatory material with study questions and projects
Standard programmed instruction materials
Audiocassette (or disk) learning packages
Audio and slide presentations
Videocassettes on specific topics and large subjects
Films, usually on key generic topics (for example, time management)
Computer-aided instruction materials
Interactive video-computer packages

These packages are available from many different sources. Frequently elements are combined to form a series of generic lessons for self- or group study that might include a combination of expository materials, study questions, projects, and programmed instruction. There are some companies that even offer films or video- and audiocassettes matched to self-study programmed instruction. There are programs like these for most subjects with a sufficiently wide base of occurrence in industry to make them commercially viable. For example, they can be found in such areas as time management, negotiation skills, sales, business writing, basic supervision, telephone techniques, banking skills, health care techniques, presentations skills, or basic finance. In fact, most general business skills are covered by one or more such off-the-shelf packages.

The Benefits

Without exception, the prime benefit of off-the-shelf programs is that they are ready to use. Just give them to your trainees and turn them loose — at least that is the impression we are given by the advertisements that sell them. The off-the-shelf programs are at least convenient. While such programs seldom train to the extent promised, they are easy for trainers to apply. And sometimes they do work well, particularly the packages computer manufacturers sell to teach basic software. By their very nature, these packages require trainees to put in much hands-on practice, so they learn despite sometimes poorly written (occasionally, even incomprehensible) manuals.

Off-the-shelf programs are not, however, maintenance-free. They can be worthwhile supplements to your tailor-made programs. This is, in essence, how textbooks are used in schools and colleges. A text is seldom the entire course itself; instead, readings and exercises are selected from it and used to illustrate or add greater depth to classroom topics. Used this way, off-the-shelf packages can be an asset.

Another benefit of off-the-shelf programs is that they provide standardized training in scattered or remote locations. Many times it is not feasible to bring workers to a central location for training. Sometimes, too, there are not enough people needing training to justify a centralized program.

I hesitate to mention a frequently touted benefit: price. Off-the-shelf packages can be economical, certainly when at the level of a textbook. But at the other end of the spectrum are many companies that waste a great deal of money purchasing off-the-shelf programs that cannot solve their problems. I know of a company that spent $150,000 for a set of videotapes which ultimately proved of little value. Such expenditures are hardly a savings.

The Limitations

The limitations of off-the-shelf programs fall into two categories: management and educational. Of the management limitations, we've already mentioned, but would like to stress, that such programs can be very expensive, yet not achieve the results you want. Also, there is a tendency to use off-the-shelf packages as a way for people to train themselves. They cannot do this. Even the best packages are far better when used by an instructor. Off-the-shelf programs simply do not self-start, self-teach, or self-evaluate as human interaction can.

Off-the-shelf packages are designed to be sold. Consequently, there is always puffery in the advertisements and accompanying literature. Be a careful and thorough consumer. There can be hidden costs, also. Many standard self-instruction and programmed instruction packages come with only one set of workbooks. Since it is a violation of copyright law to photocopy them, you will have to order new workbooks each time you use the program.

In addition, you need to schedule your uses of these packages. One of the benefits of programmed instruction is that everyone can work at his or her own speed. But because these programs de-motivate, you must set deadlines by which time everyone must finish the program. If you are training a disparate group (one of the best uses for off-the-shelf programs), you'll need a fairly complex scheduling and monitoring system to remain aware of their progress. Lastly, if you must add your specific applications onto the package, you will have to work out and write up those parts of the program.

The educational limitations, likewise, are many. Foremost is the fact that the off-the-shelf programs are generic, but we've already discussed this problem. Because they are generic they can only achieve generic results. Unless your training objectives are also generic, off-the-shelf packages may be of no help — even be counterproductive.

Second, in nearly every case, these off-the-shelf packages tend to de-motivate learners. Textbooks are frequently dull to all but the most highly motivated; test packages tend to create anxiety; self-study programs are usually as monotonous as an assembly line. Many people have trouble concentrating on pure audiotapes since radio stations shifted to providing primarily background sound. Because of movies and television, darkened rooms signal to us that we are going to be entertained, so we relax and stop thinking. Only computer programs appear still to hold our interest — and they can be very frustrating when they don't work.

These are serious problems. As we've pointed out throughout this book, good training — effective training — consists of creating environments that make it easy for trainees to learn. All the off-the-shelf packages have some sort of learning de-motivator inherent in their format, which is counter to good training and for which you must compensate.

Lastly, while most textbooks, tests, and programmed instruction units are written by educators, most audio, video, film, and many computer-aided instruction packages are not. Furthermore, many academics are not familiar with the demands of industrial training, thus their teaching objectives may not be to produce action-oriented, measurable skills. As a result many off-the-shelf packages lack industry-oriented objectives and do not aim at creating change that can be evaluated.

Evaluating the Programs

I am not saying that there are no good off-the-shelf packages. What I am stressing is that a great number of them are not very good and a few are really bad. If you need a purchased program, be a careful consumer. To ensure that you get what is best, always measure the package against your training objectives. For each aspect of learning in the program, ask yourself which measurable, specific, action-oriented objectives this will satisfy. If the answer is few or none, don't buy the program. If you feel satisfied that it will address a sufficient number of your objectives (at least two-thirds), then buy it.

Always try the program before you buy it. The sales literature is not enough to judge how effective or flexible the program may be. Remember that the literature is intended to sell first and inform second. It is usually written by marketing or advertising people and almost never by trainers or by those who designed the package. Ask for a free evaluation copy of the program. If the supplier can't or won't give one, offer to rent a copy. If they can't or won't do that either, don't buy the package.

Frequently, the supplier will give you a list of previous purchasers whom you can call. This is useful, but remember that the supplier is only going to provide you with clients who are pleased. In addition, you have no way of knowing how reliable that reference is. Even large corporations with significant training departments often train poorly, and their trainers sometimes know very little about effective training. A recommendation from such a person is insufficient reason for purchasing a generic package. Instead, check the promises of salespeople or advertisements with your own network of trainers. Also check with the American Society for Training and Development or an independent rating organization. (See the Appendix.)

If time is a problem and the package you are considering costs more than $5,000, hire a training consultant to evaluate the choices and make specific recommendations. It will add to the total cost but could limit the possibility of buying a useless or ineffective program. As the cost of these packages increases, the expense of a consultant becomes more and more reasonable. Any package above $20,000 almost demands an independent evaluation as a safeguard.

When comparing packages estimate their shelf life. Ask yourself how susceptible the material is to becoming dated. This is particularly important in high-tech fields and for technical training packages. Also consider these questions:

1. What will be the cost of updating it?
2. Does it lend itself to easy updating?
3. Who owns the rights to this material?
4. What rights do you acquire with the purchase?

For example, there may be hidden costs involved in duplicating or adapting the material to your operation. Or there might be unanticipated costs in repeat orders of supplies. Know what is included in the initial cost.

Ask the suppliers of the off-the-shelf packages you are considering: What is their philosophy of learning? What theory of learning is the basis of their instruction? This book, for instance, is based on the theories of British contemporary philosopher Sir Karl R. Popper, who believes that all learning is (1) tentative, (2) iterative (that is, by repetition in ever-expanding contexts), and (3) the result of the interaction between what a

learner brings to an event and the environment in which he or she interacts during the event.[1] Consequently, teaching is the creation of semantic, emotional, psychological, and physical environments that engage the
learner's mind. If your supplier cannot answer such a question, have the
person find out who at the company can answer it. If their philosophy is
not in accord with yours, don't buy the product. If you are not familiar
with the theory, research it at your local library or college to find out
whether or not it will work for you.

Here's a final tip on off-the-shelf programs: Justify the cost *before* you
buy. There are always two dimensions by which to measure effectiveness — results and cost. As a trainer, you are responsible for results; as a
manager, you are responsible for costs. Effective training management
reflects a balance between the two. To justify costs, follow these steps:

1. Divide the cost of the training by the number to be trained.
2. Factor in all costs, including hidden ones such as administrative
   time, lost work time, space requirements, incidental supplies, and
   the like. Do this for each of several ways in which you might obtain
   the program (for example, with a consultant, off the shelf, developed in house, and so on).
3. Tally the costs of maintaining the *status quo* (no training at all).
4. Project the savings from training or other economic impacts your
   proposed program will have on future operations of the company.

In preparing your justification, remember that all off-the-shelf packages, no matter how disparate, can be compared to each other on a cost-
per-person basis. In essence, you are measuring the effectiveness of each
option for its economic impact on future operations. Diagnose the
strengths and weaknesses in your justification in terms of cost effectiveness, and compensate for shortcomings or play down the problem areas.
(See Chapter 13.)

External Consultants

A consultant is a specialist who has developed a reputation for being
good at something. For the trainer, there are two types of consultants:
internal and external. An internal consultant is usually a subject-matter
expert who is only incidentally likely to have training skills. An external
consultant, on the other hand, should have both subject matter and training expertise. Frequently a training department functions as a consultant
itself. Consultants are resources for advice, analysis, skills development,
and information. They perform specialized tasks at which they excel or for

which the regular staff has either insufficient time or no ability to perform.

There are three general areas in which consulting is done.

- The consultant may act as a subject-area resource — someone you seek out to gain special knowledge or information on a procedure. You might seek a subject expert when preparing a task analysis, for example.
- A consultant could research and prepare documentation for you. You might hire a consultant to perform a needs analysis or write a training program or a trainer's manual. Perhaps you need a feasibility study done or a powerful proposal written. You might want a consultant to prepare a series of evaluation tools. Or a consultant might be engaged as a ghostwriter, in which case he or she would work closely with the client to get an understanding of the material, then work independently to prepare the documents.
- A consultant most commonly becomes a resource for supplying live training quickly and efficiently. The training consultant tailors his or her expertise to a company's requirements and writes or adapts a program for it. Starting with a list of the company's needs (with or without a formal needs analysis), the consultant works with the company to create training objectives and then writes and delivers a program to meet them. In many cases the program becomes an on-going feature for employees and managers. It can be given each time by the consultant or taken over by a company trainer.

In effect, then, you may seek out a consultant as either an information resource, a documentation resource, or a performance resource.

The Benefits

There are at least ten reasons why you might want to hire a consultant.

1. Consultants are (or, at least, are supposed to be) experts. You may be able to write a good program for yourself but a consultant has written literally hundreds of successful programs. He or she will be able to do so more efficiently, in less time.
2. You may find yourself frequently too busy to develop a new training program or you may not know the field. You could hire and train someone to do it, but that would take time, too. Consultants are a ready-made talent pool from which to draw on short notice.

3. Consultants have verifiable credibility. By being experts and working with many organizations, they gain credence from vast experience. This is particularly important if you are training senior management. Division heads usually are not very comfortable being trained by their subordinates, but they relax and learn from an outside expert.
4. Consultants are politically neutral. An interoffice squabble often can be resolved by hiring an outside person to research or perform the training.
5. Consultants represent the state-of-the-art in their field. To stay in business, consultants must remain fully current.
6. To stay in business, consultants must be able to produce results. If you hire a consultant, you'll get the job done quickly and well.
7. Frequently, a consultant is the most cost-effective way to achieve your results. On a cost-per-person basis, hiring a consultant is nearly always less expensive than preparing the program yourself. Because a consultant tailors and delivers the program, it is also more effective than an off-the-shelf package.
8. Working with a consultant usually is an excellent opportunity to learn new skills and gain new competencies.
9. Your degree of input and advice to the consultant is completely flexible. You have whatever level of control and involvement you want.
10. Your commitment is to the contracted service only. If you are not satisfied with a consultant's performance you need not rehire that person. Get another, better consultant. You have not committed large resources to a useless program that you are stuck with. Hiring consultants on contract allows you to shop around until you find exactly what you need.

The Limitations

There are some drawbacks to hiring consultants. First, as in any field, there is a great range of competence. Someone who was excellent for the ABC Company may not fit your organization at all. Merely talking a good game doesn't make one a good consultant. Evaluate a consultant's current work to assess his or her competence before you draw up your contract. (In fairness, remember that, like all of us, consultants have great days and not-so-good days; a poor performance is unacceptable, but a fair one deserves consideration.)

A second limitation to hiring consultants is time. You are hiring expertise, but the consultant is selling time. For a consultant to devote full time to you, he or she must charge the maximum. To remain competitive, most consultants practice "streaming" clients (working on more than one project at a time) or they "boilerplate" (patch courses together from already existing programs), "modularize" (plug in standard learning modules whenever needed), and use other shortcuts. The more generic the subject, the more efficient they can be. If you need completely new material, with exercises created just for your application, you will have to pay considerably more because it will involve exclusive use of the consultant's time and creative talents.

A final limitation to hiring consultants is that, as in many fields, you pay for glamour as well as quality. Consultants range from newcomers (who can be excellent) to the world famous (almost pop culture figures). Expertise can be found at all levels, but you pay more for it from big-name stars.

At present, the range stretches from $250 per day to $25,000 for a single one-hour presentation. As with anything else, you get what you pay for. As a rule, $250 to $500 a day gives you the relatively untried or unskilled; from $750 to $1,000 you get solid performance with limited experience; from $1,000 to $2,000 per day you get the greatest expertise, seasoned with solid experience. Beyond $2,000 you begin to pay for a consultant's overhead or for the organization that is brokering his or her services. Beyond $2,500 you enter the world of glamour and pay for star quality. Consultants sell their time to whoever will pay the most for it. They are truly free marketeers.

To hire a Peter Drucker or a Tom Peters at their peak is to hire someone at the cutting edge of what's happening in management. You are getting instant credibility and guaranteed impact. A Rolls-Royce is indeed different from a Honda, and a major part of that difference is intangible — image, reputation, exclusivity, and so on. Are these intangibles important to your objectives? Sometimes they can be important, and this is one of the considerations in hiring a consultant.

How to Evaluate Consultants

With so wide a variation in price and considering how many of them there are, it is essential that you be able to evaluate the performance and quality of a consultant. Here are some guidelines:[2]

1. Try before you buy. Most consultants give public seminars as audition pieces in which to "strut their stuff." If you like what you see, talk to them on the spot. If you don't, leave quietly and no one will be the wiser.
2. As with off-the-shelf package salespeople, ask the consultant what theories or rationale justifies his or her approach to train-

ing. Someone who can answer that question at least has given thought to the matter.

3. Ask what the training objectives are for the program you've just observed.

4. Ask for a list of present clients, particularly those with on-going relationships. A one-time seminar may or may not have been good, whereas a series is likely to be done well.

5. Find out what the consultant knows about your company and, even more important, about your industry. If it's little or nothing, you will have to spend time and money supplying background if you want the work to be customized.

6. Once you've described your problem, ask the consultant to describe how he or she would address it from a training point of view. Look for answers that lead to positive changes, not just information.

7. Ask the consultant how he or she would tailor the work to meet your specific requirements.

8. Get the consultant to explain how the results of the training program would be evaluated.

9. After discussing a potential program, ask the consultant for a written proposal that specifies the rationale for the program, the training objectives, an agenda (content), the methods to be used, the materials needed and who is to provide them, and the costs of the program.

10. Request biographies of all key people working with the consultant to deliver the work you require.

11. Check out the key people with organizations that rate speakers. For example, the American Society for Training and Development currently is preparing such a referral service. Another organization that performs such a service is Seminar Clearing House International (see the Appendix for addresses). Both organizations require membership. If you aren't a member, network with other trainers at organizations similar to your own.

12. Ask for samples of the consultant's written work, then gauge whether it meets your standards.

Of course many of these questions apply only to seminar services. If you are hiring a consultant as an information source or to research, write, or advise, you need only those questions which apply to your purpose.

Negotiating with Consultants

Principles of good negotiation are covered in Chapter 14, however, there are a few additional points to consider when negotiating with consultants. The most important element in any negotiation is knowing how badly the other side wants what you have. Coupled with that is a correct estimate of what they value most and therefore would be willing to bargain.

Consultants, for the most part, are stars. What they do makes them special, and they like to be treated accordingly. Second, what they are selling is their time. It is most precious to them and they cannot give it away. Third, most consultants are self-employed or work for rather small organizations. They constantly must seek new business. Most consultants have about a six-month operating horizon; beyond that there is no business — yet. They forego the sense of security that most company trainers enjoy. Fourth, most consultants travel a great deal, which makes travel in itself unrewarding, even undesirable.

These four aspects of consulting are probably the most effective tools you have in negotiating with consultants. For example, time is the consultant's pressure point. You become more attractive when you save him or her personal time. You can do this by being very well organized yourself. Offer to gather and supply data, handle duplicating or typing arrangements, make effective use of time during consulting sessions. However, to pressure the consultant during the negotiations: negotiate for more time to be included or set a package price that includes extra hours or longer days at the regular per diem. If you hold a hard line and then give in on it, you should gain concessions in exchange. Use this strategy carefully however, because a hard line makes you a less desirable client.

One of the most attractive things you can offer is future work in a sizable volume. If you schedule a year in advance and have more programs in mind, you make yourself an important client, and the consultant is more willing to make compromises for you.

Finally, if you can offer special attention, a travel-weary consultant will want to work for you. Suggest transportation to and from the airport, flights in a company plane, first-class travel and lodging at a hotel, a fancy rental car, dinner at home or in a favorite restaurant, and so on. Most of these are not brought up openly as negotiating chips, but let the consultant know of them. Perhaps a little less money will be a favorable exchange for being treated royally. In addition, a married consultant usually leaves a spouse behind. The chance to bring that spouse (and even the children) along on a trip, especially to an interesting location, doesn't come often. If you can include the family in the travel expenses, you make a very attractive offer. Many consultants trade in first-class air tickets in order to take their spouses along; others work for much lower rates in order to have an expense-paid vacation with their families.

All consultants' fees are negotiable. Your task is to find something the consultant wants enough to concede the fees to you. Use these elements to negotiate that concession.

Public Seminar Organizations

Public seminars are a multimillion-dollar business. It is a high-risk operation but potentially an extremely profitable one. This profit potential has motivated many organizations to compete with each other in holding public seminars on different business topics. The oldest and largest such organization is the American Management Association, a nonprofit member operation serving management through its public seminars, business library, publishing arm, private in-house seminars, and conferences. Most others are profit-making private companies, which derive at least a portion of their income from seminars and conferences.

There are three types of organizations. Some, like Gerard Nierenberg's Art of Negotiation Seminars or Dale Carnegie, are straightforward seminars designed to promote a particular approach. A second type capitalizes on a name and puts on seminars under that banner. For instance, the Dun & Bradstreet seminars are run as a separate division of that leading financial organization. The third type is different only in that the name or sponsoring organization is not responsible for the seminar. Seminars are mounted by a seminar-packaging organization in a client's name through a conference center, or as a part of a conference, or to follow a particular theme, such as genetic engineering or the care of the aging. The client, conference center, or sponsoring organization has no responsibility for the seminar.

The pattern for the seminars, however, is much the same. The organization engages consultants in various fields to deliver seminars. Consultants agree to do so for less than their normal rates because of the exposure as well as the guarantee of steady employment for a period of time. The organization handles the advertising (nearly always direct mail), coordination and administration, as well as arranges the details of the seminar itself. The consultant simply shows up and delivers it.

These organizations also book in-house seminars, in which a consultant tailors a public course to a client's individual needs. The client is billed by the organization who, in turn, pays the consultant's fee. In effect, the seminar organization acts as a broker for its consultants. Thus, the organization takes on the responsibility for the consultant. Ineffective consultants are simply dropped from the roster, guaranteeing top experts on the cutting edge of their subjects.

Consider these seminars as an alternative to an in-house training program. Seminars are an excellent way for people to become acquainted with generic skills and requirements. If you have fewer than six or eight people to train, there is no less expensive way to do that. Once you have more than six or eight people, it becomes more cost-effective to hire the consultant to tailor an in-house course. It should also prove educationally more sound, because you can incorporate much more practice and evaluation.

These seminars can be evaluated in many of the same ways as off-the-shelf packages and consultants. In addition, it is usually easiest to evaluate a program simply by going to it. All organizations I've seen or worked for give excellent seminars. From time to time, each must have a dud. Don't judge the entire organization by one seminar; see a few and then decide.

The Benefits

These seminar organizations could not survive unless they continued to provide worthwhile services. Because of the competition among these organizations, you have a tremendous selection from which to choose. It is a buyer's market. Also, because of this stiff competition, the seminars are usually quite reasonable.

Constant evaluation following the seminars means that you are being offered the topics that are in most demand. It also ensures that what is being taught is up to date — indeed, the latest in its field. This is especially true for technological areas. In addition, most organizations stand behind their seminars and will refund or give you free admission to another seminar if you are not pleased with the one you've attended. Lastly, as mentioned in Chapter 7 the promotional materials for these seminars are a quick and easy way to keep up with what's going on in a field.

The Limitations

Nothing is perfect, and of course these seminars have their limitations. For example, by their very nature they must be generic. The seminars are most profitable when large numbers attend, so they are intentionally geared to as broad an audience as possible. The most popular format is a one- or two-day program. This is almost never enough time to do more than provide an information meeting. The meeting will be informative, but little will be learned unless you develop practice exercises to follow the seminar.

Some seminar leaders tend to be better performers than trainers. They are highly entertaining — great to listen to — but they only put on a show. Unless your trainees will learn something, don't send them to a public seminar.

Unprofitable topics get dropped while profitable ones attract more competitors. Consequently, for all of the plethora of courses offered, there is frequently little choice of topics. Coupled with that problem is the tendency of seminar organizations to play fads. It's hard to find a course today in Transactional Analysis or Management by Objectives, both still excellent management tools but out of fashion right now.

The least expensive programs are usually attended by the largest groups. This is the way the organization makes a profit. The larger the group, however, the less interaction there can be and the more it becomes a blank-slate, information meeting. As a rule, the more expensive the seminar, the fewer will attend and the greater the opportunity for real learning.

Employees away from home and in a new town have been known to play harder than they work. I've even had people approach me as the seminar leader to ask if it is okay for them to sightsee rather than attend the seminar. Protect your investment by giving them an assignment based on the seminar.

A final word on seminar organizations. All the organizations I've done work for have been very conscientious and honest. However, if you should ever feel the need to sue a seminar organization, don't be misled by the name. The legal entity may be a very small corporation, a partnership, or a sole proprietorship even though the seminars are given under the banner of a well-known name. You can be sure the famous name has protected itself. On the other hand, it is sometimes very difficult to enforce a suit and collect from a small entity.

Summary

In this chapter we explored the various alternatives to the lengthy process of writing a training program. One of the major alternatives is the off-the-shelf programs, which are available in a wide variety of topics. The benefits and limitations of these programs were discussed, along with some tips on evaluating individual programs. Also given were some suggestions for incorporating these programs into an in-house training program.

The chapter discussion then proceeded to uncover the benefits and limitations of working with outside consultants, either to research or actually develop in-house training programs. Consultants' fees were explained in connection with the different ways they approach their work. There were tips given for evaluating the work of consultants, as well as suggestions for successful negotiations.

The final part of the chapter was devoted to professional seminars, including a discussion of the types of seminars that are held and the organizations who offer them, plus some tips on how to use these seminars as an alternative to or as part of your training program. We also commented on the benefits and limitations of these seminars.

CHAPTER 10

Setting the Physical Environment

I have stressed that one of the keys to effective training is a positive learning environment. While the physical situation doesn't teach us, it makes it easier or harder to learn. As a trainer you need to look at ways of making learning easier by improving the physical setting.

Comfort Factors

If your trainees are comfortable, they will be able to concentrate on what you are teaching them. Let's consider the five comfort factors.

1. *Temperature.* Few things kill a seminar faster than a room that is either too hot or too cold. If it is too hot, participants fight to stay awake. Even if your lesson is dynamic enough to keep them awake, they have to work at concentrating, so they miss vital points, are exhausted much too early, and generally feel dissatisfied with the training. A room that is too cold, on the other hand, keeps everyone awake but distracts terribly from the material at hand. People are too uncomfortable to learn.

It has been found that 72° Fahrenheit is the optimum temperature for a training room. The closer you are to it, the more comfortable participants will find it.

2. *Chairs.* If you have ever attended a seminar where you had to sit on hard, wooden-slat folding chairs, you know how distracting it can be. Use the most comfortable chairs available, short of lounge chairs.

3. *Lighting.* A dingy room throws a pall over your training. Participants must always be able to see you, your visual aids, and their notes clearly and comfortably, without effort. A room can be lit dramatically for effect, but participants still need to see those three elements. Be sure the lighting is sufficient before you begin your program. If necessary, bring in extra lights.

4. *Writing space.* A steady surface is a must for each trainee, so he or she can take notes. If you need to use an auditorium with chairs but no foldaway writing arms, make the sessions shorter. Most people can't remember a day's worth of instruction without notes to remind them; make it easy for them to take notes.

5. *Sightlines.* When a participant can't see you or your visual aids, he or she will move or shift to one side, or squint to see better — once, usually twice, sometimes three times. Each time, the person tries a little less than before, and after that, he or she simply gives up. You've lost a listener. Check the entire room before your program to be sure no one has even a partially blocked view. If there are such blocked views, correct them or suggest no one take those seats.

These five considerations are the basics, regardless of what you are teaching, where you are teaching, or whom you are teaching. Take care of these and you'll have an environment where learning can take place.

Room Setups

The seating arrangement of a room may vary, depending on the purpose of the training. Figures 10-1 and 10-2 show the most common ones.

Classroom Arrangements

Aptly named, these seating arrangements are formal settings familiar from school days. In the straight classroom arrangement, the tables or desks with chairs are in neat rows in front or alongside one another. There can be individual desks or tables seating two or more people. Usually there are aisles between the rows (see Figure 10-1). The classroom ar-

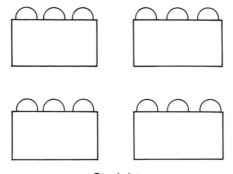

Straight

Chevron

Theater

Figure 10-1.   Classroom setups.

rangement has one strong advantage. Because it is formal and isolates each participant, it is the most authoritative setup for training. This is especially so when you use a raised platform or stage at the front of the room. If you need this authority, the classroom style will help. In addition, you might need to use the classroom style if you have a large group. For example, I use it whenever I have a group of more than 60 or 70 people. It lends itself well to a blank-slate delivery.

The drawbacks of the classroom arrangement are strong, however. It creates a "school" environment, and unless your trainees loved school, this will be a negative. Soften the arrangement by using a chevron effect, whereby tables are slanted at an angle toward the center aisle (see Figure 10-1). Or use a theater, where everyone sits in anchored seats, raked so that everyone can see clearly (see Figure 10-1). But even these modifications do not break the isolation and formality of this setup. Each participant sees only you and the back of other heads. There is little chance and no inducement to interact with others. Use the classroom setup for large groups and when you need extra authority, but when you can, soften it with a chevron arrangement.

Horseshoe Arrangement

Any arrangement that seats participants at tables along both sides and across the back while leaving the front and center areas open for the trainer is usually referred to as a horseshoe. This is true whether the configuration is rounded or squared (see Figure 10-2). The horseshoe setup is excellent for demonstrations and role-playing. It has excellent sightlines and, because participants face each other, it fosters good interaction. Furthermore, participants can be broken into teams readily, and you have easy access to each participant. For these reasons, it is the most common training arrangement.

There are, however, some drawbacks to the horseshoe. First, the number of people it accommodates is limited. Twenty people is usually the maximum, though it can be pushed to 30. After that, the horseshoe becomes too crowded and unwieldy. Second, participants really only interact with the two-thirds of the group they are facing. The closest people to them—those on the same side of the horseshoe—never get to see one another or interact. Third, if you work your way closer into the central area, you lose those trainees sitting on the ends. If you use this arrangement make an effort always to include the end people.

Circle Arrangement

The circle setup is simply a circular grouping of desks, tables or chairs (see Figure 10-2). The advantage of the circle is that it has the lowest

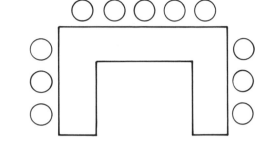

Horseshoe

Circle

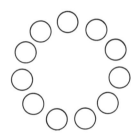

Conference Table

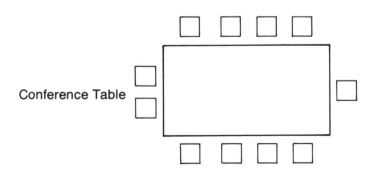

Figure 10-2. Other setups.

authority position. If you want to encourage low-key participative leadership, the circle works well. If you still want some formality, use desks in a circle or a large round table. If you want complete informality, have just chairs. In other respects, the circle has almost the same advantages and limitations as the horseshoe. One word of caution, though; if you are working inside the circle or doing role-playing or demonstrations within it, take care to move around so no one is excluded. In the circle, there can be no "front of the room" for focus.

Conference Table Arrangement

We are all familiar with the rectangular conference table (see Figure 10-2). Perhaps the greatest asset of a conference table is its flexibility. It can be formal and authoritative when you sit at the head, or informal when you sit to one side. It allows you to use visual aids, yet keeps a feeling of intimacy among the group.

The major drawback of a conference table is its size. Few tables are workable with more than 12 people seated at them. In addition, conference tables are not particularly useful for role-playing, though they do foster discussion.

Team-Style Arrangements

I use team-style arrangements a great deal. Participants are seated at tables in groups of from four to eight. Tables can be round, square, or oblong and can be arranged casually or formally around the room (see Figure 10-3). There are several distinct advantages in these arrangements. First, team-style is the least threatening environment for trainees. It creates small, intimate groups and makes no demand for interaction with the whole group. At the same time, it doesn't leave participants feeling isolated because it demands engagement within the group at each table. Second, from the trainer's point of view, it quickly fosters group spirit and encourages a relaxed atmosphere. It is very "unschool-like," yet formal enough to allow for strong leadership. Third, the arrangement breaks immediately into teams for projects, and helps those projects along with a pleasant degree of team competitiveness. In short, the team-style arrangement makes a pleasant yet businesslike atmosphere in which to conduct training.

There are several disadvantages, however. Size is a major consideration. I've handled 65 in one of these arrangements, but that is too large a group. You tend to lose the tables farthest away. The optimum number is about 30 to 35 people. Another possible problem is sightlines. Using square tables in a horseshoe arrangement, for example, puts the people in the middle with their backs to the trainer. It is possible for them to sit

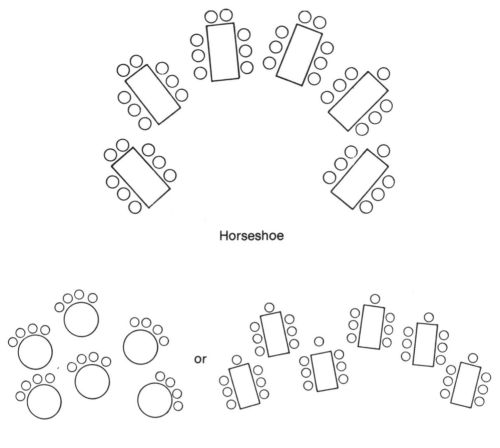

Horseshoe

or

Random

Figure 10-3.   Team-style setups.

sideways, but without swivel chairs (say, in a hotel setting) it is awkward. If using round tables (usually available in hotels), everyone has to crowd together at one side of the table. Putting fewer participants at each table helps, of course.

I occasionally hear people voice a desire to get to know others in different groups. You can help this by shifting the tables and the groups each day or each time period, but this makes it harder for you to get to know everyone by name.

Workstations

Many trainers instructing machine operators and computer workers choose this option. It is similar to school science labs, where each person has his or her own workstation to perform what is being taught (see Figure

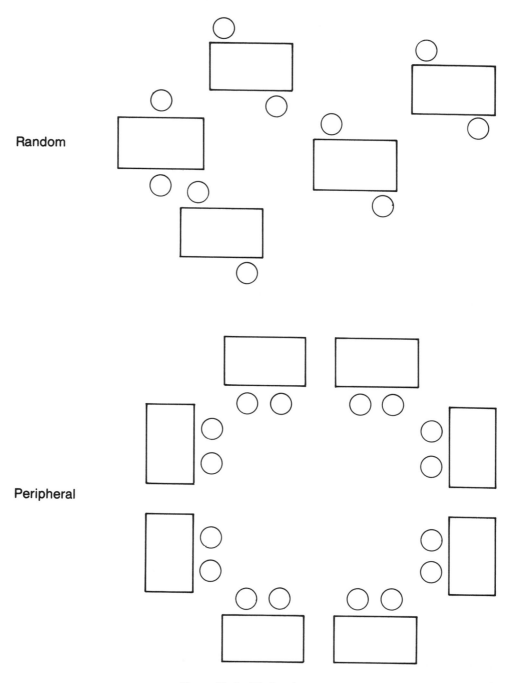

Random

Peripheral

Figure 10-4. Workstations.

10-4). Of course, its advantage is the hands-on involvement it promotes. The limitations are that the arrangement usually is very expensive, so only small groups can be trained, and it leaves the individual working alone. An answer is to combine both problems for a single solution: train groups of two or three people simultaneously. While this approach gains group feelings and more trainees, it loses some of the hands-on opportunity and requires tighter task-scheduling.

The tradition is a classroom arrangement for workstations, but it needn't be for your training program. To have access to everyone's workstation, arrange the units around three or four walls, with you in the middle. Team feeling can be fostered by putting several units in a group or cluster. Finally, if there are several units or pieces of equipment to learn, use a sequential setup and rotate different teams working on different units at any one time.

Designing and Equipping a Training Room

We don't, unfortunately, often have the luxury of being able to design our own training facility. Sometimes, however, we do get that chance — or at least get an opportunity to redecorate one. Let's look at some prime considerations.

Design Considerations

Architects are not trainers. Even if your input is sought, it has been my experience that an architect will design a beautiful building, not a training facility. This is not to complain about architects; they are hired to create beautiful buildings, and they do so very well. But architects simply are not usually knowledgeable about training needs so their thinking is spatial and conceptual, not necessarily practical.

If you are given the opportunity, or have the political clout, insist upon working with the architect. Pay frequent visits to the construction site as your facility takes shape. Remember that you will have to live for a long time with whatever they build. Be sure they get it right. This is the case whether the company is building you a new complex or is remodeling or redecorating your existing facility. You are responsible for the effectiveness the facility will have. Work to make it right.

In the beginning of the chapter we discussed the importance of proper temperature in the training room. In your new facility, make sure each room has individual temperature control. You want a temperature control system with a minimum two-degree variation. That means that with the thermostat set at 72°F., the heat comes on at 70°F. and turns off at 74°F. (or the air-conditioning comes on).

If you have a say in design, go for broad rooms. Long and narrow ones feel constrictive. Unless you have very large groups or need them for other purposes, avoid amphitheaters and formal theater seating with a raised stage. Rooms need to be large enough to accommodate your largest training classes with several smaller breakout rooms located nearby. Flexible space is a consideration, too, but be sure you have fully sound-proof dividers between seminar rooms. Breakout rooms could have half walls and could be *in* the seminar room, but that can create scheduling problems. Few things are more difficult than trying to teach when loud neighbors overwhelm your every word.

Be sure there is adequate power to run all conceivable audiovisual configurations. Locate controls at the front of the room, where you will have easy access to them. These controls should include a dimmer switch for the lights, remote controls for projectors, projector screen controls, audio system controls, microphone and sound system controls (if you use them), and video controls if you use a permanent installation such as a big-screen projector. Plan outlets, switches, and controls for your convenience, not to make the electrician's job easier. If your use of audiovisuals is extensive, consider creating an audiovisual station. Traditionally, projectors occupy a separate cubicle at the rear of the room. These are nice, but consider a modular unit (all electronics on one stand) that is self-contained and movable or set up a central control room for all your audiovisuals except overheads, flip charts, and models. This means extra staff to work the room, but in a large organization, with several seminars going on, a central control room with individual room controls for slides, film, and video makes sense.

Put everything on videotape and use a large-screen video projector. The airlines use this approach with the projector attached to the cabin ceiling. If you do a lot of videotaping, consider installing a hidden or remote-control camera to sidestep participants' inhibitions about being taped. Whatever you decide, remember to allow for the convenient and safe storage of audiovisual equipment.

Also brought out in the beginning of this chapter was the importance of adequate lighting. Provide for bright lighting (fluorescent is fine), with dimming capability for showing slides and films. Having some indirect incandescent lights to supplement is useful. What you want, however, is universal bright light throughout the room.

Windows, while nice, are distractions in a training room. You have better control of the lighting and of trainees' attention without them. However, the absence of natural light for long periods can get depressing, so be sure there are windows in areas used for breaks or lunch.

As to room color, cool pastels are best. You and your materials should stand out, not the room decor. Grays, browns, creams, and perhaps pale greens could be used as a base color, with creams, pale oranges, yellows, or blues as highlights. Dark blue is very formal and authoritative, and could be used if that is your message. Gray is a very neutral color, associated with work. Brown is a warm color, and cream is neutral. Lastly, carpeted floors add a warm and comfortable touch while keeping noise to a minimum.

Furniture and Equipment

The importance of comfortable chairs was brought out earlier. The chairs you choose should swivel, tilt if possible, and be on wheels. The seats should be padded and textured for comfort. There should also be padded, comfortable arms. Lumbar support is excellent, height adjustment is a plus.

Tables should be designed for flexible use. They can be permanent rather than folding, but should have a drop leaf that lets you change them from narrow to wide. Tables should be rectangular, but able to be made into square or near-square configurations by extending one or both of the leaves and joining two tables together.

Install an accurate wall clock on the back wall of each room, not in the front. You need to be able to see the time; your trainees don't.

Avoid artwork on the walls, but if you plan to use posters or to post sheets from your flip charts, cover the walls in a material that makes posting easier. The best is to run a two-inch-wide metal strip around the room within easy reach but above head level (say, 6 feet from the floor). Use magnetic vinyl strips to post anything you want.

Choose your audiovisual aids and other equipment with care. If you use whiteboards and chalkboards, get those on wheels so they are more flexible and you don't have to turn your back to use them.

See Chapter 11 for planning and purchasing audiovisuals; however, minimally you should have:

- at least two sturdy flip-chart easels and a selection of markers for your charts
- one overhead projector with scrolling attachment, pens for the overhead, and a stand, cart, or table for the projector
- a projection screen of sufficient size to be seen clearly from anywhere in the room
- a table (not a lectern) for your notes and supplies

In addition, I recommend an electric projection screen (instead of the standard one) and a complete videotaping package including a camera, recorder (½-inch), monitor, microphone, necessary hookups, a cart or rack, and a tripod for the camera. If possible, get a second viewing unit with another monitor, tape player (recorder), hookups, and cart or rack. (See Chapter 11 for details.)

Beyond these minimums, however, you will want to purchase any other special equipment you favor. Obviously, if you don't like flip charts and prefer whiteboards, then substitute one for the other. If you train on computers, clearly you need one for each workstation. If you train *only* on computers, you probably won't need the video equipment but instead should look into a projection device that lets you project any computer screen in the room (including your own) onto a large screen in front.

Finally, be sure you have cupboard and shelf space for supplies like paper and pencils, handouts, name cards, and the like. If you serve refreshments, have a table for them. If your trainees come from outdoors, have a closet either in the training room or just outside it. At the very least, provide a coatrack.

Multi-Use Facilities

It would be nice if we could reserve our training rooms exclusively for our training programs. In the real world, however, this is not always possible. If you use rooms that are also used for other functions by other people, there are several considerations that might help you.

- If you have input into the design or re-decoration of the room, insist upon a closet for overnight storage of equipment. If possible, try for permanent storage space in the room.
- Institute a monthly scheduling system for room use. Post the schedule outside the room and keep it up to date.
- Lock-in your room times early. If someone else wants the room and you can make other arrangements, make it a fair trade. In return, get other time you need. When people have to pay a price, they ask for fewer favors. Remember, however, that the room impacts heavily on trainees. Don't give up your time if the alternatives are not sound for training.
- Always leave the room clean. Come early to be sure it is clean. Set it up the way you want it; don't assume cleaning personnel will do it. If need be, offer the cleaning people some small consideration to guarantee the room is immaculate when you want it.

In regard to the last item, a small gift at Christmas (say, a bottle of cologne or liquor or a bar of nice soap) or an occasional lunch is usually enough to ensure cooperation, even special treatment, from maintenance staff. Be careful to make it appear as a grateful thank-you, not a bribe. Of course, what you give and how you give it depends on the people involved. Consider them, and be prepared to reward them for extra service.

Breaks and Meals

People cannot sit still and learn indefinitely. We talk about the need for breaks in Chapter 8, and now we discuss what to serve on those breaks. Heavy foods, high in protein and fats, are fillers. They do not energize us; they make us complacent and sleepy. Carbohydrates and sugars give energy, but only temporarily. For seminars, a temporary lift is excellent. The following suggestions should keep your trainees bright and active throughout the day.

Pre-seminar

Coffee (regular and decaffeinated), tea, and hot cocoa are highly recommended. Fruit juices are an excellent plus. Fresh fruit is great, too (sliced is better than whole). Assorted danishes and doughnuts are good lifters but not as good as fruit.

Morning Break

Refill coffee (regular and decaffeinated) and tea, and provide more fresh fruit.

Lunch

Light seafoods and salads are best. Cold cuts and cheese rank second, followed by sandwiches. Chicken is next best, soups and stews next.

Avoid beef, pork, and other heavy meat dishes. Avoid pasta (except in cold salads), baked potatoes, and other heavy starches. Avoid heavy desserts like pies and puddings. Fresh or stewed fruit, cake, cookies, or tarts are possible.

Afternoon Break

Coffee (regular and decaffeinated), tea, and cold soda—especially diet soda—make good afternoon refreshers.

Off-Site Facilities

While it is excellent to have good training facilities at your plant, there are many advantages to going off site for training. Foremost among these is that a new place lends a festive air to the training event. Just as dimming the lights signifies entertainment, a trip somewhere means, at the very least, a pleasant change of pace, and, at the most, a working holiday. The second advantage is that when you take people away from their workplace, you minimize, even eliminate, interruptions. Furthermore, if you choose carefully and follow a few simple precautions, you can take advantage of superior training environments. Finally, depending on the place, an off-site seminar can be a welcome change of pace for you, too.

Usually the best sites for training are those built as training-conference centers. Many hotels have jumped onto the conference-center bandwagon with varying degrees of success. However, full training-conference centers do not admit the public. They take in only those who are being trained (though some don't have housing). They specialize in handling training, and most are excellent. Look for these centers in your area or in the areas where you wish to travel.

As indicated, this has become a highly competitive business. Hotel chains like Hyatt offer the public special weekend discounts because so much of their regular business is weekday seminars and conferences. You are in a buyers' market. Shop around and look for the best facilities at the lowest cost. I have found most hotel staffs ready and willing to deal.

Although you may be in a favorable position, don't buy sight unseen. Facilities differ, and even in glamorous hotels the training facilities can be minimal. Look over the facilities. Check for the following:

1. Several rooms in the sizes you will need. Contract for specific rooms only.
2. Soundproof walls, if the space is flexible with movable walls.
3. Heating and air-conditioning controls. If need be, talk to the maintenance engineers to achieve the levels you want.
4. Lighting and decor. These multipurpose rooms often are quite inadequately lit for training or too plush and overdecorated.

5. The menus if you are supplying lunch or snacks. Use recommendations given earlier.
6. The surrounding area. Is recreation available on premises or nearby? Is there too much recreation available?
7. The sleeping accommodations and room rates.

Negotiate a package deal including seminar rooms, meals, accommodations, and services. Set up a master billing account so that the hotel bills you directly. This makes charging and subsequent payment easier, however limit the charges or the number who have authority to charge to the account.

The hotel sales staff is not usually the same as the people who will set up your room. A few hotels have sales staff who personally oversee your needs, but that is rare. Talk to the banquet manager and the catering staff to be sure they have enough people to set up and serve your group. A few dollars or personal considerations can ensure the service you need.

Arrive a day early and let everyone know you are there, making sure everything is set. Check with the catering staff to be sure it has a copy of your needs, your schedule, and so forth. Large hotels, like any large organization, tend to standardize. If you don't want the standard setups, say so and make sure you don't get them. I've been charged $2.50 per bottle for Perrier water along with the sodas because "they always include it." The participants loved it but the boss didn't!

If possible, request full setup the night before your training. If you can't get that, insist the room be completely set up by 7 A.M. Specify exactly how you want the room set up. Hotels are used to setting up for banquets, but not seminars so make sure tables are at least 4 1/2 feet apart, double that if people are to sit on both sides of them. Check sightlines.

The standard tip is still 15 percent; however, different parts of a hotel may be billed separately. Catering and room service frequently add 15 percent automatically, so check before you add on a tip. If you make special demands, take special care of those who supply them. Praise people who do good work for you, especially to their bosses. It ensures good service next time around.

As a rule, you don't get better service because you pay higher rates. Some very expensive hotels provide minimal service and space. By way of contrast, I know of one company who uses the YMCA for off-site training because the facilities are excellent, the service (minimal, true enough) is adequate, the recreational facilities are first-rate, and the costs are very reasonable. You might look into such service organizations. Normally, however, institutions that cater to well-to-do clients, such as large and well-established hotels, also provide the most considerate and tasteful service. Convention centers and conference centers are probably the most efficient, while international hotel chains are not consistent. I've had poor service and excellent service and everything in between from all the major chains. It seems to depend upon local management, staff, and facilities. Try before you buy, and take care to ensure you get what you need.

Before the Session

Whichever setup you choose, you need to check several other things before beginning your program. If it is a multi-use room, check at least one week in advance to ensure that you *do* in fact have it booked for the correct time.

Arrive at least one hour ahead to make sure everything is in order. Check the temperature setting, check the chairs to see that they are safe, comfortable, and attractive. Walk around the room and check sightlines. Are the room lights satisfactory? Be sure you can operate them if you are planning to do so. Also see to it that all audiovisual equipment (including the marking pens) is operating properly. Position and focus projectors; get other equipment ready to go.

If it is your policy, create smoking and nonsmoking sections, label each accordingly, and equip the smoking section with ashtrays. If there are to be refreshments, see that the right ones will arrive at the right time.

Be sure each participant has his or her workbook, name card, pencil or pen, writing paper, refreshments (ice water, candy) if desired, and any other handouts.

Post your agenda and set up any other materials you plan to reveal later in the program. Arrange your notes, slides, charts, overheads, pointer, and clock (always have one) for your convenience, then re-check the sightlines. Check yourself for open zippers, loose buttons, dandruff, messed makeup or hair, loose coins in pockets, distracting jewelry, and the like just before beginning.

Summary

This is one of the shorter chapters in the book but it touches on many important aspects of effective learning. At the outset, we established the need for a comfortable learning environment, and we discussed five important factors that contribute to that comfort. The chapter then focused on the various setups or arrangements for effective learning, from the traditional classroom pattern to the popular horseshoe, from the familiar conference table setup to the different workstation arrangements.

With these considerations in mind, we explored the possibility of designing our own training facility, and elaborated upon various design considerations as well as furnishings and equipment for the training rooms. Multi-use facilities were also discussed, with suggestions for keeping this a smooth operation. We briefly discussed the types of food to serve at breaks and for lunch, then moved on to cover the ways of selecting and using off-site facilities for your training. The chapter concluded with a review of last-minute things a trainer should check before beginning a training session.

CHAPTER 11

═══════════════

Aids to Training

THE key to the term "audiovisual aids" is the word *aids*. American managers have a history of throwing money at problems in the hope that it will solve them. However, it isn't the money that solves a problem, but rather how that money is spent.

Why then is pouring money into visual aids such a common practice? Purchasing videotapes, films, slides, off-the-shelf packages, slide and audio extravaganzas, and the like benefits the manager because it provides visible evidence that something is being done about the problem. And because the aids are tangible things, they are manageable. Furthermore, when the aids fail to solve the problem, the blame for their inadequacies can be put on the suppliers of the aids. From a political standpoint these are sound reasons for purchasing visual aids. But from a training standpoint they are not.

Audiovisual aids are just that—aids. They cannot and should never be acquired to train people. They are effective and powerful helpers to learning, but they are no substitute for teaching. To use them as a way to solve a training problem is a waste of both money and good audiovisual aids.

Audiovisual Aids as Learning Tools

In Chapter 2, we examined the ten key principles of adult learning. One of them, the multisensory principle, is based on the premise that what we perceive with more than one sense has a greater impact on us than what we perceive with just one sense. Furthermore, out of habit each of us depends more heavily on one of the senses to provide our information. Some like to read and understand written material best. Others find it easier to learn by listening or talking. Still others learn best by doing something physical. Audiovisual aids provide the opportunity to address and capitalize on these aspects of learning.

In addition, audiovisual aids provide for another of the principles of learning: They create a built-in form of redundancy. In Chapter 3, we discussed the need for building patterns of redundancy into your lessons. One of the easiest and most effective ways of doing this is to use audiovisual aids for the presentation of key concepts, clarification of points, and review of topics concerned. In short, an audiovisual aid can accomplish one or more of the following five functions. If it fails to do these, it should be discarded. It must:

1. *Simplify.* One of the most important uses of an aid is to simplify complex or obscure material. A picture, graph, diagram, or model is worth a thousand words. The reverse is not true, however; a thousand pictures are not a substitute for words. Often a concept or process is comprehensible only when diagrammed or illustrated. This is certainly true with blueprints and schematics in the building and mechanical trades. Furthermore, complex relationships are often immensely simplified by spatial diagrams. If your visual aid simplifies what you are teaching, keep it. If not, create a new one or do without.

2. *Focus attention.* A second key function is to focus attention on the essence of a topic. Frequently, discussions get sidetracked. Use a good visual aid to keep what's important in front of the trainees at all times, so everyone stays on the topic.

3. *Make points memorable.* Audiovisual aids should be hooks on which to hang the memory. A striking slide, model, film, or diagram, a sign, poster, or sound event can be retained far longer than words. From a simple acronym built up on a flip chart to a two-hour documentary film, visual aids create an impact; they can make what you are teaching unforgettable. Anyone who in high school ever watched the chemistry teacher make rotten egg gas, demonstrate the effects of laughing gas, or drop phosphous into water, will never forget the experience. Devising memorable graphics or producing audiovisual effects is a challenge, but it's also fun — and it pays off handsomely when you succeed.

The aids covered are as follows:

- Slides
- Charts and posters
- Boards (chalk, white, and flannel)
- Overhead projectors
- Films
- Audiotapes
- Models, cutaways, and actual items
- Video
- Computers
- Handout material
- Pointers
- You — the trainer

---

4. *Take you where you cannot otherwise go.* Of course this use of visual aids isn't essential, but visual aids that can do it are invaluable. Movies and videotapes are best, but slides also can be very effective. Sounds are wonderful for setting atmosphere and mood. You can tour the plant without leaving the room, hear the president welcome trainees, enter into minute spaces, and watch processes that cannot be brought into the room. But when using aids in this way, remember that your purpose is to get trainees to learn. If you lose sight of this, your visual aids become merely entertainment. This happens all too often with commercial films and tapes. They try so hard to entertain that they have a negative impact and there is no learning at all.

5. *Create variety.* Too much of anything becomes boring. A film, tape, or unit of slides, a story, or other change of medium can help concentration by creating a refreshing change of pace, a feeling of newness. The danger again is overuse. Too much variety becomes just as dull as too little, and variety for its own sake wears thin after a while. Your visual aids should have challenging learning content as well as variety. For example, I use two flip charts instead of one, with a variety of colors. That allows me to hold trainees' attention for a longer period, while enhancing the impact of new material by changing the colors and switching from one chart to the other across the room.

There are many types of audiovisual aids. In the pages that follow we discuss each in terms of its uses and problems (see Table 11-1).

Slides

Slides are an ubiquitous, easy-to-use medium that makes things memorable through color and variety. They are effective in simplifying mate-

Table 11-1. Types of audiovisual aids.

	Advantages	*Disadvantages*	*Best for Which Purpose*
Slides	Colorful, varied, easily transportable; give uniform presentation.	Require darkened room; no personal contact; possible mechanical problems; overused; passive, not active.	Take us where we cannot otherwise go (close-ups, enlargements, other locations).
Charts and Posters	Flexible, simple, readily available, colorful; show organization of material; enhance interaction in the group; can be referred to several times.	Limited sightlines, limited viewing distance; replacement costs; markers dry out; awkward to transport.	Can develop material interactively with the group; can refer back to earlier material.
Boards (Chalk, White, Flannel)	Can be colorful, flexible; familiar; universally available.	Limited sightlines; messy, smelly; must be erased; associated with school.	Best when you need to add or remove things in a diagram. Excellent for chart development; good scratch pad; useful when reinforcing school atmosphere is desirable.
Overhead Projectors	Universal, readily available; simple to use; flexible, colorful; great with large groups; easy reference to past materials; enhance interaction.	Limited sightlines; distracting if used sloppily; keystoning of projection.	Overlap of transparencies to show layers of complexity in a simple form; good for systems presentation, flowcharting, and developmental materials.
Film	Colorful; shows action; readily available; gives uniform presentation; lends credibility and professionalism.	Requires darkened room; covers generic principles only; easily dated; not always focused on training.	Takes us where we cannot otherwise go, *with action* (other locations, fantasies, dangerous or noisy sites, and so on).
Audio-tapes	Effective for sound-oriented training; portable; create mood.	Limited aural attention span; talks at trainees, not with them; no interaction; limited sensory input.	Let you hear yourself as others hear you; let you listen and learn while traveling.
Models, Cutaways, and Actual Items	Real thing, larger than (or as large as) life; help visualization of the abstract; take you where you cannot otherwise go; some easily made.	Limited sightlines; initial cost; unavailability; storage and breakage problems; maintenance; distracting if used sloppily; tendency for information overload.	Demonstrate how things work, look, or will look; show complex relationship of parts in context; show internal movements; allow close inspection and hands-on practice.

Table 11-1. *Continued*

	Advantages	*Disadvantages*	*Best for Which Purpose*
Video	Dynamic; takes us where we cannot otherwise go; easily updated; easily transported.	Incompatible formats can be a problem; fairly high initial cost.	Lets us see and evaluate our own performances; action-oriented like film but can be homemade and is easier to update.
Computers	Self-paced instruction; interactive; exciting future.	Mechanical process with no human contact; high initial expense; time-consuming to program; tied to commercial software; monotonous to use; tendency for information overload.	Hands-on practice; can be used to give trainees practice on equipment they will actually use; excellent for simulations.
Handouts	Can be referred back to after the course; no sightline problems.	Distracting if distributed while you are talking.	Useful for hands-on practice and for giving assignments.
Pointers	Can be used to enhance several other aids (slides, boards, posters, and so on).	Distracting if played with.	Excellent for focusing trainees' attention on one specific detail at a time.
You	You can adapt any training method to suit the exact needs of your trainees.	None!	To train: for everything, you are the main message. You can motivate trainees as nothing else can.

rial with graphs and charts and in focusing attention on key data in an organized sequence. They take us where we cannot go, and they provide considerable variety.

Slides are relatively inexpensive, particularly if you shoot your own. They can be changed and updated easily, too. If you travel to your training sessions, they are easily transported and projectors are readily available.

The Uses of Slides

Slides are at their best when they take us where we cannot go. We can see other locations, people, or equipment that would otherwise be unavailable. Close-ups and enlargements present detailed views of material, particularly when it is microscopic or enclosed.

Using Slides

1. Preset projector and screen. Mark their positions with tape if you intend to move them during the lesson.
2. Load slides into projector.
3. Check that all slides are right side up and all slides are in right order.
4. Focus projector. Check that there is a spare bulb.
5. Check that all mechanical equipment is working properly.
6. Check your control of room lights.
7. If using audiotape, check if it is cued up correctly and that it is synchronized with slides.
8. If you use a microphone, check that it is working, set at the right volume, is where you can find it, and has a place where it can be put down.

Working with Slides

If you use audiotapes and slides in a synchronized presentation, your presentation gains the added effects of music to create an environment, and you standardize your material. However, you sacrifice flexibility in updating and changing the program, and you eliminate your interaction with the group, leaving them passively viewing a mechanical show. Weigh this trade-off and choose which alternative corresponds to your training objectives.

In assembling your presentation, make sure each slide is top quality, that each is inserted properly in the tray, and that all are in the proper sequence.

When making your presentation, preset the projector and screen and focus the projector before your session. Test the room lights. Check the operation of the projector. Have a spare bulb and know how to install it, should you need to.

If you will be speaking along with the slides, practice ahead of time to be sure your slides have maximum impact in context. If you are using an audiotape with your slides, run through it before your session to ensure that it works properly.

Problems with Slides

The major problem with slides is that the room has to be at least partially darkened for them to be exciting. The darker the room, the more striking the slide, but as soon as you turn down the lights you trigger an

"It's showtime!" response. They become prepared to be passively shown something, not to actively learn something. Remember the time your neighbors invited you over to watch slides of their recent vacation? Training slides usually draw the same response, even more so when the voice is recorded and therefore impersonal.

To correct this problem, don't dim the lights all the way. Leave the room lighter than it would be in a "show." Keep the slide sessions very short—stay under ten minutes. Five minutes is good and three minutes even better. Provide the trainees with work to do during the presentation. Ideally, give them map lights so they can see to take notes. List key points they should look for and respond to during the presentation.

A second problem with slides is that they have been seriously overused. Slides are everywhere, and trainers have come to rely on them too much. Weigh your use of slides against your training objectives, as well as the five things visual aids should do. If your slides aren't accomplishing at least two of them, drop the slides.

In addition, remember to keep your slide presentation short. Avoid trying to use slides to depict motion. They are a static medium, and even multiple-screen razzmatazz fails to create the impression of motion. If motion is important (for example, to show how a machine works), don't use slides. Lastly, avoid being sold a bill of goods by an off-the-shelf package salesperson or by someone who makes a living selling slides. Always ask, "What are my training objectives? Does this aid help to meet them?"

Charts and Posters

Charts are wonderful visual aids. They are ubiquitous, flexible, and uncomplicated, and serve four of the five functions of audiovisual aids. If you are not using charts, find a way to do so. They will enhance your training.

Actually, there are three types of charts: the standard flip chart, sometimes called newsprint (a pad of blank paper suspended on an easel); prepared charts, which may be in a flip format or in separate sheets; and posters, which are displayed in the training room or workplace.

The Uses of Charts

Charts simplify, focus, and make material memorable. They also provide variety. They can be used to prepare the trainees for training, to present material, to document practice activities, to organize evaluations, and to provide redundancy in the form of summaries and reminders. Indeed, charts are the most universal and versatile of audiovisual aids.

Using Charts and Posters

1. Check sightlines. Walk around the room and be sure you can always see the charts.
2. Make sure you have enough paper on each pad you'll use for flip charts and that each pad is firmly attached to a solid easel.
3. Make sure you have enough markers in correct colors. Check that each marker is neither dried out nor smashed.
4. For prepared charts, check to see if they are in the correct order, if they are all right side up, and where you will place each one when you are finished with it.
5. For posters, check that they are firmly in place and unlikely to fall down during your presentation.
6. If you will tear sheets off a flip chart to hang up as posters, be sure you have tape, tacks, magnets, or other adhesive materials.

Flip charts can be prepared ahead of time and then used to forecast a series of points you will cover in the session. They can provide a simple framework of notes to keep you on track as well as form the basis for trainees' personal notes. They are very effective in posting elicited responses from the group and building each point with trainees' input. They are also useful in illustrating concepts that are getting bogged down in language. One of their greatest advantages is that you can refer back to them from time to time simply by flipping the pages. Or tear several key pages from the pad and attach them around the room as posters.

Perhaps the best use of charts, however, is in developing both your own and the participants' materials. Charts can function as a giant scratch pad on which you and the class figure out processes. This lends an immediacy, a freshness, that no other medium can give you. Such charts reflect the group's responses, which become principles they have *built* rather than things they have been told. This approach demands Socratic interaction with the group and so enhances your training effectiveness by creating effective participatory learning.

The value of prepared charts is that they can be done professionally to produce striking visual impact. Colored base stock can be used to heighten the effect, too. However, they are awkward to transport, and eventually they show wear and tear and have to be replaced. If the charts are separate cardboard sheets, you must have a place to stack them neatly as you finish with them.

Posters are not used as often as they deserve to be. They can be placed around the room and referred to from time to time. For example, I once observed a trainer who posted a series of quotes from related literature around the training room like an eye-level ribbon or band. Then he systematically referred to each quote as he covered the material. Posters can serve as review tools or as reminders of key concepts. One of the most effective uses of a poster is as a reminder in the workplace after training is completed. These reminders can range from epigrams to steps for performing tasks. This reinforcement is, oddly enough, not common though most workers could benefit from it.

Working with Charts

In general, rules for using charts, especially flip charts, apply as well to prepared charts and posters. To begin, plan the content and layout for the charts in advance. In planning, list the key ideas and then ask whether a visual aid will help convey those ideas. (This is a good question to ask of *all* aids.) If so, develop the chart always keeping in mind that "less is more." Don't overcrowd the page. Limit yourself to seven points per page. Omit *all* unnecessary details, particularly in diagrams and pictures. Being a technical expert, you may want to ensure that the diagrams are correct. Indeed, they must be correct but also must be simple. Caption or title every page except poster slogans. (They can stand alone.)

Write large enough for everyone to see. This usually means using uppercase letters; however, if your lowercase lettering is neater and easier to read, use lowercase or mix the two. Only if your penmanship is exquisite should you even consider script. Print larger for larger groups. If what you've written can't be read from 50 feet away, print larger still. Also, avoid abbreviations, if possible, or use only standard ones. Use numerals rather than spelling out numbers.

Make your drawings large, too. Use flowcharts to illustrate processes, procedures, or organization of elements. Use bar graphs to show comparisons or to weigh advantages or disadvantages. Try to avoid line graphs unless they are exceptionally clear. These tend to be harder to read and interpret.

Use color to identify main parts or movements in diagrams and in general to emphasize key points. Color also provides simple variety. When I use two flip charts I use black on one and blue or green on the other. After lunch break, I swap colors, solely for visual variety. With black lettering I use red, blue, or green to highlight. (Some theorists argue that red should never be used because it is inflammatory—I have no problem with it.) With green lettering, I use black, blue, or dark brown to highlight. Purple is possible, too. With blue lettering, red, black, or brown make the best highlighters, though dark orange is possible. Avoid light colors; they are hard to see from a distance.

Practice with the aids before using them. If you are developing the charts with the class, practice writing (printing) from the side of the chart so you don't cover it as you write. This both enhances your professional style and allows the group to read as you write. If you have prepared charts, keep them covered until you need them. If you use two flip charts, place them on opposite sides in the front of the room so your trainees make a physical shift when you move from one to the other. Or place them side by side (with room for you to stand between them to write) if you want to compare or contrast the two. Put them alongside one another (or use a special double-width chart and easel) for a horizontal diagram. Needless to say, if you are using two charts in this manner the charts and easels must be of the same height and design. With two charts you can use them apart or together at will for even more visual variety.

Avoid talking to the chart. Look at it briefly in silence if you need to, but then face the group and talk to them. This maintains your leadership role and keeps alive the personal involvement. Lastly, give the group time to read and absorb the information on the chart. Don't dispose of an aid too quickly.

Problems with Charts

The main problems with charts are sightlines and distance. A visual aid is useless if it cannot be seen. Check all sightlines before you begin by standing in front of each chart and looking at all the seats in the room, particularly those to your extreme left and extreme right. In addition, walk around the room and check whether each participant will be able to see the charts clearly.

Avoid wall-hung flip charts. They may look good but usually are inflexible and can't be adjusted to accommodate the group. Furthermore, they force you to turn your back to use them, hiding what you are writing and breaking eye contact with the group. In fact, *never* stand in front of your charts.

The maximum reading distance for flip charts is 50 to 60 feet. If, because of numbers or room configurations, you have participants sitting farther away than that, don't use flip charts except as posters with one- or two-word slogans. Switch to an overhead projector or slides, instead.

In addition to the problems of sight, there are a few things to watch for when using flip charts. For example, if you are using charts developmentally, be sure you have enough paper on each pad. Delays to change pads are a waste of time. If you tear off a sheet (or use prepared cardboard charts), have a place nearby to stow each one neatly as you finish with it. Remember that your trainees will react to how you treat the sheet. If you crumple it or drop it on the floor, they will mentally do the same.

There are physical problems as well. Frequently, when you turn a sheet over, the top edge won't fold down neatly and will crinkle or bulge in an unsightly manner. Take the time to smooth it out. Your respect for the material will be transmitted to and reflected by your trainees. If you talk while holding an open felt-tipped marker, sooner or later you will go to print and the pen will have dried up. Prevent this unprofessionalism by checking all pens before you begin, having backup markers on hand, and *always* replacing the cap immediately after making an entry on the flip chart. Never leave the cap off a marker for longer than it takes to write on the chart.

Boards (Chalk, White, and Flannel)

Blackboards, or chalkboards, are the precursors to charts. Though "black" boards are still found today, most are now green or brown, but all use chalk as the writing medium and so are called "chalkboards." Whiteboards are a much newer invention. These are smooth white boards with a surface that you can write on with erasable alcohol-based markers. Flannel (or felt) boards are just that: wooden boards wrapped in flannel. Cutouts of felt in brilliant colors can be pressed onto the flannel surface. Anyone who has attended a Protestant Sunday school is familiar with flannel boards, but they are not often used in training programs. Their possibilities in training, however, are not lessened for that.

The Uses of Boards

Chalkboards by far have the widest application in training. They were borrowed years ago from education, where they had evolved from the personal slates pupils used in 19th-century schools. Chalkboards have the advantage of being very familiar to all trainees and the disadvantage for some of a negative association with school. With chalkboards you can do most everything you can do with a flip chart except refer back to earlier material. Chalkboards also provide a larger format for your diagrams and notes. Usually chalkboards are mounted on a wall, but are also made on reversible, rolling frames.

Chalkboards are best when you want to reinforce the school-like aspects of your training. They are also useful in planning or developing materials not meant to be saved. They make excellent scratch pads.

A major limitation of chalkboards is that any attempt to use color turns out pallid pastels. Another drawback is that chalk creates dust, which pervades the room. This is why whiteboards were invented. They are used in the same ways as chalkboards but the surfaces accept brilliant felt-tipped colors. In fact, whiteboards are most effective with brilliant

Using Boards

1. Check sightlines.
2. Be sure all boards are clean.
3. Check for ample chalk or markers in the colors you want. Check markers to see they are not dried out or crushed.
4. Check that there is a clean eraser and other tools you'll need (compass, ruler, and so on).
5. If you have a scrolling whiteboard, make sure it is in working order.
6. If you have a flannel board, brush it against the nap to ensure a fuzzy surface for gripping.
7. Be sure all your cutouts are in their proper order where you can reach them.
8. Check to be sure you have your lab coat or chalk holder, if you use them.

colors. They are excellent for diagrams, flowcharts, and graphs. Because they don't have wide use in schools, whiteboards are useful when you want to show a difference between your training and most people's schooling. Whiteboards are usually wall-mounted, but can be acquired on wheeled frames as well. In fact, state-of-the-art whiteboards allow several "pages" of board that can be accessed at any time by scrolling forward or backward. Furthermore, a "page" of whiteboard can be photocopied with the push of a button. Almost instantly, a hard copy in black and white emerges in the copy tray. To my mind, the scrolling device to some extent solves, albeit clumsily, the problem of referring back to earlier work, but the hard copy capability, though amazing, seems to have little practical application for training. It appears excellent, however, for preserving work in progress, such as new design ideas or mathematical formulas.

Using flannel boards is a bit different in that you must prepare cutouts in advance and rehearse your presentation to be effective. They might be used for variety, for color, or for fun. Their application is limited to presentation, however, and would probably be best for a change-of-pace illustration of a logical progression or a spatial relationship.

Working with Boards

Here you can refer back to the section on working with charts. The major difference with boards is the size of the surface. Give some thought ahead of time to your use of this increased space. Remember also that, with more space filled, you must allow trainees more time to copy or absorb the material before erasing it. Obviously, you will need to stand in front of the board to write, so take extra care with sightlines.

Problems with Boards

I prefer not to use chalkboards or whiteboards (and I confess I've never used a flannel board) because I feel the problems they create outweigh their advantages. For the most part, anything you can do on a board you can do more easily on a flip chart. However, you may prefer to use a chalkboard or whiteboard, or may have inherited them and have no choice. If so, remember that chalkboards are messy. If you don't want your clothes full of dust, wear a lab coat or duster and keep a dust rag handy for wiping your hands. In addition, you might want to use a chalk holder, which is a handle that holds the chalk. In theory, it keeps your hands clean. Likewise, don't let chalk dust build up on the erasers or on the ledge at the bottom of the board. Clean both daily and wash the board with a damp cloth at least once a day.

Always have spare chalk with you; you will surely need it. Break a new piece of chalk into fairly small pieces. Large chalk causes a high-pitched shriek that annoys many people.

With whiteboards, there is a tendency for the colors to imprint permanently if left on too long. Always erase the whiteboard within 30 minutes of writing on it. Clean the whiteboard erasers regularly. A dirty eraser smears color. Be careful how you use the markers too. You can get high from sniffing them. Again, these are felt-tip markers and they dry out very rapidly if the cap is left off. Replace the caps instantly after use.

If you use flannel boards, keep track of the various cutouts after you use them. They are easily lost and a bother to remake.

One of the worst problems in teaching with boards is talking to the board. Often it takes time to fill that large space with notes and diagrams. Few things break your contact with the group more quickly than talking with your back to the group. Instead, write on the board and then turn to face the trainees to discuss what you have just written.

As mentioned earlier, be aware that it takes time for trainees to copy the material. Don't be in a hurry to erase the boards. Finally, take special care always to start with a clean board each day. A clean slate creates a strong impression; a smeared or partly filled one gives a negative impression.

Overhead Projectors

Overhead projectors shine a beam of light through a transparent sheet to a mirror suspended above, which projects the image on the

Using Overhead Projectors

1. Preset projector and screen.
2. Focus projector and adjust screen for keystoning.
3. Mark floor with tape if you are going to move either.
4. Check transparencies for correct order and positioning.
5. Check that you have a spot to stack transparencies to be used and those which have been used.
6. Check that you have a pointer, pencil, or marker if you plan to use one.
7. Make sure electrical cord is taped down to floor.
8. Make sure you have a spare bulb.
9. Check sightlines.

transparency onto a large screen. They are almost as common as flip charts and are used in much the same way. Overhead projectors have a built-in problem, however. Usually the projector must be placed between the screen and at least one of your learners, seriously affecting sightlines. In addition, they tend to be used carelessly and distract attention from a presentation as much as they focus it. With such problems and the fact that overhead projections usually duplicate what can be done more easily on a flip chart, why would anyone want to use them? The first answer is size. When people in the back can't see your flip chart, the overhead projector is ideal. The second reason is that an overhead provides visual variety, particularly if you use color on the transparency. An added plus is that you get a large-screen projection with little or no dimming of room lights.

The Uses of Overhead Projectors

There are basically two uses for overheads: to project a ready-made visual onto the screen, and to use it as a large tablet on which to develop your points. In effect, you have a giant chart, and you can use it as you would cardboard or flip charts discussed earlier. The transparencies can be professional or your own, though better artwork conveys greater professionalism. If you want to combine the two and develop material on prepared transparencies, you have a very effective use for overheads. For example, this method would be particularly useful if you wanted to show how to fill in a form. You project the blank form, which is identical to handouts each participant has. As you describe what is to be done, you fill in the form while the trainees follow suit. Upon completion, you can erase your entries with a damp sponge or cloth (assuming the form itself is printed in indelible ink). As an alternative, you could use a scrolled transparency over the top of the permanent one. (Most projectors will take a scrolling attachment, which is simply a rack that holds a roll of transparent acetate, stretches it across the glass projection tray, and allows you to "scroll" it from one side to the other.) You can then write, correct, and rewrite on the top sheet without ever writing on the form itself.

By far the best—and almost unique—use for overheads is with multiple overlays. With a series of acetate sheets placed one on top of the other, you can show the development of a process or operation or the complex interrelationships in a system. Each overlay can exhibit one step, phase, or system, the way diagrams of the human body are shown in some encyclopedias. One sheet shows the skeleton, the next has the vital organs, then the circulatory system, after that the nervous system, followed by the muscular structure, and finally the skin. No audiovisual aid shows this kind of layering as well. Computers can do it, but not for a large group at once.

If you use transparencies in this fashion, you will need to create accurate registration. That is, each sheet must fit in place exactly over the prior one. You can ensure this by binding the acetate sheets together with tape or by using a projector with registration pins at the side or bottom of the glass projection tray. These half-inch-long pins hold the sheets in proper alignment. Such an arrangement allows you to use a dozen or more layers and still get good projection. The diagrams are more comprehensible if you use color codes—for example, a different color for each new system or process you are showing.

Working with Overhead Projectors

Always set up the screen and focus the projector before the seminar. If there are participants present and you don't want them to see the first projection, use any relatively flat object to focus the unit. I use a coin, paper clip, even a comb. When preparing the projector, also be sure you have a spare bulb. Most modern machines have a built-in spare you can engage by simply moving a lever or twisting a knob. Familiarize yourself with the projector ahead of time.

Check the room for sightlines. Be sure everyone can see.

Make sure you have space near the projector to stack the acetates to be used as well as those you will have used. Arrange the transparencies in the order in which you will use them. They are easier to handle in cardboard frames, but if you don't have frames, slip a sheet of paper between each transparency so they don't become confused.

When you finish with each transparency, turn off the projector, then remove the transparency to the used stack and place the next one on the projection tray. Do this even if the next one won't be needed for hours. It makes you seem prepared when you have the correct projection already in place when you switch the unit on. There is an exception to this method, however. When you are using two or more transparencies in immediate succession, leave the light on, remove one transparency with one hand while at the same time replacing it with the next transparency in your other hand. Make this a smooth motion — practice until you can do it easily from either side of the projector. Few things are more distracting than a bright blank screen or a sloppy shift from one visual to the next.

A relatively new aid in the transfer process, available for some projectors, is a time-delay dimmer switch. When you want to change a projection, push the button. The projector fades to black, allowing you to change your visual and walk away from the unit. In the desired number of seconds (preset by you), the projector comes back on again automatically. It is a frill, but a nice one that adds a professional touch to your presentation.

In developing the transparencies, remember that "less is more." Don't put more than seven points on an overhead projection unless you are showing a form or data sheet identical to one each participant has. Then walk them through it and explain how it is used.

Use a pencil or pen to point at the transparency on the projector tray rather than at the projection on the screen. When you point at the screen, you turn away from the group, sometimes touching the screen itself and making the projection wobble. Also, you might walk into the projected image with at least your hand, which never fails to look ridiculous. Remember, though, that sightlines are vital. Whenever you stand beside the projector, someone can't see the projection. Instead, leave the pen or pencil on the tray pointing to what you are stressing and walk out of the sightline to discuss your point.

Problems with Overhead Projectors

We have touched on most problems already, but the main one is sightlines. Pay careful attention to where you set up the screen and where you place the projector. Sometimes it helps to set them up on a diagonal or to one side of the room. In any event, be very careful not to stand between the screen and participants when the projector is on.

Another problem is keystoning; that is, since the projector is lower than the top of the screen, it throws a broader beam of light at the top than at the bottom. The effect is a keystone shape, but because this distortion is so common with overheads, most participants will ignore it. You can correct it two ways, however: tilt the screen forward so the bottom is farther from the projector than the top (many portable screens have an extension hook on the top for just this purpose) or tilt the projector until it throws an even picture on the screen. A combination of both techniques often makes a perfect picture. If you tilt the projector, though, be careful that your transparencies and pointer don't fall off the tray.

Avoid walking through a projection on the screen. If you must cross from one side of the room to the other, either walk behind the projector (that is, the end which is not projecting) or turn it off, step through, and turn it back on again. Either of these is far less distracting than walking through the lighted projection.

Projectors are usually in your way when not in use. Wherever possible, use a rolling table for the projector so you can move it to one side when you don't need it. If you do this, mark its position on the floor with tape so that the projector will be in focus when you use it again.

Lastly, you will look clumsy if you trip over the cord. Tape it to the floor with wide duct tape. If you are going to move the projector, use an outlet to one side so the cord is not in your way.

Film

Above all else, film takes us where we cannot go. It can be used to show how something operates or to take us into the inner workings of the boardroom. Film shows action and interaction. Films are usually professionally produced, so they lend an aura of professionalism to your training. In some cases, when they use big-name performers or spokespeople, they also lend considerable credibility. By crystallizing certain key actions film can clarify concepts and make ideas memorable. Finally, film is a wonderful change of pace. Used well, it can be an effective break from a single speaker, even an amusing bit of fun in the middle of the seminar.

The Uses of Film

As mentioned, film is excellent for taking you outside the classroom or into other environments. Hollywood was built on this simple yet powerful attribute of film. From the beginning of the film era, we have seen romance, history, fantasy, science fiction, and mystery. Film can take us to dangerous sites or show us infrequent events such as the aftermath of real accidents (for safety training), or operations in which noise level would normally hamper training, or situations where training groups would interfere with production.

Films are usually much more action-oriented than slides. Apart from this aspect, however, films suffer many of the same problems and enjoy many of the same benefits. They are readily available. Projectors are simple to operate and always available to rent. Films usually cost far less

---

Using Film

1. Preset projector and screen. If you will be moving them during the lesson, mark their positions with tape.
2. Thread film. Make sure you have the right film loaded.
3. Focus projector.
4. Check and adjust sound levels.
5. Check your control of room lights; be sure they dim.
6. Check for a spare bulb, and know how to change it.
7. Rewind film after use.

---

than writing a program would and can be rented for even less money. As we've said, they can be glamorous, amusing, and provide a change of pace. Sixteen-millimeter seems to be the preferred format, in terms of both sound and picture quality, though 8-millimeter would be effective if materials were available in that size.

Films are best for the presentation step of a lesson. They can be used for the preparation stage, but have very limited potential for practice or evaluation, except perhaps to test ability to spot or identify key behaviors.

Working with Film

Always preview a film before you buy it. Many distributors will allow a free trial. If they don't, rent the film for a single showing to determine if it meets your needs. If you order a film from a distributor or rent one from the local library (often an excellent source, by the way), arrange for timely delivery and return.

Before your session, preset the projector and screen and focus both the picture and sound levels. Have a spare bulb handy and know how to change it. Run the film before the meeting to ensure it is in working order, that it is the film you ordered, and that you can run the projector.

As with slides, leave enough light on in the room to allow viewers to work while the film is on. Assign key concepts for them to look for during the film, and then discuss the film afterwards.

Problems with Films

We've already discussed the problem of a darkened room. This is further compounded by the fact that training films are usually less entertaining than their commercial counterparts, so there is a built-in disappointment factor.

In addition, films become dated very quickly. If styles change, your film appears to be out of date. This may not seem serious, but look at most films made before Equal Employment Opportunity regulations or before we became sensitive to sexist treatments. If you use one of these today you will step on toes, and a discussion of biases will ensue. Equally important is that if your procedures change, so must your film, and that is expensive.

A third problem is cost. To make your own film is prohibitive. Even if you rent the equipment, it costs $50,000 to $100,000 to produce a ten-minute film. And, of course, the film would soon become dated. The alternative is to use generic films, but this brings up another problem. Are the films really applicable to your situation? Some industries, such as insurance, banking, and health care, are large enough for filmmakers to profit from films that address their specific problems. (And even these films are not completely specific.) Films are fine for generic topics, but to make them specific to your application, you must build a lesson around them.

Moving beyond these problems, when you consider buying a film don't let yourself be sold a bill of goods. Remember, salespeople are in the business of selling, not training. Don't be sold a pig in a poke. Always preview before you buy and measure the film against your training objectives and the five functions of a visual aid.

Once you've selected your film, avoid depending on it to teach for you or to entertain your trainees. You *must* integrate the film into your lessons by discussing it, assigning material from it, bringing it into future lessons as part of your redundant patterns and, if possible, using materials from the film for role-playing or projects. Often you can use the same characters, but suggest alternative scenarios that customize the material to your company's application.

Audiotape

If you are training people who will work primarily with sound (radio operators, telecommunication engineers, telephone operators, safety inspectors who use sounds for diagnostic tests, and so on), audiotapes are vital; otherwise, these tapes have limited application to training. As pointed out earlier, ours is no longer an oral culture. Radio in the 1920s and '30s was one of the last vestiges of purely oral experience, and it has been supplanted by visual television. Radio today is largely background. We no longer attend well to what we only hear. Consequently, it is difficult for people to learn just by listening.

The Uses of Audiotapes

There are still, however, several legitimate uses for audiotapes in training. If trainees are being taught to listen, then audiotapes can be

Using Audio Tapes

1. Make sure tapes are rewound and cued up.
2. Make sure machine is in working order.
3. If your player uses batteries, make sure they are fresh. Have a spare set with you.
4. Check sound levels.

valuable. (In addition, many people swear by audiotapes as a way of learning while driving or flying.) For those in jobs where the voice is important, the tapes can be both a model for and a reflector of personal performance. In addition, audiotapes frequently are coupled with slides for a multimedia format that grabs and holds attention.

By far the most powerful use of audiotapes is as a reflection of trainees' own voices. People learn when they can hear themselves. Use audiotapes to allow trainees to hear themselves as others will.

Working with Audiotapes

Use good-quality equipment. Cheap equipment distorts sound, so if you want your trainees to hear themselves as others do, you have to use equipment that can do the job. This doesn't necessarily mean a top-of-the-line sound system. Usually, top systems have features you won't need, like multiple mixing and editing, but get good microphones and recorders.

Keep taped material short, and follow it with immediate coaching. Play a sequence, then analyze and critique it. One-on-one development with a trainee is best when feasible. People can and do learn to listen. As you progress with the tapes, increase the demands on your trainees by lengthening the content. If you use tape to present examples, direct the trainees to listen for specifics. Play the tape, then discuss with them what they heard. If need be, play the tape again. If you use audiotapes to instruct individuals while they travel, encourage them to listen by assigning homework based on the tape. Brief them on what specifically to listen for and provide for interaction on what they have heard.

If you are dealing with telephone fear (a frequent problem when training telephone solicitors), it may help to play examples of supervisors doing a less-than-perfect job. Hearing the mistakes supervisors have made helps get trainees past their initial fears to the realization that even role models make mistakes. If you are training in areas in which recognition of key sounds will help trainees perform, record several instances of the sound. If, for technical or safety reasons, you can't do this, then ask a sound recording expert to reproduce the sounds with parabolic microphones, stethoscopes, and multiple tracking with filters, or even special effects.

Problems with Audiotapes

There is one big problem: inattentiveness. Everything you can do to heighten and maintain interest will help. For example, avoid segments longer than two to three minutes. Anything longer runs the risk of boring your learners.

There are some other things you should be careful to avoid. For example, few things are more annoying than turning on a tape and finding it not cued up. Always rewind tape after use and check it before you use it again.

If you use a portable cassette player, make sure before your lesson that the batteries are good. Keep a spare set handy, especially if you plan to record, because weak batteries record at a slower speed, producing playback that sounds like a cartoon character.

Models, Cutaways, and Actual Equipment or Real Situations

When you are training people to operate a tool or a vehicle, or to use certain hardware, it helps greatly to have the actual thing on which trainees can practice. The problem, however, is that it is often prohibitive to supply each trainee with a real unit. The situation is compounded when the units are likely to be damaged easily by beginners. The answer is to build or buy models or simulations that let novices make harmless errors or show in some depth the operation of the real unit. Thus, full models, cutaway models, simulations, and actual practice models are an important aid to training.

Cutaways are models that show a cross-sectional view, as if you had sliced away the outer part to reveal the inner workings. Cutaways are frequent in fields like medicine, mechanics, architecture, and mechanical design.

The Uses of Models

Often the major use of models and simulations is to show what the real thing looks like, how it works, and what the parts are. Better than any other aid, models show the often complex relationships of parts to each other. In areas in which conceptual work is done, like mechanical design, computer modeling, or architecture, a model shows what something will look like as well as allows trainees to troubleshoot problems before they appear.

Working with Models

1. Check sightlines for all demonstrations.
2. Make sure all parts are labeled correctly.
3. Make sure all moving parts work properly.
4. Test actual equipment to see that it is in working order.

Cutaways are best for showing movement, location, and function of internal parts. Both full models and cutaways are used often to enlarge or shrink elements to a size that allows for easier viewing. Thus doctors are trained on larger-than-life cutaway models of the eye or the ear. Aircraft technicians fly model airplanes in wind tunnels to diagnose airfoil problems. Of course, the actual item provides the best opportunity for close inspection, hands-on practice, and real adjustments of parts. A special case is the working model, which combines the cost and safety advantages of a model with the hands-on practice and adjustment advantages of the real thing.

Working with Models

Give careful thought to the model you use. Ask yourself whether it is the best visual aid for the lesson and whether you really need a model. Consider whether there is a less expensive alternative that would work almost as well.

If the model is the best way to go, consider making your own model. If it is an operating principle you are illustrating or the relationship of parts, any reasonable facsimile can be used. We are all familiar with the stereotype of the retired military officer retelling glorious exploits by manipulating knives and forks, saltcellars, and glasses to represent the model battlefield. Often it is the concept you need to teach, so you don't need the real thing, only objects to simulate it.

Before class, check that your model is in working order. Practice your performance until it is smooth. Make sure the model will illustrate exactly what you want it to.

Often the best way to use a model in class is to have an assistant (perhaps one of the trainees) demonstrate it while you explain what is happening. In presenting the model take special care of sightlines. Be sure everyone can see it, and don't allow the trainees to crowd in close, excluding others.

Don't pass the model around while you explain it or anything else, for that matter. You'll split the trainees' concentration. Talk about it while you show it, then allow free time for it to be passed around. Provide time for the model to be handled or used by each learner until you are sure all are familiar with it.

Lastly, beware of information overload. If you have set your objectives and know what you want your trainees to learn, you can pare your demonstration down to the essentials. When possible, use models to show processes and relationships rather than technical details and "nice-to-know" information.

Problems with Models

We've already touched on the two major problems with models: limited visibility and nonfunctioning equipment. These are easy to avoid if you plan ahead. In addition, try not to let your model upstage you. You can make it the centerpiece of your lesson, but always remember that it is what the trainees *learn* that counts, not what they see or enjoy.

Video

Video is probably the most dynamic and exciting invention for training since the overhead projector. It solves nearly all of the problems inherent with slides and film and creates completely new opportunities for training. It is relatively inexpensive, easily updated, portable, action oriented, flexible, easy to use, instantly replayed, reusable, and doesn't require darkening the room to see it. Furthermore, both films and slides can be transferred to videotape at nominal cost. Add to this how videotape gives the ability to tape and review a trainee's performance, and you can see why I hold it in such high regard. There is no more flexible or useful training tool.

The Uses of Video

Once again video takes us where we cannot otherwise go. As with slides and films, video presents views or interactions of absent characters. It can be used for professionally produced programs, and special effects can be produced with multiple screen projectors.

More important, it can present very precise up-close views. This is probably demonstrated most clearly in the field of medicine. There was a time when interns hunched over viewing windows in a gallery high above the operating table to catch glimpses of a skilled surgeon performing an intricate operation. Today every nuance and gesture of the surgeon can be caught in close-up detail, with three or four cameras creating a demonstration tape of superb quality and usefulness.

Using Video

1. Run tape to check for operation of unit, that tape is properly cued up, that sound is working, and that color looks natural.
2. If recording, test recording process to be sure everything is properly hooked up and working.
3. Check sound levels to be sure microphone is working and that you are recording sound.
4. Check that you have enough tape.
5. If trainees are to operate equipment, make sure they know how.
6. If trainees are to view themselves in another room, have a set of instructions on how to run the viewing equipment. Include how to load and start the tape, adjust the sound levels, and rewind the tape.
7. Upon completion, rewind tape, cover camera lens or point it down to a neutral color, and turn off all power to camera, tape, and monitors.

In addition, thanks to fiber-optic technology, the video camera lens can enter the body to show students and diagnosticians internal conditions which once would only have been revealed by a full-scale operation. Coupled with the microscope, video takes us into the world of molecular science. Used with X-rays, it allows us to watch our own hearts, lungs, brains, or circulatory system in operation. I use medicine as an example only because it is an area in which the full potential of video has been used. With imagination these uses may be applicable to your training.

The third boon of video is that it allows us to review and evaluate our own performance. It gives us the gift "to see oursel's as ithers see us!"—a wish expressed by Scottish poet Robert Burns more than a hundred years ago.

It is hard to decide which use of video is best, but if pressed I'd opt for its reflective capacity. Video is used by every professional athlete in every sport to troubleshoot and analyze technique or play. Watching ourselves make a mistake increases learning many times over. You can tell me I'm doing something wrong and show me a better way, but nothing drives the point home so powerfully as seeing myself do it wrong! Find a way to tap this use of video and the effectiveness of your training will increase.

Because cost is low and many photo and video shops have the capability, use a professional to convert your slides or film to video. With slides, give careful thought to sequencing and the sound track but the video professional will help you match these with your training objectives.

Working with Video

Set up and test the camera, microphone, tape player(s), and monitor(s) well in advance of use. Be sure you are familiar with the operation of all pieces of equipment.

If you are using video to have the trainees view themselves, you have several options. First, you can tape the performance prior to your seminar. For instance, you could tape your trainee salesclerks, operators, or customer service personnel at work. In the seminar, you would show them the tapes and critique their performances either individually or with the group.

A second approach is to tape role-playing. For instance, you could set up a realistic "office" outside the training room (a *Candid Camera*-like arrangement), tape the performances, then show the tape in the seminar for critiquing. This helps to solve the problem of role-playing sometimes being unrealistic when done in front of a group.

Third, you can tape a performance in class, critique the performance, then let the performer view the tape privately later on. In this instance, while the last performer is viewing his or her performance, the group is taping the next individual. This is an efficient way to tape large numbers of participants, but it requires two tape players and monitors (but only one camera and mike), two rooms (seminar and viewing), and three tapes (one in use, one being viewed, and a backup tape in case a viewer takes longer than the next performer).

A fourth option is to tape all participants in sequence, critique their live performances, then schedule times during breaks or before and after the seminar time for them to see themselves. Alternatively, you could play the tape back immediately and use the playback as the basis for a group session.

When you have more than ten participants or when you are taping role-playing or are at a distance from the participants, use a separate microphone. Most cameras have microphones built in, but these are effective only at moderately close range. Since you will be watching the performance, have a participant operate the equipment and another keep track of time.

Taping itself is not enough. Critical feedback must accompany the taping, either before, during, or after viewing. Most effective but time consuming is critiquing while viewing—stopping the tape to discuss a problem. Critiquing before viewing is the next most effective.

Plan your time carefully, and assign time limits for each sequence. As a rule, a follow-up critique takes twice as long as a performance. To figure times, take the total available time and subtract the times for breaks. Divide the resulting time by the number of people to be taped. Then divide the result by 3 (1/3 for the performance, 2/3 for the critique). Don't be too concerned if the first few take longer to critique and you get off schedule. Usually there are general principles to be made in the beginning which occur frequently thereafter. As you go along, you'll pick up time by concentrating on individual performances rather than general principles.

When critiquing, follow a few simple rules:

1. Don't overload. Limit critical comments to no more than three things (skills), and indicate the order to follow in improving them. Remember, "less is more."
2. Balance negative feedback with positive. When people's feelings are hurt, they stop learning. Be supportive.
3. When work is excellent, say so. Don't feel you always must be critical. As a learning exercise, however, ask the group (or the individual) how it might be done differently. This way even the best work presents a challenge and forces them to think creatively.
4. As the group becomes more expert, let them critique more while you do less. This breaks monotony, keeps them involved, and makes them more observant.
5. Center your critique around a few (say, five) key skills or variables. This creates redundancy and uniformity. It also allows you to establish at the beginning what the standards are.

Purchasing Video Equipment

You will have to give some thought to format and equipment. For example, you have to decide between a Beta format and VHS. By far the most popular and widely accepted is VHS; however, Beta produces superior quality recordings and is backed by Sony. Because of Sony's size, market clout, and steady innovations, Beta will be around for the indefinite future. There will also be less costly Beta equipment manufacturers because Sony keeps the market alive. The one drawback to Beta is that the recording process is more complex than VHS, so is much more difficult to service. Half-inch VHS is certainly adequate for the uses we've mentioned, but regardless of which you choose, avoid mixed-format equipment. All video equipment is not compatible. When you decide what to use, stay with ½-inch (unless you plan to produce training tapes, in which case go with ¾-inch to ensure across-the-board compatibility). You will not need the new ¼-inch or 8-millimeter minicam formats presently being marketed.

There is no point in throwing money away on top-of-the-line equipment with capabilities you won't need or use. However, you will need:

- 2 monitors (perhaps a third for backup, if you use them a lot)
- 2 videocassette recorders (perhaps a third for backup)
- 1 camera (1-color tube is adequate; a zoom lens is useful; a second camera for backup, if needed)
- 1 tripod, preferably with a floating head or other smooth action
- 1 power transformer for camera
- 1 microphone (2 for choice and backup), either lavaliere or standard table type; omnidirectional, not unidirectional
- Necessary cables and hookup cords, including at least 20 feet of microphone cable

In purchasing these, look for brand names of products that can be serviced locally. There is usually no need to go for the most expensive, but don't buy the cheapest, either. Consider what size and price range rental car your company allows you, then go for the same bracket in video equipment. Take the advice of knowledgeable salespeople, however. You will have fewer problems and be more likely to get good service.

Remember that the simpler the equipment, the less there is to go wrong with it. You do not need a tripod with wheels; a Neuman or Telefunken microphone; three-tube color cameras; character generators, automatic focus, or electronic zoom in the camera; edit features on the tape player; extra lighting; or other frills. A wheeled rack or stand in which to carry all this equipment and to hold the players and monitors would be a plus, though.

Be wary of sharing your precious equipment with other departments. Scheduling becomes a major problem, and when others use it, equipment may not be functioning when you need it again. If you must share, set up guidelines for scheduled use, maintenance, and repair.

Problems with Video

Video is so useful that there are few problems associated with it. There are a few things you should avoid, however. For example, an all-too-frequent situation arises when people want to save the tapes and you've been rotating them, erasing each performance to record the next one. To avoid this, make your procedures clear in the beginning, or record all the participants on one tape and have them scramble to find time to see themselves. As an alternative, let each person have his or her own tape on which *all* their training performances are recorded. This is costly but of great educational value because each participant has a record of his or her progressive improvement.

One frequent mechanical problem is sound. Few things are more annoying than recording a performance only to find that the sound wasn't turned on. When you set up and test your equipment, pay attention to the sound, too. In addition, I usually check sound when recording my first participant.

Incidentally, I have deliberately avoided the mechanics of setting up equipment because each brand is different. The person who sells or installs the hardware will be happy to explain everything. If you are unsure of your requirements, rent before you buy to become familiar with what you are getting before you are stuck with it.

Computers

I include computers as a training aid because in recent years educators have made much of computer-aided instruction (CAI) — using the computer as a kind of teaching machine. See Chapter 8 and the end of this chapter for more information on these programs. Many training departments exist to train in the use of computers or in new software applications. In this case, computers are "actualities" in that they are not simply aids but rather the real thing themselves. For these reasons computers today are a rather special and important training aid.

When coupled with laser disk storage and fiber-optic linkage, computers may become an even more dynamic training tool than video. Laser disks will allow video to be programmed into the computer so that learners can watch the results of their actions carried through to total failure. People learn best by making mistakes. Through laser technology, the computer will supply an array of animated or acted-out options, *each* of which can be played to its logical conclusion. Errors can be made, the consequences demonstrated, and corrections learned and practiced, all through interaction with the computer. Such devices are presently in operation (at great expense) to train airline, jet fighter, bomber, and helicopter pilots. Fiber optics will make this laser technology linkable with PCs and mainframes, so that training will be possible simultaneously in several locations.

We are not there yet. However, the basic technology is in place and test operations are already functioning. The future is very real. We need, therefore, to look at computers as an aid to training.

The Uses of Computers

A frequent use of computers in training is with simulations, in which the computer is used to respond to and manipulate data to produce answers to hypothetical questions. These are most often part of case histo-

Using Computers

1. Turn on all units; check that all are working.
2. Check that correct disks are loaded (unless this is a trainee task; if so, check if correct disks are in place).
3. Test the command sequence (for example, log on and off) to be sure equipment is working correctly.
4. Have a manual handy in case you need it to troubleshoot a problem.
5. Upon completion of class, be sure all disks are unloaded and computers are shut down.

ries or simulated training exercises. It is in these hypothetical situations that computers are best used. They become a problem-solving tool producing results based on the data fed into them. This gives you the opportunity to devise exercises involving decisions structured around realistic data. Simulations or in-basket exercises become much more realistic.

The second-best application of computers to training is as the actual equipment trainees learn how to operate. They learn from the machine while also learning to operate it for consistency. This is one form of programmed computer-aided instruction (CAI). Standard programmed instruction (covered in Chapter 8) is a series of questions put to the learner in a carefully organized sequence, each building on information contained in the answers to previous questions. A correct answer moves the learner to the next question; a wrong answer stalls the learner at that question or moves him or her to some remedial material. Self-tutoring software programs follow this same pattern, but the programming is very interactive, and the CAI format works exceptionally well because the errors are real and the results are immediately measurable. In fact, the immediacy of results is one of the best features of computers.

What computers do *least* well is CAI in its present state of development. As programs become more realistic with the growth of laser storage capability and the responses to questions more dynamic and less artificial, this situation will change. For the present, CAI programs do a commendable job training basic processes and relationships to already motivated trainees. They also succeed with theory and in bringing operational skills to acceptable levels of understanding (such as recognition, recall, and discrimination). If a simulation program can then be added to test for judgment, you may be able to create an excellent package, but only to the degree of reality you can achieve in the simulation. Except for simulating computer operations, computers themselves provide artificial environments, and that is one of their drawbacks.

Working with Computers

Later in this chapter we examine how to construct a basic CAI program. For now, let's assume you have purchased one and are about to use it. Promoters of CAI sell the programs on the idea that they are completely self-paced. Trainees learn at their own rate. This is true, assuming the trainees *want* to learn. For unmotivated trainees, "their own rate" is not at all. This is one of the major problems of CAI.

Therefore, to use CAI effectively, follow these tips:

1. Work in groups. Find ways to share answers and problems. Try the buddy system. The more human you make the environment, the more dynamic the training becomes.
2. Use those trainees with aptitude to help those who are slower or de-motivated. Keep their interest alive with coaching assignments or other projects.
3. If you need to work with separate individuals in remote locations, keep in frequent contact by telephone and, where possible, by computer. This way you can monitor progress and personalize the instruction.*
4. Use computers as an aid to training, not as a substitute for your instruction.
5. Mix technologies. I've always found it advisable to use a large-screen projector to display your own or one of the trainees' screens for the whole class to see. This allows you to solve the problem together.

Problems with Computers

The principal problem with computers is not their lack of interpersonal skills, but their cost and availability. If you must instruct on a mainframe, operating time is almost nonexistent. Try writing a simulation of the mainframe operations for a personal computer, instead. Save limited mainframe time for final tests or pinnacle exercises.

For most of us, even the cost of individual personal computers prohibits classes larger than five or six, which is great for individualized instruction and more effective coaching. If you are going to acquire com-

---

* I sound like a Luddite crying out against computers in the world of training. It is not that I don't admire computers; I have great hopes for them in the future. It is just that human beings are social animals. We can learn to use tools and come to depend upon them without human interaction, but it is harder. All learning is faster, more thorough, and easier when human interaction is involved. The problem with computers is inherent: they are mechanical. Research into artificial intelligence has come a long way toward alleviating the problem, but it hasn't solved it — yet! Until that time keep your computer training as interactive and supportive as you can make it.

puters, check if you can train on less expensive hardware. Atari hardware costs far less and runs many IBM-compatible programs. The transfer to IBM configurations becomes relatively simple once the program capabilities and operations have been mastered. Regardless of what you purchase, don't share the equipment. Make sure any hardware you buy is reserved for your training use only. This will save you much trouble down the road.

If you are buying generic CAI programs, remember they have all the problems of other off-the-shelf packages. They are generic and can only teach the basics, so you will have to teach any in-house applications. Be very careful of copyright, however. Software manufacturers are becoming increasingly vigilant about any pirating of their material. It is unethical. Write your own CAI programs, or buy ones you can't write — even adapt the ones you've paid for — but don't copy, use, or sell anyone else's program without permission.

Here's a final note on computers. They have wonderful training advantages. Whatever you do on the computer gets an immediate result, and this enhances learning. However, they also have disadvantages. Computer programs are rather dull — long strings of command sequences in not easily comprehensible language. Information overload and monitoring are constant dangers. Concentrate instead on working your computer instruction around the principle of "less is more" and on changing the pace as often as possible. Both will help make your computer training easier.

Handouts

Handouts are too commonplace and familiar to warrant more than a note or two here (they are also discussed in Chapter 8). Self-study materials, workbooks, textbooks, or illustrations can be used as teaching aids. Here are a few pointers on their use:

1. Distribute your materials before you refer to them or after you have covered the topic — never while you are covering it. Allow time for people to look over the materials.
2. Make the handouts more important by assigning homework based

---

Using Handouts

1. Count to be sure you have the correct number.
2. Make sure they are in the correct order.
3. Check to be sure you've planned when and how to distribute them.

---

on them. At the very least, walk the group through the handouts so they will be familiar with them.

3. Keep the material relevant. Many people feel frustrated when given more material than will be covered or needed. If you give out material that will not be covered, explain its applicability to the course.

4. "Less is more." If they have to read a book, they don't need you. Keep your handouts to a minimum.

5. Prepare neat and attractive materials. It helps make the learning easier.

Pointers

A pointer is an extension of your arm. Its main purpose is to focus attention on a particular detail. The problem with pointers is that trainers use them idly. They lean on them, play with them, wave them about. In doing so, they distract attention from the matter at hand. All eyes are on the pointer, not on the topic. This is particularly true of lighted pointers used with slides. A wobbly pinpoint of light can flutter about like a firefly.

Using a pointer well takes self-discipline. Point *once* to the object, words, visual and then either hold that point or put the pointer down until needed again. Used with this discipline, a pointer is excellent. Used without it, it is a disastrous distractor that does more harm than good. If you can't control your use of a pointer, don't use it at all.

The easiest kind of pointer to use is the collapsible type, but be very careful not to open and close it too frequently or it, too, will become distracting.

Yourself

You may not be used to thinking of yourself as a visual aid. But you are the main message, and it is your attitude toward the material that the trainees will buy. Make it good. This is why I stressed personal appearance, dress, and manner in Chapter 4. If you have been reading this chapter separately for audiovisual ideas, please spend some time with Chapter 4. It will pay off for you.

Using Pointers

1. Be sure your pointer is where you want it.
2. If it is collapsible, check to be sure it collapses and opens properly.
3. Remind yourself not to play with it.

You: The Trainer

1. Make sure you have a clock or watch, not on your wrist, that you can see easily. It is best if the trainees can't see it.
2. For women, check to see that your make-up is correct and that you are not wearing jewelry that would distract trainees.
3. For men, be sure all zippers and buttons are done. Button your coat jacket.
4. Go over your opening remarks to be sure you are comfortable with them.
5. Check your agenda to be sure you are on track for the day.
6. Check *all* your audiovisuals.

Remember that because you are the message, you should enjoy yourself. Have fun; get psyched up about what you teach. You have set affective training objectives as well as cognitive ones, and trainees won't feel good about the material if you feel poorly toward it. They'll love the subject if you are excited about it, too. So work at smiling, gesturing and using other forms of animation, and generating personal enthusiasm, especially late in the day. You'll become the best audiovisual aid you can use.

How to Acquire Audiovisual Aids

Having discussed the uses of audiovisual aids, we need now to spend a little time looking at how to acquire them. Remember, the measure of an AV aid is its usefulness to you. Does it help you to produce the results you want? To answer that question, first you must weigh any audiovisual aid choice against your training objectives. Then ask yourself:

Does this aid simplify material for my trainees?
Does this aid help me to maintain focus?
Does this aid make material memorable?
Does it take us where we could not otherwise go?
Can it be used to create a change of pace?

It must do at least two of these; otherwise, as mentioned earlier, it is a waste of training time and money.

Is the visual you want more complex or fancier than it needs to be? Is there a simpler way to explain the idea? Also consider how quickly the material will date itself. When will you have to replace it? Give thought to the level of quality you need. What levels are unacceptable? Do you really need the top-of-the-line product?

What are the costs involved? Are there extra costs this new aid will incur? I once worked for an organization that accepted an offer of two free broadcast-quality television cameras from a local station, which was upgrading its equipment. With great excitement we laid plans for using them—that is, until we realized we also needed control room equipment, cables, lights, dollies, and other equipment that would drain our training budget for the next eight years. As far as I know, the organization still has not used the cameras.

Consider what usefulness the equipment will have beyond the course for which you are considering it. How can you adapt it for other functions? Can it be used for more than one course? In more than one department?

Answering these questions will prepare you to negotiate for the best audiovisual aids. They should protect you from purchasing a disaster. There is one other tactic, too. If you are in doubt, rent before you buy. I have never found hardware that couldn't be rented. Most commercial packages, films, slides, tapes, and the like, can be rented easily. If they won't rent, insist on a 30-day free trial. If they won't give you that, there may be something wrong with the product. It is amazing to me how many trainers have been stuck with materials they don't use or don't like. Always try it out before you buy it.

If you use an aid only once or twice a year, you may find it is more reasonable to rent than buy. If renting, avoid the audiovisual groups who serve the large hotels and conference centers. They usually have excellent equipment and fine service, but they charge exorbitant prices. Instead, go to a good electronics or camera shop—one that provides full repair and customizing service—and ask where you can get rentals. It may well be one of the hotel service facilities, but at least you'll know they are the most reasonable available.

For prepared visuals such as films or slides, membership in the American Society for Training and Development will put you on the mailing lists of everyone in the country who sells these aids. Actually, you'll be put on the mailing lists of everyone who sells *anything* to trainers. Excellent! There is no better way to keep abreast of the marketplace. In addition, your membership brings you a subscription to *Training and Development Journal*, the professional magazine of the American Society for Training and Development, which is filled with ads for every imaginable audiovisual aid. Another magazine is *Training: The Magazine of Human Resource Development*, which does not require membership and which provides much the same service. (See the appendix for more information.)

Finally, an excellent, highly recommended source is your company purchasing agent. A good purchasing agent is expert at ferreting out sources and pursuing the best possible prices, delivery, service, and so on.

In most large organizations, purchases have to go through the purchasing department anyway and, because their job is to get the most for the least, they may override your order and purchase something of lesser quality than you want. Don't fight them; befriend them so they can help you acquire the best aids at the best price. By working with them, you'll ensure you get what you want.

An excellent source of rental films is your public or college library. Most libraries participate in a statewide central lending agency that gives them access to almost every film available. The libraries are inexpensive and efficient; you need only institutional membership to participate.

When planning audiovisual purchases, consider what you'll use. If you dislike overhead projectors or never train more than five or six people, you certainly wouldn't want to buy one. On the other hand, every trainer needs some kind of board or chart to write on. I recommend flip charts on portable easels as the most versatile and easiest to use. The pads, of course, are a constant supply cost. Using a chalkboard or portable whiteboards eliminates this, but is not as flexible. A good compromise is oilcloth- or acetate-covered sheets for the flip chart easels; they can be erased and re-used many times. These materials are more costly than newsprint, but are less than whiteboards.

A good movie projector and screen are nearly always useful. Both can be rented if you use them infrequently. If you buy them, go for the most user-friendly equipment you can find.

Video equipment is so useful that I recommend highly that you consider purchasing a unit. Even if you don't use it at present, weigh how you might be able to in the future. Unless you train only on actual equipment, like computers, you will find video a tremendous help. There is more information on purchasing video equipment in the section on video earlier in this chapter, and later on when we discuss making your own training tapes.

Other visual aids are strictly a matter of preference or need. Computers are vital for computer training. A slide projector is necessary if you want to use slides. Models are a great help if you train in subjects for which they can be used. Give some thought to what you are now doing, and ask yourself if an audiovisual aid might not simplify or enhance your training.

In fact, at least once a year, probably approaching budget time, evaluate where you are and where you want to be in one year, in five years, and in ten years down the road. Weigh your needs analyses against your present capabilities and future projections. If your department is going to be growing (and I hope it is), you will need to give thought to expanding your audiovisual and equipment needs. Plan your acquisitions in one-, three-, five-, and ten-year cycles. Let management know well in advance what your budget requests will be (see Chapter 12).

If you have a large capital expenditure coming up—say, buying a number of personal computers—go to the accounting and purchasing departments and explore with them the possibility of leasing rather than purchasing the equipment. Leasing will increase your operating budget, but it completely avoids a large capital outlay, which might have both tax and operational advantages for your department. Alternatives might include a rental with payments toward purchase; a limited-time lease with a buy-out upon completion (most car leases are of this sort); or a phased-purchase system whereby new items are added each year, purchased by a fixed amount in your annual budget. Discuss the pros and cons of these options with the accounting and purchasing people, and seek out the best alternative that provides what you need, has a realistic acquisition schedule, and is the most painless option for the company.

How to Create Audiovisual Materials

An alternative to purchase or rental is to create your own aids. Of course, I'm not referring to hardware; I wouldn't want to try to build an overhead projector, let alone a video camera. But you can prepare much of what we use the hardware for.

There are three important advantages to doing it yourself. First, your materials are totally customized, hand-tailored to your needs and to suit your company. Second, while the cost of your time and effort is high, making the aids yourself often saves money, freeing it for acquisition of hardware. Third, you gain a wonderful feeling of accomplishment and pride when you can create something and then use it successfully.

There are, of course, drawbacks and limitations. Paramount is the cost of your time and effort. Unless you are prepared to spend a good deal of your work time and most probably a lot of your personal time, this isn't the route for you. A second large liability can be an amateur result if you aren't used to this kind of work. A third drawback is that once you've done one and it has been successful, you can get hooked on it all and want to do more. Furthermore, as the word spreads around the company, other divisions will approach you to do media for them. You can get far busier than you ever intended to be.

A good response to the first two problems is to seek professional or semiprofessional help. You can keep your time commitment down and the professional level up with someone else's expertise. I have a client who wrote a great script for a 20-minute training tape on employee assessment and goal setting. He hired a local producer to shoot it; the producer hired local professional actors, used in-house sets, and came up with an excellent training tape for under $10,000. Even more money could have been saved by engaging the local college filmmaking or television instructors. They love to work with business, are reasonable, have considerable expertise, and produce work with maximum quality in mind. So these options help solve the time and quality problems. As to the third drawback mentioned — becoming too busy making other aids — you'll have to deal with that problem when and if it happens to you, but Chapters 12, 13, and 14 will help.

We've already discussed elements involved in preparing charts and posters. It is unlikely you will make your own boards, so let's move on to making models.

How to Create Models, Cutaways, and Other Devices

Often you can hire a retired artist or model maker who will be thrilled to create a professional model for you. Today computers have taken over many of the functions of models, and model makers are either forcibly retired or working at something else. These people were trained artists who could use any suitable medium to create desired models. The models were used by companies involved in mechanical or structural design, automobile design, engineering, construction, architecture, aircraft design, shipping, furniture design, and the like. To find an expert model maker, check with a local mechanical engineering society or association, ask an architect, call up a theatrical designer or set maker, or contact schools of mechanical engineering or architecture. For a reasonable fee you can get any model you can imagine, built professionally.

Failing that, remember the retired military man refighting his triumphs. You can make a model using anything you have on hand. First, plan the model in your head, then on paper. Gather the best (that is, the least costly, the most adequate) materials for your project. Keep the model simple. Only show relationships or basic processes; don't get stuck in details. Use color codes to highlight parts.

If your model is fairly easy to construct, consider assigning it to one of your children or young relatives (11 to 17 years old) or offer it to a class in design, business, art, or science (grades 6 through 12). They'll have fun, you'll have a selection of models to pick from, and the school can apply the money to a cause, say, a scholarship, new band uniforms, dance decorations, and so on.

If your model has working parts, it is probably best to seek a design expert. Alternatively, convert the real thing to a working model. Take an old piece of equipment and restore it to the point at which you can use it to illustrate basic principles or operations. This is frequently done with engines, presses, guns, and the like. You can also make a cutaway model by slicing an old unit in half and then color-coding its parts.

How to Create Simulations

The simulations to which I refer here are participatory ones such as management games, role-playing, case histories, and so on. Here are some guidelines when setting up simulations:

1. Whenever possible, base your simulations on real events. I recommend the critical-incident method, in which you select a situation either you or the trainees have just experienced. Alternatively, select an incident that is ongoing or about to happen. I use this frequently in courses on negotiation techniques.
2. Have desired answers and approaches, but don't cover all the bases. Leave some questions unanswered. Challenge the group by letting their work exceed the standards you've set.
3. Provide all the background information in detail. If part of the training is selecting data, provide the trainees with irrelevant and excess data to challenge their ability to discriminate. Give them choices.
4. If possible, let the choices play to their natural or logical conclusions. Let the group err; they'll learn from their mistakes.
5. Games work well. Simulate popular television game shows by paralleling their steps or events. I've used *Let's Make a Deal*, *Jeopardy*, and *Family Feud* very successfully.
6. As an alternative to real situations, set up artificial ones to illustrate a point. And keep them short. An example of this is an exercise designed to demonstrate the teamwork involved in listening. Each participant, paired with another, is instructed to do anything and everything but listen while his or her partner talks. After three minutes the roles are reversed and the exercise is repeated. In the ensuing discussion it becomes apparent that both sides of a conversation need to share the listening responsibility. For further considerations, see Chapters 6 and 8.

How to Create Computer-Aided Learning Modules

We discussed the value of CAI (Computer-aided Instruction) early in this chapter and also in Chapter 8. There are a number of excellent programs on the market, but like all such programs they are generic. Yet the methods for writing your own self-paced programs are relatively simple.

Unless you are a designer of computer languages or a highly skilled computer programmer, don't tackle the programming phase of CAI design. Follow the outline given here to create the instructional modules and computer guidelines, then seek a computer pro to create the program for you.

There are two types of computer-based instruction: computer-aided instruction, in which the computer actually instructs and the learner interacts with the computer; and computer-managed instruction, in which the computer directs the learner to perform specific tasks, such as to read a chapter of a book, perform several steps on a machine, solve a set of problems, and so on. Upon completion of the task, the computer tests the learner as to what has been learned. Depending on the answers, the computer either directs the learner to remedial work or moves on to the next level. This latter format requires a resource library of structured tasks to which the learner can be directed (which doesn't really have to be assigned by the computer), a series of tests on that material, and a remediation program.

Computer-Managed Instruction

To create such a program, you need three items:

- An organized, progressive set of reference materials and/or tasks to be assigned to the trainee. These should be structured from least to most difficult in an inverted funnel pattern (see Chapters 3 and 8), in much the same way mathematics is taught in school: simple arithmetic to algebra and up through advanced calculus. None of these is actually programmed into the computer — only the assignments are.
- A series of tests (see Chapter 6) administered by the computer. It asks a question; the trainee answers. The computer asks the next question, and so forth. Upon completion, the computer gives the learner the score and offers advice on remedial work to improve it.
- A remedial program that can be planned by following the Response Analysis Format covered later in this chapter.

Such a program, relatively easy to build, is most useful where you have only one or two trainees at a time and when you have the necessary resource materials for them.

Computer-Aided Instruction

This program involves four principles of lesson design: (1) it requires clear-cut objectives; (2) it requires trainees to be active; (3) it allows trainees to check themselves for corrections and relevance (they can make errors); and (4) it allows trainees to develop mastery of the subject.[1]

To create a program, begin with a very detailed task analysis (see Chapters 5 and 7). To review, there are four basic steps:

1. Acquire or write an accurate job description.
2. Break the job down into separate tasks. That is, what are the various things someone with this job would do? A task is defined as having a clear beginning, a discernable end, and a product or result.
3. Break each of these tasks down into the steps that must be performed to accomplish that part of the job.
4. Break each step down into all the substeps or individual actions that go into completing the task.

Using the task analysis and your training objectives, plan a series of learning modules or lesson plans following these six steps:

1. *Select tests for each topic (task) module.* That is, write a test by which you will measure whether the trainee has learned a particular task (not the substeps, yet).

2. *Outline the steps to mastery for the task.* For each step, create a test. This test frame is the climax of a learning unit. Each unit instructs and then tests the mastery of each substep leading to the performance of the task. Each such unit consists of a set of instructions (how-to's or explanations), called an *instructional frame;* a series of problems to solve based on the instructions with coaching or prompting from the computer, called a *practice frame;* and a minitest question or problem, which is not prompted by the computer.

3. *Each unit is a miniature lesson plan.* It follows the four-step method (Chapter 3) by preparing the trainee to learn, presenting the material to be learned, providing skills-building practice, and evaluating how well the trainee has learned the material.

4. *Enlarge the unit patterns by writing out the instruction steps.* Write them out in full and verify (with others) that they are clear and comprehensible (the instructional frame). Then, based on those instructions, devise one, two, or more problems (depending on complexity), with hints or prompts and directions to help the trainee solve them (each is a practice frame). Here you might also write in praise for right answers.

5. *Set up a series of units like beads on a string (subtask units).* That is, write a brief statement of what will be learned. Then plug in "unit 1," which, as we've seen, consists of an instruction frame, practice frames, and one test frame. Next come units 2 and 3 and so on, up to unit 6 (or until the complete subtask is learned. More than six units usually require more strings of learning units). At this point, write a posttest drawn from materials covered in all units. What you have at this point is each task broken

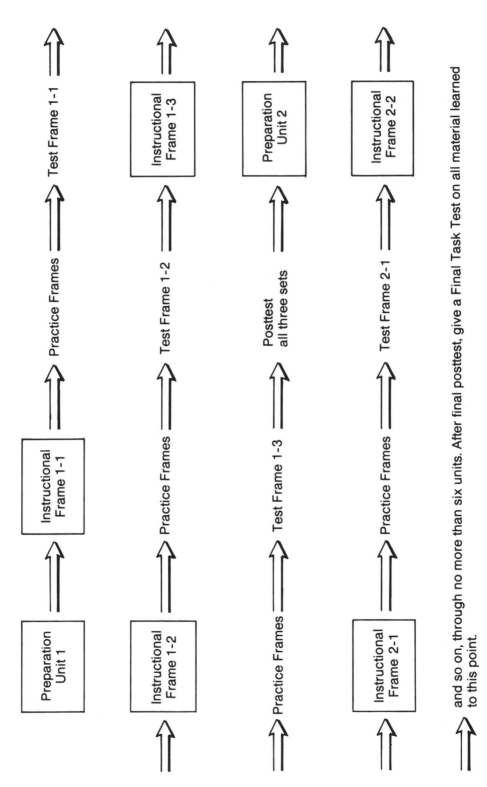

Figure 11-1. Computer-aided lesson plan format.

into subtasks or steps, and each step broken into learning units (see Figure 11-1). Upon completion of each unit, the trainee is tested for mastery. Upon completion of each step (string of subtask units), the trainee is again tested for mastery. Upon completion of instruction for each task (all the subtasks making up the task), the trainee is tested with the original test devised in Step 1 above.

6. *Go back over the entire string.* For each test frame, create a series of remedial instruction frames and practice frames leading back to the test frame again. This is, of course, only for those who got the test frame wrong and need extra practice or instruction. Until they get the test frame right, they cannot progress to the next unit.

You now have a self-paced instruction program, but you still must get it into the computer. To ensure that the programmer produces your instructional package in a workable form, he or she will need the following documents: mainline chart, flowchart, Response Analysis Form, and screen layout form. Let's look at each in turn.

- *Mainline Chart.* Essentially this is the same as the string of units you've just created. Add to it reference material (so you will have it documented for future use) if applicable, and give tentative suggestions for where screen changes should come.
- *Flowchart.* This lays out the program. It allows both you and the programmer to keep track of the remedial units (which will stack; see Figure 11-2). This should be kept as simple as possible.
- *Response Analysis Form.* This is a breakdown of each frame and all of the allowable (predictable) responses, plus what the programmer must program the computer to do (see Figure 11-3). The response analysis form must do this for *every* practice frame and *every* test frame.
- *Screen Layout Form.* To ensure that the program does what you want it to, use the discussion from your tentative screen requests in the mainline chart and type out an exact copy of what you want each screen to look like. Use one separate page for each screen layout.

Armed with these four forms, your programmer can provide you with the CAI package you've designed.

How to Create Videos

Film and video are fabulous in taking you where you cannot otherwise go. But the commercial films and tapes are so generic they lack specifics. An answer to this problem is to make your own movies. You can

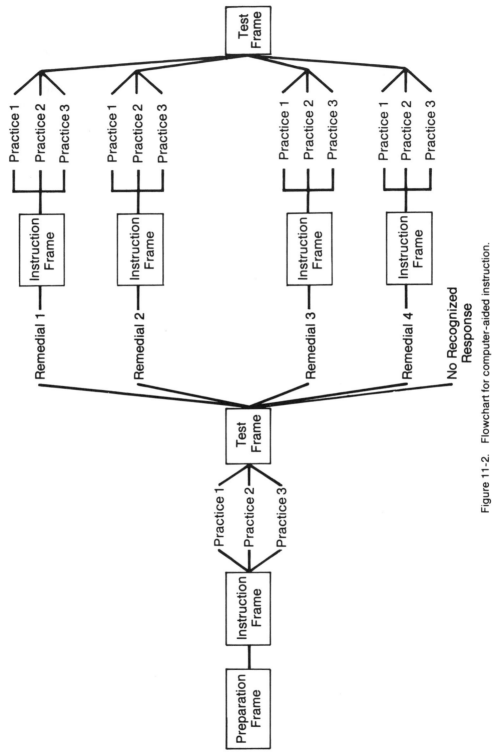

Figure 11-2. Flowchart for computer-aided instruction.

Frame 1. If response is (a) go to (e) and give the following feedback (i)
(b)   (f)   (j)
(c)   (g)   (k)
(d)   (h)   (l)
No recognized response go to (1) test frame
(2) next unit
(3) repeat this unit

Figure 11-3.   Response analysis form.

use film, but that's much more complicated and expensive. Video is feasible, however, and can be very cost-effective.

Your first concern is your training objectives. Will video help bring about the changes you desire? Why video? Are there other media you could use? Create a rationale for the video and relate it to your training objectives.

Establish what equipment you will need.[2] It will vary with your applications, budgets, and needs. If you need to have copies to distribute to various locations, do everything in ¾-inch tape. Home video is ½-inch; it's good, but doesn't hold up to copying. Each copy loses quality until, after four or five copies, the picture is poor, colors fade, and sound becomes muffled. The best is 1-inch broadcast quality, used by television stations. You can shoot in ¾-inch or even ½-inch, transfer to 1-inch, and then edit and make copies in 1-inch. But 1-inch equipment is very costly. Sony has a relatively inexpensive Super Beta ½-inch format they claim is as good as ¾-inch; the disadvantage is that it is not compatible with any other system. I recommend a ¾-inch system.

Equipment

To make your own videos, you will need:

1 camera (at least)
1 tape editor (simple is fine)
1 character generator (simple is fine)
2 tape recorders
3 monitors
1 sound mixer
1 to 3 microphones, depending on your application
1 fluid-head tripod
1 four-piece lighting unit
cables, batteries, cassettes (as needed)
several rolls of seamless paper in various widths and colors

You also will find useful a commercial music library.

Minimum Video Equipment

For See-Yourself Taping (½-inch format)

1 camera (1-color tube)
2 tape players
2 monitors
1 microphone
1 power converter for camera
1 tripod
2 wheeled racks or dollies for equipment
connecting cables, extension cords, tapes, and so forth

COST $5,000 to $12,000

For Do-It-Yourself Production (¾-inch format)

1 camera (three-color tube)
1 tape editor
1 character generator
2 tape-recorders
1 fluid-head tripod
1 four-piece lighting unit
3 monitors
1 sound mixer
1 to 3 microphones
cables, batteries, cassettes, tapes, and so on as needed
commercial music library
several rolls of seamless paper, in various colors and widths

COST $30,000 +

Cameras. As of this writing, equipment costs range from $4,000 to $10,000, depending on the quality and the number of picture-generating tubes in the camera. One tube is least expensive, three tubes (which produce much better color and pictures) are more expensive. Cameras are made by Sony, JVC, Panasonic, Ikegami, and Hitachi. The Hitachi, at about $8,000, is very near broadcast quality. The JVC at half that price is not as good. There is one saving grace: second-hand cameras can be excellent and are far less costly. Buy a used Hitachi for $5,000 (in good condition, of course) and it will pay off.

Tape editors. An editor is used to link together electronically all the pieces of tape you've shot. Each scene or still photo can be shot in any convenient order and edited into its proper sequence. Tapes can be changed and updated by editing or material can be deleted. Having the power to fade to black means you can fade out on one scene and fade in on the other. It makes for smoother transitions. Mix these fade-outs with straight jump-cuts from one scene to the next. Incidentally, an inexpensive way to include slides or still photos (these normally require a special camera to be edited onto a tape) is to project them on a wall in a darkened room and then tape the projection. This tape can now be edited normally.

Editors need not be fancy. A simple cut and paste unit that will fade to black is fine. Buy good-quality equipment but don't go for fancy capabilities such as a special effects generator or a switching unit. Editors are made largely by the same manufacturers as the cameras and range from $8,000 to $15,000. Again, you can save some money by buying a second-hand unit in good working order.

Character generator. This unit lets you write captions, titles, and so forth, either on a choice of colored backgrounds or superimposed on the picture. Your equipment need not be fancy. A simple character generator will have one or two fonts (particular style and size of type), a possible mix of up to 250 color combinations, and the power to superimpose and justify (that is, to move the print around on the screen). You won't need more than this. These run about $3,000 and second-hand ones are usually fine. You could use a computer to do this as well, but you will need special software and have to cope with compatibility. Telecomp 1000 is a $400 computer-video combiner available from Universal Video Catalog (an excellent sourcebook, by the way).

Tape recorders. Do *not* buy these second hand. Of all of the equipment mentioned, tape recorders are the easiest to break, require the most service (full service every 1,000 hours of use), and suffer most from neglect. Tape recorders work like the ones you have at home (only ¾-inch ones are larger) and don't need to be fancy, either. They must have a separate "audio in" port to allow you to dub sound. I recommend two tape recorders because when you are editing, one must play your tape while the other (your master copy) receives and records the new edits. With three machines, you can alternately feed material from either tape, through the editor, onto your master tape. Costs are $1,800 to $4,000 per machine.

Monitors. Monitors are plain television sets. You will probably want more than one, though you could get by with that. I recommend two: one for what's being put into the editor and one for what's being recorded. You can get a small audio board and record/cassette player. This allows you to mix in voiceovers, or outside sounds such as music or special effects. (In this regard, I would recommend buying a standard musical background library for about $400. This is a set of records or tapes of mood, effect, and background music. It adds a very professional touch to your tapes.)

Microphones. One microphone is enough but can get cumbersome when you have more than one person talking. Ideally, have one lavaliere mike (small ones that clip onto clothing), one shotgun-type mike (which is very directional and allows you to control background noise; it only picks up sound in front of it), and one omnidirectional table mike for use on a desk or on the floor with several people around it. Again, these don't have to be first quality. Expect to pay about $150 each, though the shotgun may be more. And remember that you'll need cables and extension cords, too.

Tripods. These are used to hold your cameras. Don't stint on them. Buy one with a fluid head, which allows you to pan the camera back and forth, to tilt it up and down, and to raise and lower it for special angle shots — all without jiggling the picture. Spring-mounted or plain tripods are simply not smooth enough to ensure good quality. If you plan on doing tracking shots (in which the camera moves horizontally along with people who are walking, or moves around those standing still), you'll need wheels for the tripod. Tripods cost $1,000 to $2,000 new, but a second-hand one in good working order is fine.

Four-piece lighting unit. Even though most cameras will shoot in natural light, colors are dropped and details are lost under these lighting conditions. You should have a four-piece kit consisting of two lights and two stands and the cables for connecting them. A company called Lowell, Inc., makes a production kit available in photo shops and video stores, as well as in catalogues. These cost around $1,000. Set them up one on each side of your subject, one higher than the other to control shadows. To create shadows, hang a venetian blind in front of one of the lights or use a branch with leaves, or whatever. You can create silhouettes by lighting the background rather than the subject, or backlighting by setting one light to shine from behind the subject but off camera. You can even create a soft-light effect by shining the light on foil or a sheet of bright white paper and bouncing it indirectly onto the subject. Use your imagination.

Paper rolls. One of the handiest supplies you can buy are rolls of seamless paper in various colors and widths. These allow you to change your background simply by hanging a different color or texture from the wall and shooting in front of it. You can cover windows and doors, create rooms, or make neutral areas. One very effective, prize-winning industrial training tape I've seen uses black paper to create a multitude of scenes in a limited space. The furniture becomes the setting, the background is totally neutral.

A final few words about hardware. The Uniforce facility (see footnote 2 for this chapter) has all the equipment I recommend here. They have a full studio operation (but not a studio facility, in that they work out of an office and a conference room) to produce one or two 30-minute tapes per month for distribution to all their offices. These tapes are done in a news program format and contain company news, current events, motivational materials, and training how-to's. The entire Uniforce facility cost under $40,000. However, to produce the volume of quality material they put out, they have a full-time production and operations person to run the studio. Using ½-inch minimal industrial equipment, you could produce a worthwhile videotape with $15,000 worth of hardware. Uniforce is excellent at $40,000. You can get superb quality work of professional caliber but may have to go as high as $140,000 for top-of-the-line hardware. In video, cost impacts directly on quality.

A final word of caution. You will need an expert! Manuals on video equipment are written by engineers and are very confusing to the nontechnical person. Furthermore, there is a plethora of hardware available, much of it of no use. Hire a consultant to help you design, purchase, and learn to operate your facility. It will be money well spent. I know of a major American company that sidestepped the consultant and spent $400,000 on video equipment which is gathering cobwebs today. Know what you want (your training objectives), and get expert help in acquiring it and learning to use it.

Writing and Shooting

Consider your staffing capabilities, too. Do you have time to produce a tape yourself? Determine the distribution and number of copies you'll need, as well as the production style you want. Do you want a dramatic script? A documentary? A series of involved graphics? Simple head shots? A news format? I had a client who limited his time to writing the script and then hired professionals to do the rest. He brought in an excellent 20-minute training film for under $10,000. And he had no equipment overhead.

Draw up a budget for equipment purchases or rentals and extra staffing costs (overtime, and so on). If you don't yet have the money, justify the cost. Show how what you're asking will be repaid many times over by the use of your tape.

Draw up a script. In film or video it is less effective to tell something than it is to show something. The worst videos are "talking heads," in which one person stands or sits and talks to the camera. Video is an action medium. When doing the script, visualize how it will look. Whenever possible show us something happening or have dialogue taking place. Talking heads are okay occasionally for short periods but keep them to a minimum. The entire video should really be no longer than ten minutes maximum.

Once you have the rough script, ask yourself whether it will meet

Making Your Own Videos

1. Review your training objectives and create a rationale for the project based on those objectives. Justify your costs in terms of company goals.
2. Determine what equipment and how much staff you have and what you'll need.
3. Establish the end use of the tape: distribution, number of copies to be made. Decide on the best approach: drama, documentary, news format, and so on.
4. Write the script. Keep it active; don't tell, show through action. Use dialogue, very little monologue.
5. Draw up the budget for equipment, staff, and so forth.
6. Storyboard the script. Break sequences down into specific shots. Keep shots varied and short.
7. Scout for or create sets and locations. Be creative; have fun.
8. Schedule your shooting, people, use of sets, and the like.
9. Shoot your video.
10. Edit to a finished copy, adding sound and graphics.

your training objectives. How will it fit into the lesson? Can it be used for more than one subject area? If your answers are satisfactory, break your script down into specific camera shots. This is called a "storyboard," and it is often done in cartoon fashion. The storyboard is a step-by-step portrayal of what will be on the screen every second of the final tape. The average length of a shot (a single camera view or take) on commercial television is three seconds. The more shots, or takes or camera moves, you have, the faster paced the final product will look; the fewer shots or takes the slower it will be. When you have lots of action, this alone will hold the trainees' attention. When you have only one or two people talking, add the appearance of action by breaking the dialogue into many shots. Try close-ups, full master shots (the whole physical scene or set in one shot), and medium-range shots. Vary them and mix them up. Make each a different length. Professionals create dramatic rhythms this way and so can you. One word of caution, though. Don't overdo it! If you jump around too much it will put your audience on edge and make them uncomfortable. Work on variety with a smooth blending of angles, types of shots, different lengths of shot, and so on.

Plan and, if need be, scout or create your sets and locations. Schedule your shoots, actors, equipment use, crew, and so on. One time- and money-saver that Hollywood uses is to shoot all the scenes that take place in one location at that location regardless of when they occur in the script. For instance, say you're using your company president's office. There is one scene in the beginning of your film, two midway through, and one at the end that take place in that office. Don't schedule four separate visits; that would drive the president crazy. Schedule one visit and shoot all four scenes, out of sequence. This means having different actors sometimes or having frequent changes of costume, but it saves time and bother in the long run.

A logistics problem needs to be addressed here, though. Keep careful track of what scene is shot where on which tape. Keep a log of your takes. When you come to putting it all together, you'll find it very frustrating when you cannot find footage you know you shot or when you need footage you meant to shoot but simply lost track of. Movie companies have a person whose only job is keeping track of footage.

Finally shoot your video. Be flexible and creative. Sometimes the shot called for simply doesn't work, so try others. Maybe a better idea will occur to you while you are shooting. Try it. Shooting is the best part of moviemaking. It's work, but try to enjoy it. It can be exciting. When you've finished shooting, edit the tape and add sound and graphics to the edited version. Now you have your own training tape. And every one you make will get better than the one before.

Summary

In this chapter we have taken a close look at audiovisual aids and their application to training. It was pointed out that a trainer must consider each aid in connection with training objectives. Effective visual aids perform at least two of five possible functions: to simplify material, to focus attention, to enhance memory, to take us somewhere we cannot otherwise go, and to provide variety. We examined the audiovisual aids available, discovered their best uses, how to work with them, and what problems might be anticipated.

As cost is a factor in any business, we discussed the question of rental versus purchase. Too often trainers buy unsatisfactory media, so we established some criteria for evaluating aids. We looked at sources of audiovisual materials, and considered some ideas on budgeting for media acquisition.

The final section of this chapter dealt with alternatives to readymade, mass-produced materials. We described how to get help in building models, and gave guidelines on creating meaningful simulations. One of the key topics here was step-by-step instructions for writing computer-aided training packages. Finally, we examined the costs and considerations of setting up a video production unit, plus how to script and shoot your own training films.

PART III

Managing the Training Function

Introduction to Part III

PART III addresses problems that training managers are likely to face, whether they are managers of large and active training departments or run small one-person operations. I've divided the problems into three broad categories: managing the training department (scheduling, budgeting, handling subordinates and so on); selling your training ideas to management and other departments; and negotiating with outside vendors, other departments, management, and subordinate staff. These tasks must be mastered by a training manager, whether experienced or just recently promoted to managing the whole training function. In essence, this material is a checklist on how to function as a training manager.

The approach here is consistent with the rest of the book, in that it provides simple "how-to" information and avoids complexity wherever possible. There are more involved (perhaps even more accurate) systems available for accomplishing these tasks, but none is more effective for normal operations.

In Chapter 12, we look at the everyday tasks of managing people and money. Included here are general budgeting formats and a specific budgeting format for a single seminar or training program; a breakdown of different training tasks, forms of employee (that is, trainer) performance evaluations, with discussion of familiar formats such as Management by Objectives, and approaches to praising, motivating, and criticizing subordinates; and Hersey and Blanchard's Situational Leadership system for developing employee skills and abilities.

Chapter 13 describes the steps to take in putting your training programs on the map in your organization as well as maintaining a high profile once you've achieved that. Because the marketing of training involves written communication, I've also included some guidelines for good writing.

Chapter 14 presents some general principles of negotiation and then applies those principles to specific situations such as working with vendors, negotiating with subordinates, or arranging agreements with peers to train their people. Negotiations are viewed in terms of variables: time, information, and power. I also provide a set of questions to help you prepare for negotiations, and a checklist of specific tactics to use.

As with the rest of the book, this final section can be used as a convenient reference to refresh your memory and as a basic textbook of fundamental techniques. It is also a resource for developing training personnel, so they can eventually accept management responsibility on their own.

CHAPTER 12

Managing the Training Department

THE duties of management can be broken down into three arenas of activity: physical resources, human resources, and financial resources. Most managers tend to be good at one or two of these and regard the remaining one as a chore — something to struggle through when the time arises. We've discussed the importance of physical setting in Chapter 10. And being a trainer, you know that the human resources arena is paramount. If you are like most trainers, you probably concentrate on these two arenas and save financial management for budget time. This chapter discusses both human and financial resources, but begins with the often-neglected topic of financial management.

Managing Your Financial Resources

Are you one of those managers who neglects the financial aspects of training? It needn't be so. Nothing gains the respect of financial people (for whom training personnel are a liability, remember) like careful allocation of financial resources. It's a good way to develop political friends.

Benefits of Budgeting

1. Promotes analysis of existing activities
2. Focuses on future planning
3. Establishes reference points for measuring performance
4. Motivates you to achieve your goals
5. Focuses your attention on priorities
6. Fosters timely action

In fact, budgeting benefits you in several ways. It promotes an analysis of existing activities, forcing you to take stock. It places your focus on the future and on future planning. And it provides a reference point for measuring performance (yours and your subordinates'). Budgeting also motivates you by forcing you to set goals and inspiring you to reach them. It focuses attention on priorities, and makes you work for what is most important. Lastly, it fosters timely action to deal with upcoming operations.[1]

The first thing to recognize is that anyone can make up a budget. The challenge lies in making a budget that reflects your circumstances and that plans accurately for future needs. As with computers, if you put garbage into a budget, you'll get garbage out. So the first step in making a budget is to gather accurate information.

The budget information you gather should answer three questions: (1) What is your cost history? (2) What is the present state of affairs? and (3) Where do you want to go? Based on the answers to the first two, you can determine how much you will need to get there.

There are two recognized types of costs to be budgeted: fixed and variable. Every budget format takes both into consideration, but they don't all do it equally well. If you mainly have fixed expenses (that is, wages, contributions to overhead, amortization of equipment, material costs, scheduled maintenance, and the like), then a fixed-cost budget format is best. If, on the other hand, you have a large number of variable costs (that is, new equipment, off-the-shelf package purchases, last-minute consultants, off-site locations, responses to management's re-active training requests, unscheduled maintenance, equipment rentals, and so on), you'll need a budget format that accommodates variables and makes them easier to predict.

Fixed-Cost Budgets

There are two common formats for this type of budget: planning, programming, and budgeting; and zero-based budgeting.

The Planning, Programming, and Budgeting System

In this approach there are five steps to preparing a budget.

1. Define and analyze your objectives. Trace last year's performances and compare them with present levels of performance. Determine what changes you want to achieve in the next year.
2. Analyze anticipated output in light of each objective. In effect, list the benefits to the company, in terms of money saved or increased dollars earned; that is, show the impact of each objective.
3. Using items 1 and 2 above, project the anticipated total costs for several years ahead (say, five years).
4. Put forward and analyze the alternatives to achieving your objectives. This is a vital step. It helps you develop convincing reasons for accepting your budget and training plans. It also encourages you to create contingency plans; these are vital because, in the event your budget isn't approved, you may have to accept one of these alternatives.
5. Break down dollar figures into interim and total costs. If approved, this will be your budget.

The Zero-Based Budgeting System

This approach was made popular in the late 1970s by the Carter Administration. It assumes that there was no last year. You start from scratch (base zero). There are three rather simple, direct steps:

1. Break down all your activities into "decision packages"; that is, define and list the activities, clustering the related ones.
2. Evaluate each decision package and rank it on a scale from Most Important to Least Important.
3. Allocate your resources according to your rankings. If you want to accomplish all of them, it will cost more and so you must ask for more money.

This system forces you to set clear priorities and then fund items in accordance with those priorities. The most important things get done, the least important are not so costly if they don't get done.

Variable-Cost Budgets

The greatest problem with fixed-cost budgets is that they usually can't handle contingencies. The variable-cost budget does deal with contingencies, but for that very reason it is less accurate. There are four approaches:

Direct Estimates

This is actually contingency planning. You base your estimates on past years' operations. If you are just beginning and have no past history to draw upon, use industry standards, data from your training network, or information from similar departments in your company. You can estimate flexible costs within a range, and budget for the top of that range. For example, this approach is used by some city governments to budget for snow removal. It works best with a carryover fund to draw against in shortfall years and to contribute to in surplus ones.

Minimum – Maximum

In this system, you address the problem of variable costs by creating two budgets: a minimum budget to keep you afloat, and a maximum budget to allow you to grow. You ask for the minimum, but are allowed to draw up to the maximum as conditions dictate. Monthly operating expenses are figured on a formula based on the difference between the minimum and maximum amounts divided by the degree of fluctuation (changes, training days, travel costs, off-site location expenses, and so on). You use the minimum budget as the baseline and the maximum as the limiter.

Correlation, or Historical, Standard

This is perhaps the most common type of variable-cost budget. You take the cost for each month and compare it to the equivalent month last year. Desired changes are forecast and accounted for. You are, however, linked to last year's patterns, which your training may change. It also assumes that while there are month-to-month variations, the monthly patterns themselves are not variable. As you know, this is not always the case.

Cost per Unit

A variation on the correlational format is to break all costs down to a per-unit measurement. For training, that breakdown would be a cost-per-person amount. Based on past costs, it is possible to project a fairly accurate budget by estimating the number of employees to be trained. This offers the added advantage of backup evidence from attendance records to show that you are on target. Such systems are used by public seminar organizations, by advertising agencies, and by direct mail marketing groups.

General Budgeting Considerations

These are some budgetary considerations that should be helpful to the new training manager, and may be food for thought for experienced managers, too.

1. Keep closer tabs on expenses by segmenting budgets into weekly, monthly, and quarterly goals. Thus, a very costly month can be balanced by a frugal one to keep the year in line.
2. In setting interim goals, use past data to predict where you should be at any given period. However, adjust the data and your goals to reflect projected trends and changes. This is especially useful when planning long-range, gradual growth.
3. Build attainment of major objectives into these interim milestones. Equipment purchases, for example, can be spaced out in planned intervals to look less costly in the annual budget.
4. Consider the budgetary impact of leasing versus outright purchase. Your accountant and company purchasing people can help you here. Purchase is a one-time variable capital expense. Leasing is a constant fixed expense that comes out of the operating budget.

Program Budgeting

So far we have talked only about budgeting for the department. Another separate, and vital, budget is the one drawn up for each training program. There are two sets of information you need: direct training costs and company costs. The first we refer to as raw costs, and the latter as both gray-area costs and hidden costs. Which costs you include in your budget depends upon how you want to use the budget.

Raw Costs

In all cases you need to look at the raw cost — or training budget — first. This is the simplest budget format, and it is a tally of the costs to your department of a given training program. For comparison, it is also useful to divide the total cost by the number of participants you will be training. This gives you a cost-per-person figure that can be used to justify alternatives, prove the bottom-line value of training, call for departmental budget increases, and so forth.

The raw costs include such variables as:

Preparing and duplicating handout materials
Creating new audiovisual aids
Obtaining outside materials (consultants, off-the-shelf packages, and
  the like)
Renting off-site facilities
Providing service setups on-site or off (coffee breaks, plus tips for
  serving personnel)

Gray-area Costs

These don't usually come out of a training department's budget but
are, none the less, important factors for the company. Gray-area costs
usually come out of budgets for those departments or divisions sending
people to you, and include:

Trainee travel (including transportation, room, meals, and entertainment)
Lost work time of trainees

Hidden Costs

These are usually limited to the overall costs of maintaining training.
For example, putting on a seminar involves a portion of the training
department salaries to cover both actual training and preparation time. In
addition, the costs of space (heating, furnishing, lighting, and so on) are a
percentage of company overhead. Such costs are monitored by the accounting department, so you should be aware of them

For purposes of comparison and persuasion, all training program
budgets should contain a list or breakdown of the costs per trainee.
Whether you include gray-area costs depends upon the purpose of the
budget. If it is to be seen by managers upon whom those gray areas impact,
then by all means you must address them. If management looks at larger
costs, then you will have to include those larger costs.

Hidden costs are usually of little direct concern outside the training
department. In cases of cost justification, however — particularly if you
are under fire from cost-cutting movements — it pays to be able to detail
the costs of maintaining any training function. It is most effective to be
able to compare these costs (raw, gray-area, hidden, and total) with the
costs of not training or of less training.

Managing Human Resources

For the rest of this chapter, we look at the management of human resources — those who work for you. The content is designed as a way of approaching management problems; as a series of workable answers to those problems; and as a refresher on creative resources for the experienced training manager.

The management of human resources requires overseeing the process of getting things done by other people, motivating people to enjoy doing things well, and developing those people into more competent workers for the company — in short, preparing them for management themselves. The first of these we call staffing; the second, assessment and motivation; and the third, development. Let's look at staffing first.

Staffing

Staffing is simply the division of labor.[2] When the job becomes too large for you to handle or, preferably, when you can predict that it will be, it is time to hire one or more subordinates to take over some of the tasks. Coordinating and controlling their efforts — that is, knowing who is doing what and when — is the manager's task.

The question of when to hire is answered by asking what you are hiring that person to do. In training, there are twelve categories of jobs. In very large organizations several people may work at the same job, with a supervisor or manager for each category. In many organizations only some of the twelve categories are pursued; however, as a rule, a training manager hires others (either on staff or as consultants) to perform one or more of these jobs.

Most trainers wear many of these hats. Only in the largest organizations is it possible for each job to be a separate position. But each is a separate task and should be viewed as such when bringing in new staff or dividing the workload among the present staff.

Technical Training

This division of training involves teaching skills to technical personnel. Skills can range from safety training or heavy equipment operation to word processing, from teller training to telephone skills and computer operation. These are the basics of your company's operations, and they are taught to entry-level, clerical, skilled, and production employees. This training often makes up the entire training effort. When the task is large, it is best subdivided into logical divisions of labor, such as clerical, production machine, customer service, and the like.

Twelve Divisions of Training

Technical training
Sales training
Supervisory training
Management training and executive development
Instructional systems design
Internal consulting
Human resources planning
Career development
Training administration
Audiovisual management
Organizational development
Training management

Sales Training

Selling is a front-line skill. It is also a specialized skill. In many cases, a make-or-break marketing approach results in a high turnover rate. So most organizations that depend heavily on sales have regular sales training. All too frequently, sales training is handled by the sales department itself, on the theory that only a sales rep can teach sales. You may want a specialist to handle it for you.

Supervisory Training

Most companies promote employees, yet skilled laborers moving into a supervisor's position may know nothing about supervising others. They need training in this field. Often the answer is to rely on a professional group such as the American Management Association, which has a course for first-time supervisors. But if your company is large or has special supervisory problems, this situation is usually best handled in house.

Management Training and Executive Development

As managers are promoted, new problems and new responsibilities demand new training. Courses such as budgeting, planning, systems design, Management by Objectives, presentation skills, negotiation, and so forth are needed. As the management level gets higher, the pool of trainees becomes smaller, and fewer courses are required. In these instances, professional organizations and consultants are used more heavily.

Instructional Systems Design

Someone has to plan and write new training programs. Much of Part II was about how to perform this function. In large training organizations, planning new programs can be a full-time job. In smaller operations, the alternative may be to relieve a staff trainer of regular work so as to perform this function. Or hire a consultant.

Internal Consulting

Many organizations are shifting to a profit-center accounting system for their training departments. In this way, the training department acts as a consultant to design programs and supply training services. Other departments who use this service are charged back for it, so training realizes a profit. To make this work, usually there should be someone to act as liaison, sales rep, marketing planner, needs analyzer, and—most often —program designer.

Human Resources Planning

This is the job you are doing when you read this chapter. It involves long-range planning and staffing for the whole company, particularly with regard to pay scales, work hours, enforcement of Equal Employment Opportunity regulations, pensions and benefits, and so forth.

Career Development

A special, relatively new area for training, this involves helping management candidates achieve their career goals. It includes both serving as a learning resource for these fast-track executives as well as creating assessment standards whereby they are selected and tested for advancement.

Training Administration

This is the job of running the training plant, scheduling the courses and personnel, and registering the attendees. It is just one more task if you train only three people a year, but it is a major job if you have an active and complex department. Usually this job is performed by an administrator who needn't necessarily be a skilled trainer.

Audiovisual Management

As demands for training expand, so do audiovisual needs. Frequently, there is sufficient demand for a manager and a staff of four to five people just to acquire, maintain, and schedule audiovisuals. It is an important task, but one easily assigned to others. Of course, if you are producing your own audiovisuals, this becomes an even more demanding job.

Organizational Development

These people are the change specialists. When a company undertakes a corporate-wide change, it is wise to hire a full-time development specialist whose job it is to plan and administer the innovations desired. An OD administrator would be advisable, for example, if you were installing a company-wide Quality Circle procedure. Such a staffer would also be useful in planning or instituting unpopular changes such as new work rules or new labor-saving equipment.

Training Management

This is the boss — the person who does the planning for, coordinates, and staffs all other divisions of training. Depending on the size of the training organization and the importance of training to the company, this position can vary from a first-line managerial or supervisory responsibility to a fourth- or even fifth-level senior vice presidency. The training manager is responsible for all training, and is the person to whom all other training personnel report.

Assessment and Motivation

The second function of human resource management is to gauge how well subordinates are performing their work and to motivate them to continue to do so or improve. There are many ways to perform these two tasks. Here we'll consider a few, first with regard to assessment, then motivation.

Assessment

Assessment is often seen as a chore by management and as a trial by subordinates. It should be neither. These people are hired to relieve you of some duties so you can perform others. Unless they are very good at what they do, you will spend far too much time helping or correcting them or even re-doing their work. That is self-defeating. The purpose of assessment is to measure how well subordinates do their work and to provide positive feedback to encourage them to improve their performance. They benefit from knowing how they're doing; you benefit by being able to trust more and more their ability to get results on their own.

To evaluate job performance you must specify precisely what the job entails. Your analysis doesn't have to be as detailed as for a formal task analysis (Chapter 7) but you do need to break each subordinate's assignment into specific tasks, then categorize those tasks to evaluate the performance on a scale from excellent to unacceptable.

There are two steps to this. First analyze the duties, responsibilities, and behaviors of the task to set up criteria, then identify the desired performance level for each specified task — in other words, the performance standards.

It is best to work these both out with your subordinates so that they become mutually acceptable goals and measurements rather than ones you have forced. Viewed this way, the assessment process is in terms of job requirements rather than individual performance. Of course, the individuals are being assessed, but the focus is on the job requirements and the assessment process is removed from the difficult and subjective interpersonal arena.

With the job requirements established, you must decide how often you will assess your subordinates, what methods and what scale you will use to evaluate their performance, and what you will do with the data you collect. The question of how often to assess your subordinates depends upon: (1) the maturity of your people (see the section on development later in this chapter) and how actively you wish to develop their capabilities; (2) available time; and (3) company policy (if there is one). Most companies assess employees only once a year, some every six months. If you are active in developing your subordinates' skills and abilities, you will need to evaluate much more frequently — at least quarterly, perhaps every six weeks or once a month.

The question of assessment methods depends on the performance standards you've set. Presumably you've worked out the job requirements together, and are keeping a performance record to compare development. The areas traditionally measured[3] are as follows:

- *Personal traits.* These are individual qualities such as initiative, leadership, positive attitude, competitive attitude, and so forth. Exercise great care to ensure that each trait is clearly job related. You need those assurances to comply with E.E.O. regulations.
- *Job performance behaviors.* These are skills required of the job. How well do the subordinates perform them? Measure their performance against agreed-upon standards.

- *Job results.* Sometimes doing the job "right" with the "right" attitude isn't enough. Job results are an important check on the accuracy of your assessment standards.

Approaches to Setting Standards

There are four approaches commonly used to rate employee performance, as follows:

1. *Comparative standards.* In the comparative approach, each employee is ranked in comparison with his or her peers. In each job category the evaluation will reflect top performers, middle-range performers, and those needing help. Our school system uses this approach almost exclusively. It is also used when you engage in motivational ploys like performance bonuses and sales contests. Those who do best win; those who don't, don't win.

2. *Absolute standards.* In this approach, the company or management—sometimes with employee input—sets the performance standards. Standards are an objective description of the job. Workers are measured as to how close they come to meeting or exceeding the standards. Training objectives (see Chapter 3) are of this type. Our school system uses this method when it sets passing and failing grades. But within this approach, there are two types of standards.

Qualitative standards measure employees for correct (established) behavior on the job, in real or simulated circumstances. Critical incidents are recorded and analyzed in the real performance of the job. Simulations (such as fire drills, airline flight simulators, war games, or role-playing) are run periodically in training. Judgment here is much more subjective, but clearly defined standards can keep the simulations meaningful. We'll look at such an evaluation system directly that you can incorporate into your training department.

Quantitative standards are specific goals that each employee strives to meet or surpass. These are defined criteria similar to the points used by judges in some sporting events; the time, speed, or distance records athletes try to break; the sales quotas set by sales managers; the admission standards established by schools and colleges. In effect, they are the level or standard to achieve or surpass.

3. *Set goals.* This approach uses a system called Management by Objectives whereby an employee and manager jointly set performance goals to be achieved by the employee within a certain time.[4] Job standards can be used as one measure of achieving these goals. Assessment takes place at the end of that time, and performance is measured by whether or not the goals were achieved. This approach can be combined very effectively with quantitative absolute standards, which were just described. In essence, you use this system whenever you conduct training to produce a

change in behavior. You specify your goals (training objectives), train them, and either fail or succeed depending on whether those goals were met. As a training manager, this is one of the easiest measurement tools to use.

4. *Direct indexes.* This approach[5] is the system discussed in Chapters 3 and 6 for measuring your own effectiveness as a trainer in achieving affective learning objectives. You relate attitudes to specific job behaviors and then observe those behaviors down the line. Measurements such as absenteeism, turnover rate, sales volume, customer complaints, use of time, and so on, are the means of gauging how well employees are doing their jobs.

I know of a training department that assesses its trainers solely by measuring trainee performance after training. If trainees have failed to change, to improve, or to meet new standards, then their trainer is viewed as having failed also. It's a tough system but a logical one. The principal drawback is that there are many factors beyond a trainer's control which can impact on trainee behavior. It is unfair to hold a trainer completely responsible, but this limitation can be balanced by using trainee downline behavior as just one measurement of trainer performance. Used in this way, direct indexes are valid for training assessment. After all, isn't this how an entire training department is measured? Senior management asks what the impact of training is. They answer that question with the direct index of results.

Behaviorally Anchored Rating Scales

In discussing absolute standards I mentioned using qualitative ratings. This approach has a motivational aspect as well as an evaluative one. It is called BARS, which is both an acronym for Behaviorally Anchored Rating Scales and a description of the system.

To make an assessment system for your trainers' work, you need to devise a checklist — a way of objectively quantifying the incidence of correct (desired) behavior. To do so you need: (1) to isolate a group of behaviors, traits, or characteristics that reflect each level of performance; and (2) to arrange them in a simple checklist or devise a differential scale by which the behavior can be judged. Your scale could be along the line of "always does," "usually does," "occasionally does," "seldom does," "rarely does," "never does," or the like.

With this checklist or scale you can evaluate performance insofar as it approaches the preset standards. While the observance is not totally objective, the standards you've set are, and the checklist or scale focuses your assessment sessions on performance of the job rather than on subjective evaluation.

The BARS system adds a motivational dimension to this basic structure. Because subordinates are measured against a standard, it is always best to engage them in setting those standards. If they have helped set them, they cannot later claim the standards are unfair. In addition, with BARS you don't just set one standard but, rather, a series of ascending layers or "bars" of behavioral standards, each for a level of performance superior to the one below. The final result will be descriptions of the following BAR levels:

> Behaviors that constitute excellent performance.
> Behaviors that constitute very good, or far above average, performance.
> Behaviors that constitute good, or a little above average, performance.
> Behaviors that constitute average performance.
> Behaviors that constitute nearly average performance, but still in need of improvement.
> Behaviors that constitute below average performance that will require a lot of work to correct.
> Behaviors that constitute unacceptable performance.

Each of these bars are performance levels toward which the participants can strive. Use positive as well as negative descriptions and work each one out carefully with the employees. To standardize the achievement levels for all employees, have them also reflect the input of other subordinates, but negotiate until the standards are acceptable to all involved. Once you have agreed upon standards, you can contract with each trainer to achieve or maintain a desired level. Each trainer's assessment is a measure of their success in reaching the BAR level they have chosen.

The key to BARS is using descriptive anchors to delineate the performance levels. Write these in much the same manner you wrote your training objectives (see Chapter 3). That is, they should be:

1. Very specific examples of behavior.
2. Realistic examples of behavior (avoid qualifying adjectives and adverbs such as good, acceptable, and so on).
3. Measurable, observable behaviors; avoid assumptions about knowing or understanding.
4. Descriptive rather than prescriptive to avoid quantifying the behaviors; describe the behaviors rather than call for how often they should be performed (save that for a related rating scale, if you like).
5. Neutral. Specify the behavior but make no demands and set no performance limits.

So to describe an acceptable performance level, you would not say, "Trainer moves well, has good posture, and gestures effectively most of the time." This is not specific enough and has too many qualifiers. Instead, you might describe these behaviors as, "Trainer does not wander or pace idly. He (or she) stands with both feet on the floor about two feet apart, and stands still and erect while doing so. He (or she) uses both hands above the waist with elbows extended and wrists firm when gesturing."

Goal Setting

BARS also can be used as a developmental tool. It fits well with Management by Objectives, a system of employee development and evaluation that has become very popular in recent years because it works so very well.[6] I treat it briefly here. The main concern is output rather than "how to." That is, this system aims solely at end results; within reason, the ends justify the means. Manager and employees jointly frame the results employees will achieve in an agreed time frame. Employees are free to try whatever methodology they can to obtain the result, and their success or failure is measured by that result.

Management by Objectives is a very pragmatic system. It appears on the surface to be very mechanical, but the human side is obvious when you realize that the end result can (and, indeed, should often) be positive behavioral and skills goals. In my experience, this system is best when it is project oriented. That is, a task is identified and then the results are agreed upon by management and subordinates. A time frame (perhaps in terms of a series of plateaus) for completion is decided and management contracts to supply the needed resources while employees contract to deliver the finished task in the agreed-upon time. Notice that the manager is responsible for supplying resources and help and, if requested, coaching to achieve the goal. The contract is not a one-way street. The manager is a resource; the subordinates get the job done.

As suggested earlier, the frequency of assessment sessions depends upon company standards, employee motivation, the developmental nature of the job, and the needs of the managers and the subordinates. On a project basis, assessments can be at every plateau. On an overall job basis, they can be annual. Final assessment standards can be based on self-improvement, on BARS, or on direct indexes.

Motivation

As I've said, this chapter is intended to give initial direction to newly appointed training managers and to provide food for thought for the experienced ones. Consequently, I touch on only one or two aspects of motivation. For more detailed information, I refer you to my cassette/

workbook series *How to Motivate for Success,* which gives complete coverage of the field of employee motivation, with directions for setting up a motivation program.*

You need to motivate yourself and your employees everyday, whether or not you have a formal motivation system. People need to feel good about what they do. When they don't, there are two major reasons: (1) They aren't receiving the recognition they would like, or (2) the job dissatisfiers outweigh the job satisfiers. Let's look at both as the keys to motivation.

Satisfiers and Dissatisfiers

Many readers are familiar with the brilliant concepts of Frederick Herzberg.[7] Herzberg looked at the things most managers felt motivated the workforce and realized that they only motivated behavior in some limited circumstances and, then, usually negatively. He called these "hygiene" motivators because, like dirty hands, they motivate us only when negative enough to come to our attention. We wash our hands to get rid of dirt, but we seldom set washing our hands as a goal. Among the hygiene motivators, Herzberg listed such things as wages (only important when we get less than someone else doing the same job), working conditions, hours, and so on.

What Herzberg believes is that there are a number of other factors that move us in positive, purposeful directions. People work hard for something they believe in (a verification of self-worth), for a sense of achievement, and for the sheer pleasure of the task. These things he called real motivators.

In my seminars I like to ask which participants have hobbies. I select a hobby that requires a great deal of time, and I ask why that person puts such effort into doing that after a long day or week of work. The answers are always the same:

A sense of personal satisfaction
A sense of achievement
A potential for growth and mastery
Recognition among peers
A perception of the task as pleasurable and challenging rather than work
A sense of personal responsibility

These things truly motivate us. Of course, other things do, too, or there would be no television game shows. But these reasons just given are triggers often left untouched by management.

Management by Objectives, combined with Hersey and Blanchard's

* Available from AMACOM.

Situational Leadership (discussed later) and **BARS**, can foster a sense of personal development on the job rather than a feeling of the grind. If emphasis is on growth and development — on mastery to succeed — rather than on assessment and evaluation for their own sake, then the perspective shifts to a motivational one. Objectives become personal challenges and evaluations are merely checkpoints to measure progress.

To achieve this perception, make your standards a point of pride (as the Marines do). Create rewards and recognitions for achievement on all levels. Set personal goals as challenges rather than as being for the good of the company. Load work horizontally, not vertically.* Express pride and disappointment appropriately and use Management by Objectives to gain a commitment to improve. Challenge employees with realistic objectives and make them a team by developing *esprit de corps*. Lastly, create formal ranks or levels of aspiration and celebrate the rite of passage from one to the next. These actions will build a sense of worth and create a need to grow, a motivation to improve and excel. One word of caution, though. Be careful not to overwhelm newcomers. Lay out a path by setting objectives and letting them achieve before escalating to a full motivational program.

Recognition

As mentioned earlier, the other key to motivation is recognition. No one ever gets enough recognition. Even top achievers, who get most of it, want more. Unfortunately, we usually wait until people have done really outstanding jobs before praising them. Or we do the opposite and praise people so often and for no reason that our praise becomes devalued.

Using the assessment systems discussed in this chapter, you can set up a schedule as follows:

- To praise highly successful people whenever they *surpass* their goals.
- To praise moderately successful people whenever they *reach* their goals.
- To praise less successful people whenever they *almost reach* their goals.

I realize this goes against common practice, but if you never praise the people who don't ever quite reach their goals, they have no incentive to try. By praising their efforts, you can raise them to the level of those people who quite often reach their goals. They gain a sense of growth, accomplishment, and self-worth, and you gain more skilled and happier subordinates.

---

* Horizontal loading means giving work assignments that broaden skills and responsibilities. Unfortunately, most of us have worked for managers who loaded vertically — that is, who increase the workload for the same task. We only grow more efficient or tired; there is no challenge, only drudgery.

In giving praise, refer to the standards or objectives you've set. Be specific in your praise, and refer positively to a trait or personal characteristic that led to that success (perseverance, effort, and so forth). Express pride — show how you feel — and refer, if possible, to how far they've grown from last time.

The other side of the coin is criticism. When you need to criticize, make it constructive. Too often, managers throw the baby out with the bath water. Being disappointed, we rant and rave, criticizing everything. Yet in nearly every performance — even a bad one — there is some part that was done well. Praise that part. It doesn't lessen the criticism, but it makes it less personal and more job oriented.

To criticize fairly, follow these tips:

1. Confirm the undesirable behavior with subordinates so you agree on what happened.
2. Express what you feel was good about their performance.
3. Explain the problems you have (make them problems, not faults).
4. Describe specifically what you think should be done to correct or solve the problems. This is best if subordinates can suggest what they think should be done.
5. Gain a commitment from the subordinates to make a change. This is to be their next objective.

Development

Using a few basic principles of motivation and assessment, you will be able to build an effective, tightly knit, loyal group of trainers. But there is a third function of human resource management: development.

Routine jobs get dull. For example, teaching the same course 20 times a year eventually becomes tedious. Stagnation results when someone does the same task over and over again. It is hard to motivate a workforce that feels its job is monotonous. The answer is to create a developmental program that tracks each trainer through the full range of tasks your department performs.

Instead of simply increasing the work load of each trainer as you become busy (vertical loading), set up a series of challenging tasks. Design the program so each task contributes to the overall effort of your department, each utilizes different training skills, and each challenges the trainer to whom it is assigned. Then assign these jobs so that each subordinate gets to perform nonroutine tasks as often as possible (horizontal loading).

Suppose that, following our "pro-active" principles (Chapter 5), you detected an area you thought mandated a new training program in the next 12 to 18 months. You could assign the needs analysis to one subordinate, the program development to another, the proposal to a third, the writing of lesson plans to a fourth, and the creation of audiovisual aids to a fifth. These tasks would all be in addition to regular training duties. You would act as coach and coordinator — be a resource for them.

Notice that this way each trainer gains experience in a different facet of training. Each time a new project comes along a different trainer performs a new task. This is development. Eventually, several trainers will become experts in all phases and are then promotable. Of course, if the only job to be promoted to is yours and you aren't leaving or being promoted yourself, you will probably lose at least one valuable employee to another company. But not really. You are a trainer, and you will have trained trainers. Be a mentor and help their careers. You'll develop loyal friends and build an effective training network.

To conduct such a development program, you will need to:

1. Divide the overall project into specific tasks that can be segmented.
2. Arrange these tasks in a developmental sequence.
3. Have resources available to aid and instruct trainees (for example, this manual).
4. Develop individual flowcharts for each trainer to help them through the developmental phases.
5. Use developmental coaching techniques that encourage each person to succeed.

Setting detailed times for completion may be useful, but since most of the tasks don't follow predictable schedules, the program should be task oriented — that is, framed within a broad time, but with no set completion date. This is truly continuing education. Of the items just listed, most are straightforward, easily worked to suit your tasks. However, the matter of developmental coaching needs to be addressed. Paul Hersey and Kenneth Blanchard's Situational Leadership Model is excellent for this purpose.[8]

Situational Leadership is based on two dimensions of a job situation: task maturity and leadership response. The first dimension considers whether the employee is able and willing to do the job. The second dimension involves the type or level of approach the manager uses to assign and assist the subordinate to complete the task. The second dimension is a reflection of the first. Immature employees need a great deal of attention, while mature ones need very little help. Let's look at each in turn.

Task Maturity

Task maturity has nothing to do with employee age or longevity of service. It relates, instead, to the task and is a reflection of whether the employee is able to do the job. To decide this, you must answer three questions:

- Does he or she possess the skills for the task?
- Is he or she able to set and achieve realistic objectives to complete the task?
- Is he or she able to take on the responsibility for completing the task?

An employee who is strong in all three areas is fully mature, described as being at Maturity Level 4. In contrast, an employee with none or few of these requirements is task immature, at Maturity Level 1. Maturity Levels 2 and 3 are judgment calls between levels 1 and 4. Notice that it is not the difficulty of the task that defines these levels but, rather, the ability and attitude of the subordinate.

Leadership Response

Each maturity level demands a different management style or approach: telling, selling, participating, and delegating. At Maturity Level 1, employees need instruction and close supervision. They either are not able to set objectives, do not know what to expect, lack the necessary skills, are not yet able to take on full responsibility for the job, or any combination of these. Such people need to be told how to do the job, be taught how to set goals, and be helped with the responsibility. This approach is *telling*, and it involves a lot of task-oriented communication and much less relationship-oriented communication.

As the employee matures to Maturity Level 2, however, the situation changes and demands a different style of management or leadership, hence the name Situational Leadership. Skills improve, the ability to set and reach objectives increases, and the sense of responsibility grows. This situation needs encouragement; relationship messages are very high, as well as task-oriented ones. You are *selling* the task to subordinates.

As employees master the job skills, become comfortable with setting and meeting objectives, and are, as a result, more responsible, they reach Maturity Level 3. You need not spend time on the how-to's of the job, but can relax and enjoy working with the subordinates. *Participating* is the mode of leadership style — high levels of relationship communication and little or no task-oriented direction. This is the team phase of development.

Finally, when employees reach Maturity Level 4, they are fully

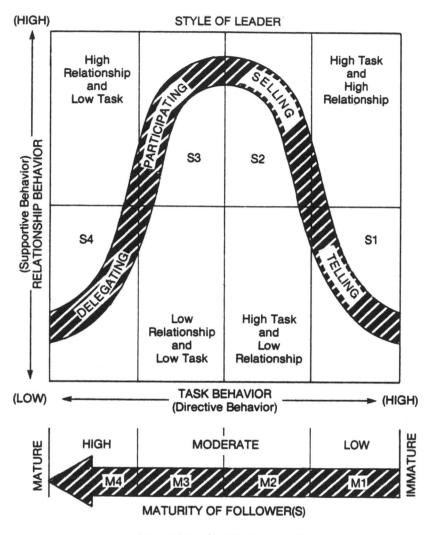

Figure 12-1. Situational leadership.

Source: Paul Hersey/Ken Blanchard, *Management of Organizational Behavior: Utilizing Human Resources,* 4th ed., © 1982, p. 200. Reprinted by permission of Prentice-Hall, Inc., Englewood Cliffs, New Jersey.

skilled, fully competent to achieve results, and completely responsible for completing assignments. Now you are *delegating* tasks and leave subordinates alone to achieve them. Communication of any kind is much less because employees are busy doing their jobs and you are free to work with others on other tasks.

So, to bring in a few abbreviations to simplify matters, use M1–4 to show maturity levels and S1–4 to show management approaches (see Figure 12-1). When you have a subordinate at M1, you match that with the S1 approach: *telling.* If your employee is at M2, respond with S2:

selling. In the case of an M3 employee, respond with S3: *participating*. And, finally, with M4, use an S4: *delegating*. Which response you use depends upon an individual's maturity at a particular task, so one person may require all four leadership styles in the same day. Furthermore, as an individual grows, the style for a particular task must change, too. If you rush ahead and delegate too soon, a subordinate will fail, and you will need to go back to the next lowest S level to bring that person up to par again.

Situational Leadership is a flexible, dynamic theory. In practice, however, there are usually three problem areas:

1. Few managers can remember all this all the time. Treated casually, the system tends to fall apart because it is easier to lose your temper when things go wrong than it is to adjust your S level.
2. Maturity levels tend to be guesswork, so the system doesn't always work.
3. It is easiest to categorize people at a certain maturity level and leave them there. You simply load them vertically at the same level, rather than advance them through horizontal loading.

The system *will* work for you, however, because I have solved each of those problems. As we discussed earlier, break down the tasks of your training department and organize them into a developmental hierarchy. Then flowchart each subordinate's progress through that hierarchy. That solves the first problem. You know exactly when to use which level of leadership with whom. If you forget, you can go back and look it up. Using the BARS system and Management by Objectives for assessment, you can solve the second problem. Gauge maturity to standardized levels and areas of performance. By creating a hierarchy of tasks and scheduling people to move through it with horizontally loaded tasks, you will see growth and development. In fact, you'll be hard pressed to maintain a static judgment in the face of dynamic employee growth.

The purpose of Situational Leadership is employee development. The end result is a staff of highly skilled, first-rank trainers. As nothing remains static, however, you will also create a dynamic learning environment for your trainers, which they will carry over to their trainees, who, as a consequence, will become highly motivated achievers.

Summary

This chapter was about two of the three spokes of management: financial and human resources management. Financial management in the training function consists of budgeting accurately and then staying within that budget. We examined the value of budgeting and gave three formats: planning, programming, and budgeting systems; zero-based budgeting; and different kinds of variable factor budgeting.

The balance of the chapter was devoted to human resources management. We covered three areas: staffing, assessment and motivation, and development. Within the realm of staffing we looked at the twelve traditional divisions of a training department to see in which areas you need help and to assist you in assigning staff to tasks in your organization.

For assessment and motivation we concentrated on ways to develop your employees' sense of satisfaction. Using goal-directed assessment tools such as the Behaviorally Anchored Rating Scales (BARS) and Management by Objectives, you can inspire employees toward self-improvement. Other contributing factors are horizontal loading of work assignments and recognition. We also provided a format for giving praise and constructive criticism.

Finally, we looked at employee development, and used Situational Leadership as a way to build trainer skills.

CHAPTER 13

====

Marketing the Training Function

IN the first chapter training was defined as the means for bringing about a change. A company creates a training department to bring about that change, and they hire or assign a trainer to produce the change. The trainer then becomes an agent for change, a management resource to be called upon when the need arises. It is at this point that we need to look at the marketing of the training function.

As a trainer, you are a management resource—a possible solution to an immediate problem. However, you are only called upon when the need arises, creating the all-too-common re-active stance— the "putting out fires" situation discussed in Chapter 5. It is part of your job to keep management aware of your position as a constant and important resource. Some managers realize this, but others don't; it is those who don't whom you need to inform.

This is not empire building, though I have seen several executives use the training function to do just that. I am talking about marketing your services in house. As a consultant I am often brought in by the training department to serve as a resource. I occasionally work for other departments because they don't know their training department could help. I am always a little sad when this happens, because it means that the training department has failed to market itself successfully. Like any good salesperson, you, as a training manager, cannot wait for people to come to you; you must go to your customers and ask to solve their problems.

Steps to Marketing

There are several steps to a marketing effort. You must:

1. Define the target market.
2. Define the product or service to be sold.
3. Research the target market.
4. Choose the most effective channel in which to market.
5. Sell the product or service.
6. Follow up on your sale.

Let's look at each from a training point of view.

Defining the Target Market

Do you know, as you read this, how every department or division in your company feels about you? If not, you need to do some marketing. Draw up an organization chart of the company (and of your division, if you work in a large organization). Check off the departments for whom you train or circle those for whom you don't. Of the latter group, fill in the names of executives from senior levels on down to supervisory ones. These individuals are your target market.

Defining the Product or Service

Once you have targeted your market, ask why you are not presently servicing their needs. There may be excellent reasons, such as if you lack expertise in that area or if there isn't sufficient staff to justify training. At this point ask what it is you can sell them. Your choices are among the following:

Seminars tailored to identified needs
Seminars tailored to needs of which they are unaware
Seminars currently offered to others from which they or their people might benefit
Expertise in hiring outside consultants for training
Needs analyses
Recommendations for outside seminars and self-study programs
Audiovisual resources

Select one for now and two more as long-range goals for each area you've targeted.

Researching the Target Market

Find out about your market. Ask those who interface with these divisions and levels of management to glean information about their operations. Also talk to the personnel department. You want to discover:

1. How they feel about training.
2. How they feel about you (not personally, but as a training department).
3. What, if any, outside seminars they have sent people to or attended.
4. If they have brought anyone in from outside to train.
5. If they are informed about courses you offer.
6. If they are affected by any current or proposed corporate-wide changes.
7. What their political position is in the company.
8. If they have a training budget.
9. If their counterparts in other companies do any training.

The answers to these questions will give you a handle on how best to present your proposals.

Choosing the Best Channel

There are many ways of approaching people. Be imaginative and have fun. For example, make appointments to ask what people's needs are. Be up-front about your request. Say that you are assessing your role as trainer (which indeed is true). Add the names on your targeted market list to the circulation list or "copies to" list for your memorandums. Then create new memorandums notifying all personnel of completed training programs. Each time a program is completed, tell everyone.

Ask for five minutes at key meetings to present a talk on what your training department has been doing. Start a word-of-mouth campaign by asking those you've trained to talk up their programs. Start a poster campaign, too, and write articles for the in-house press. In fact, volunteer to write a column.

For those who regularly send trainees to you, get together to sponsor a guest speaker and then invite target-market personnel. Lastly, create a company-wide survey of future training needs. Ask questions like:

What are your current needs?

What do you perceive as your future needs?

If we offered *xyz*, would you send people?

Are you aware that we train in *abc* areas?

Which of the following seminars or courses have you attended or sent
people to in the last five years?

Selling the Product or Service

Choose one or two channels and mount your campaign. Be careful.
You don't want to become a pain in the neck, but you do want to make
people aware of you — to put your training on the organizational map.

Following Up on Your Sale

Once you've gotten people to your sessions, follow up. Three months
down the line ask them what they found useful from the seminar. Or ask
how their people are using the information. Even if you've only sent a
survey, follow up and ask for responses. All of these build the image of
training throughout the company.

The Art of Gentle Persuasion

A major element in marketing your training function is persuasion.
Persuasion is defined as gaining the willing cooperation or agreement of
another. The important word is *willing*. You can force someone to do
almost anything if you have enough power, but though coercion may get
people to do what you want, it will never gain willing compliance. People
hate to be coerced and fight back when even an attempt is made. If you
rise to a position of power in the organization always remember that you
will get better work, cooperation, and results with persuasion than
you ever could with force.

The Elements of Persuasion

There are probably many ways to persuade people and many successful approaches to use. There are, however, three elements that you can
include in any persuasive message to ensure that it will be persuasive.
There is no guarantee that the other person will agree with you, but you
will exert great pressure for him or her to do so. The elements of persuasion are (1) logical appeal, (2) emotional appeal, and (3) ethical or authoritative appeal. Let's look at each.

Logical Appeal

Whatever you are asking must make sense. And it must make sense from the other person's point of view. A persuasive argument should be well thought out, with solid, logical reasons to back it up. Define the problem and lay out your plan of action as the most logical possible solution to it. The person you are persuading must see that you have weighed alternatives, and have chosen this one only after careful thought. Explain your reasoning, and answer questions before there's a chance to ask them. Cover the facts; make them real, not puffed-up data for the sake of argument. When you discuss alternatives, track them down to their logical outcomes, but show that your answer is better.

Emotional Appeal

Don't rant and rave or become hysterical, but do show some excitement about what you say. Remember Albert Mehrabian (Chapter 4) and the three basic relationship messages. You must exhibit a high degree of involvement, and the other party must know that the topic matters to you — that you care. Show that you like the other person; people are seldom if ever persuaded by those they think don't like them. You must show you care and that you are working in that person's best interests. On the other hand, be authoritative and exhibit a degree of assertiveness — perhaps it is best called confidence. The people you are persuading must believe you expect them to agree with you, not that you expect them to say no.

Ethical or Authoritative Appeal

To be persuaded, people must feel that what you are asking them to do is the right thing. They need to believe they are making a good decision. An ethical appeal underlines or stresses those elements of your argument that affect broader aspects of the situation: the greatest good for the greatest number; justice and fairness; those who've been deprived will benefit; help the underdog. These are strong appeals because they reach people's sense of proportion, their desire for fair play, and, indeed, their perception of ethical conduct.

An authoritative appeal, on the other hand, gains its sense of correctness from references to powerful or respected others. The president of the company wants it, the competition must be met or matched, government agencies have proved, and so on. Such expressions apply pressure on people to agree with you, and they give both you and your argument an authoritative stance.

General Rules of Persuasion

1. People are persuaded by solutions to their own needs or arguments that satisfy their own attitudes.
2. People won't change opinions by 180°. Break your persuasive arguments into smaller ideas and make them appear familiar.
3. People never give more than they are willing or able to give.

There are no guarantees, but a request that appeals on all three levels is hard to resist. Logic provides the rationale for the decision; emotion provides the desire to go with the decision; and ethics or authority provides the justification for making the decision. If people have a good reason to, want to, and are justified in doing so, they will make the decision you want them to make.

These are the persuasive elements; however, there are a few other factors you can use to enhance your persuasive powers even more:

- *Credibility.* This is a combination of belief and trust. If people believe you are an expert they will trust what you say. You have credibility with them. If, on the other hand, they don't believe you know what you are talking about, you have no credibility. According to psychologist Jerome Brunner, there are two ways in which we gain belief, and hence credibility, in the eyes of another: authority and sincerity.[1] Cite your authorities. Let people know you know what you are talking about. Use a sincere, concerned manner (not as though you were showing off), and you'll build credibility for yourself.
- *Identification.* To be persuaded, people must feel you know their situation first hand. They must be able to identify with you, and for that to happen, you must identify with them. Do your homework. Address their problems from their point of view. Let them know that you know where they are coming from, that you "done took into account what hills and valleys [we] come through befo' [we] got to wherever [we] is."[2]
- *Uniqueness.* Every commercial shown on television began with a conference of advertising writers to decide on the product's "unique selling proposition." They have considered what makes the product unique, different from everything else on the market. And the commercial reflects that difference. No one will be persuaded by "just another one of *xyz.*" To persuade people, you must show your position, approach, or solution as unique, too.
- *Data.* People believe in numbers. Gather numerical proof and they

will be swayed. Everyone knows that computers make mistakes, but look at the power of a computer printout. Do people doubt it? Use statistics, facts, data to enhance your credibility and make it almost impossible to disagree with you.

- *Specifics.* Don't deal in broad generalities like politicians do. Tie your position down with facts, examples, and solutions.
- *Consistency.* Don't be too flexible. If you bend with every opposing request you lose credibility. How can a good solution be so wishy-washy? Stick to your guns.
- *Scope.* One of the strongest ethical appeals you can make is to say that what you are asking is for the good of everyone, that it is bigger than both of us.

By using these elements of persuasion, you can gain power over other people's decisions. There are also a few other tactics for trying to persuade others. For example, people are best persuaded by approaches that fulfill their recognized needs or that grow out of attitudes they already possess. To persuade another person, find out what his or her needs and attitudes are, then couch your argument in those terms. You can find out about these attitudes and needs by talking to other people who know that person; by checking company performance records (as for the needs analysis covered in Chapter 5); by surveying needs or attitudes; or by simply talking to the person.

If you can avoid it, never ask for a 180-degree change. Almost no one will do a complete about-face. If someone believes your pen is blue, you will be very hard pressed to convince that person it is yellow. Instead, try for lesser degrees of change. For example, compromise your position to calling it a light blue or a greenish blue pen. Couch your arguments in what is familiar to people, and accentuate the familiar while minimizing the differences.

Lastly, if the request looks too big to tackle, the answer you'll get will be no. Don't ask for more than what those you want to persuade can or are willing to do. You can create the willingness, but don't ask for decisions they dare not make. Keep your requests within the range of what the other people's positions allow, what their character makeup will grant, and what the political pressures will permit.

As a final note on persuasion, here is a set of nine ground rules for making persuasive presentations to management:

1. *Talk from management's point of view.* Your boss doesn't want to approve things for your reasons. He or she will only okay them for his or her own reasons. This is human nature. Yet how often do we ask favors of others or request help or approval solely for our own reasons? Such requests carry no weight at all. When this type of request does work, it is

because the person feels obliged or sees a personal gain. You can use these tactics, but be careful; they smack of poor ethics and can undermine your argument. It is best to allow the other person to discover a personal gain rather than pointing it out. It is fair and right, however, for you to point out how your request will help the boss achieve corporate goals. Couch your arguments in terms of management's goals; as a cost reduction or containment; as reducing inefficiency; as part of a larger company thrust; as aiding the competitive position, and so forth.

2. *Base recommendations on demonstrated needs.* You must prove that there is a significant enough problem to demand attention. It can't be a general problem either; make it specific. I like the *EASE* formula:

> *E*—example: cite a specific incident.
> *A*—amplify: enlarge on how this affects others, how big or widespread the problem is, the number of cases involved, and so on.
> *S*—specify: tell what you think should be done; make your proposal; ask for money, more staff, new materials, new space, and the like.
> *E*—execute step one: plan an immediate first step that, once taken, locks everyone into your solution. Say, "If you approve, I'll go ahead and . . ." or "I have already completed the needs analysis and can create a new course for you within *xyz* weeks of your approval if I can start today," or another dynamic statement. It means that you've gotten the ball rolling and it is up to others to either let it go on (the easiest thing to do) or stop it (usually too much bother).

3. *Describe the anticipated results.* What will happen if management approves your new, much larger budget? What will they gain by giving you the go ahead? Tell them. Give solid estimates of exactly what benefits will accrue and how what you propose will solve their problem. Again, be precise and specific.

4. *Describe costs.* You must bring up costs and discuss them realistically. Costs are a constant concern of management because they minimize profits. Just as your function is to create change, their function is to manage costs to produce a profit. Sometimes trainers hide costs or sneak them timidly into their proposals. Don't do that. Put them in front and then justify them! Costs, regardless how great, are small if the benefits to be derived from them are greater. Besides, detailing your costs gains you credibility (you've obviously done your homework) and ensures that you are talking their language.

5. *Do your political homework.* A perfectly acceptable proposal can

be rejected purely for political reasons. It may not be pleasant, but a large part of management is politics. The higher you go, the more high-pressured the politics is. Do your homework; know who are your allies and who are your enemies. Talk to both sides before you make a proposal. Go to those who oppose you and ask what you can do to gain their approval. Even if their answer is an adamant "nothing," you've gained in trying. Be open to their suggestions. If your proposal is to be judged by several people, keep your allies close, avoid offending those who are opposed, and concentrate your efforts on the ones who are undecided. Strike deals for their cooperation. In Congress, this is called arm-twisting, and even the president does it. If your proposal matters to you, work at it. You ought to know the outcome of your request before you ask for it.

6. *Answer unasked questions.* An excellent way to head off opposition is to answer questions before they are asked. Knowing someone will ask you *xyz*, provide an answer ahead of time. They will see that you've thought your proposal through from their point of view (identification), and that you're fully prepared (credibility). It's hard to argue with someone who anticipates your objections and satisfactorily lays them to rest.

7. *Describe other instances of what you are asking.* Only 7½ percent of the population is truly innovative; the rest need to be reassured to a greater or lesser degree that something will work because it has in the past. Cite pilot studies (if need be, sell a pilot study as your first step), research findings, industry parallels, and, if you can, what the competition is doing. I just recently sold a seminar on the strength of having also given it to my new client's major competitor. The thinking was, "If it helped them, it should help us." Nobody wants to give the competition an edge, not even in training.

8. *Go with realities.* People will not give what they do not have. If you have been persuasive, but get management approval for only three-quarters of your proposal, accept that. If they agree, you've persuaded them; if they restrict you, they probably feel they must. If you think they are restricting you merely for knee-jerk reasons, try negotiating but be prepared to go with reality.

9. *Keep management informed.* Let management know how you will report the results of your project. You accomplish several things when you do. First of all, often just after people have approved something they suffer "buyer's remorse." They wonder if they made the right decision. Being told that you will keep them up to date on developments has the effect of a 90-day warranty. It makes them feel they are still in control; though they have made a decision, they aren't totally locked into it.

Second, it affirms and reassures that you expect solid results. It underlines the deferential relationship, saying you are acting on their behalf. It is a way of saying thank you without appearing desperate. In addition, knowledge is power, particularly at executive levels. By defining how you will keep them informed, you are letting them know that you are working to give them information (power) and are not building your own empire. Management seldom likes people who play their cards close to their chests. They want team players. Lastly, you cement the relationship and make your next proposal much more likely to be accepted.

Writing Skills

Many aspects of marketing the training function involve writing. In fact, effective writing is one of the most important skills a training manager can master. I know several executives who save samples of atrocious (and often very funny) writing that crosses their desks. If these samples were meant to be funny they would be a few bright spots in a long day. But frequently such poorly written documents are incomprehensible and fail to communicate the writer's message. There are no overt penalties for unfocused memos, unclear proposals, or badly written evaluations. I've never heard of someone being fired for writing a confusing memo. But there are direct rewards for sharpening your writing skills. Among them is that you become an important source of information (power) for your superior. Trust is a two-way street, and you enhance your position considerably just by writing effectively.

Management communications consultant Beverly Hyman points out that schools do not teach how to write to communicate.[3] We are taught to write correctly (spelling, grammar, penmanship); to produce a quantity of writing (a paragraph, a page, ten pages); to express random thoughts (what we did last summer, who we want to be) — but never to communicate with each other.

Clear writing is very much like good training, and many of the same rules apply. Like teaching, good writing is a direct result of the planning that you put into the job. You can no more write effective memos off the top of your head than you can train extemporaneously. If you don't address the reader's interests and needs, it is unlikely he or she will respond as you intend. Furthermore, you can't burden your reader with unduly long pieces. We've all received (but I hope have never written) long, rambling essays that must be read five or six times before we can glean the writer's intentions. Unclear and clumsy memos are almost epidemic in the corporate world. Proposals filled with trite or legalistic language proliferate. Don't let your training materials reinforce these practices.

The Four-Step Recipe for Good Writing

Good writing requires personal discipline to eliminate such problems. Beverly Hyman suggests a four-step "recipe" for keeping your writing on track.

Think Before You Write

Don't write off the top of your head; first decide what you want to say. Collect your thoughts. After all, as Dr. Hyman points out, every time you prepare a memo, a proposal, or a report, you are writing your résumé. While such documents usually don't go into your personnel file, they leave an impression of your capabilities with everyone who reads what you've written.

Consider Your Audience

First, ask yourself, "To *whom* am I writing?" Who do you want to reach? As in training, your potential audience controls to a large extent what you say and how you say it. Ask yourself what your reader knows about the subject. Obviously, there is no point in wasting time rehashing what people already know. A few words to set the context or refresh the memory are ample.

Second, ask yourself, "What does *XYZ* want to know about the subject?" When you write your memo, start with this premise. *XYZ* will read your memo, report, or proposal only if you include the information that's wanted. Hiding the information or saving it until the last ensures that your message will be discarded in disgust, frustration, boredom, or anger.

Finally, when you've established what *XYZ* knows about the subject and what he or she would like to know, you can concentrate on what he or she needs to know about it. That is the heart of communication; anything else is extraneous. If all this sounds familiar, that's because these are the same questions asked in Chapter 3 in connection with writing the lesson plan.

Determine Your Objective

Now ask yourself, "What action do I want my reader to take?" You've established what you need to say, but now you decide how you will say it. In effect, you are determining your objective. Never write a memo, report, proposal, lesson plan—in fact, any document—without an objective. If you can't think of an objective, don't write the document.

Have you ever received a memo and said, "What on earth am I

supposed to do with this thing?" Hyman's third step—setting a clear, personal objective—eliminates this problem.

Organize Your Information

You know what you don't have to say; you know what your readers want; you know what you have to tell them; and you know the results you want. Now you can structure your presentation. Once again, as in a good lesson plan, you must consider almost the same structures described in Chapter 3.

Remember the primacy–ultimacy principle. Put your most important message in the beginning, then repeat it in your summary. For your overall structure, try a problem–solution format or a cause-and-effect arrangement. A straight topical arrangement is workable, but requires some additional organization. Avoid a strict chronological presentation, because it provides too much detail and nearly always moves too slowly. Use this arrangement only to describe a sequence or process whereby something is done. (A cookbook recipe is an example of such use.)

Break up large blocks of writing with headings and subheadings. Headings keep the reader on track and also show your train of thought. They are signposts to your meaning. Further highlight key points with bullets, but don't overuse them lest they lose their impact.

Remember always that "less is more." Say what you want to say and then end it. In training, it is up to you to communicate with the learner. In writing, it is the writer's responsibility to communicate. If you follow Hyman's four steps, you will declare war on inconclusive and confusing writing.

"Wordsmithing"— The Power to Say What You Want to Say

The essence of effective marketing is positioning—that is, defining and describing what you are selling in a way that appeals to those you are trying to reach. This principle is also at the heart of persuasive writing.

The words that you choose limit and control the responses others make. How you talk about something defines how we should behave towards it.

General semanticists use an interesting metaphor to describe this phenomenon. They say that the words people use are a map of what they mean.[4] I like this metaphor because it shows how language functions. We all know that a map is only a representation of the actual territory. We don't drive on a road map, we drive on the road. But the map tells us which road to take and where it leads. The map, therefore, directs and controls what road we travel on.

There can be many different maps of the same area. How you travel depends to a very large extent on which map you are using. For example, the area where you live has been described in street directories and on road maps, topographical maps, political subdivision maps, and survey maps. There probably also are demographic maps, aerial maps, navigational charts (if you live near water), geologic contour maps, and, if you live in a city or the suburbs, sewer maps. Furthermore, there are state maps, regional maps, country maps, continental maps, and globes of the world, all of which cover the area where your home is.

Each of these maps allows us to behave in certain ways. In my seminars I explain how a sewer map shows a different way of getting from point A to point B than would a street map. In fact, the map can control the route one travels. When you write a memo, proposal, report, or any other document, regard it as a map and realize that those reading it will use the map to make decisions. Construct your map so that your readers end up where you want them, not lost, confused, or bored.

Another general semantics tool is the "ladder of abstraction." If you look at an object — say, a ballpoint pen on your desk — you can describe it in a number of ways. Same pen, different words. If you arrange those words or phrases in a hierarchy — a ladder — starting with the most specific at the bottom and moving upward toward the abstract, you would climb the ladder of abstraction. For example, with the ballpoint pen, you might have:

    Gross national product
    American affluence
    Planned obsolescence
    Total net worth
    Cheaply manufactured artifact
    Carelessly owned artifact
    My property
    Messy house
    Clutter in room
    Clutter on desk
    Writing instrument
    Pen
    Cheap ballpoint
    XYZ Co. medium-carbide clear-plastic ballpoint pen
    XYZ Co. medium-carbide clear-plastic ballpoint pen with black ink

If this were a listing for a chemical or design engineer, it could be even more specific with formulas for polymers. If it were a listing for a commission on international trade, the abstractions could extend to the world economic environment. But each of the expressions refers to the pen. If you sent a memo about clutter on my desk, I might leave the pen there and move something else. If you addressed me about paying more attention to my artifacts, it is unlikely I would think of the pen. If you want me to understand that I shouldn't leave cheap ballpoint pens lying on my desk because it creates a bad image*, say so! Be specific. Come down the ladder of abstraction whenever there is any chance people will not understand what you've said. In my experience, 80 to 90 percent of the disagreements I've had with others cleared up when we exchanged abstractions for specifics. This is what "less is more" means. Keep it simple.

Writing Training Documents

As mentioned earlier, good writing skills are essential for marketing the training function. There are many documents a training manager must write. For example, reports to keep management informed are a vital part of persuasion. Training manuals and handouts are also critical to training and should be written well. Memos should always be very simple, very direct. Articles for in-house publications are challenging but one of your best marketing channels available. Beverly Hyman's four steps and the other semantic tools apply to these, too. Finally, personnel records and documents are far more useful when written clearly.

Foremost among a training manager's writing assignments, however, are training proposals. A proposal is written to gain permission, get a budget approved, or build support for something you'd like to do. The proposal combines elements of marketing, persuasion, and writing. There are four parts to any proposal: (1) the introduction, (2) the rationale, (3) the description, (4) the conclusion.

The Introduction

Remember that your audience governs much of what you write. Your objective is to get a go-ahead, so your proposal must start with the answer to the question, "Why should I approve?" Begin by telling your reader what will be discussed. Your first statement is the name of the program,

---

* "Bad image" is fairly high up the ladder, too. It would be better to say "because those passing by might jump to the conclusion that you were messy, careless, and cheap."

whom it will involve (number and level of participants to be trained), and the length and frequency of the training. These should be simple statements; you don't need to elaborate yet.

The Rationale

Here you get to the heart of the proposal, the reasons why the plan should be adopted. Describe the problem from management's point of view. To do this you will have already found out what they know, what they want to know, and, therefore, what they need to know. Management must recognize that you see the problem clearly, and your rationale should let them see the problem as well.

Demonstrate the need for your plan by showing how badly the company needs the solution you propose. If you need support data, however, don't put it here. Include it as an appendix. If the plan is corrective action to solve an existing problem, state the problem, detail the costs that problem incurs (in dollars, if possible), and project the savings (again, in dollars) your solution will bring about. If the plan is preventive action or is aligned with an ongoing management thrust or master plan (always a good idea, if you can), then state the problem you foresee, project how that problem will interfere with the proposed operation or project, and describe how your plan will eliminate that problem.

End your rationale with a list of the management goals your proposal will satisfy. Management's goals are always cost reductions, more efficient operations, and higher profits. There also may be personal goals among managers, such as pet projects, promotions, or increased political power. Don't address these last two directly as such, but imply them through the other, more legitimate concerns.

The rationale is the heart of your proposal, yet it should not take more than five minutes to read. If this section doesn't grab attention in five minutes, the proposal probably never will, either. Keep it short and simple.

The Description

Once you have your readers interested, you will want to tell exactly what you are proposing and what it will cost. Start with a list of your training objectives (see Chapter 7) and follow with a fairly detailed agenda of what will be taught. This material doesn't have to include timings but must be given in sequence. (See Chapter 8.) At the end of the agenda describe how you will evaluate trainee performance, from both short and long range perspectives (see Chapter 6). Let management know

---

Training Proposal Format

1. State what is to be taught, who is to be trained, and the length and times for training.
2. Create a rationale for training from management's point of view.
3. List management goals that will be met.
4. Describe training objectives that will be met.
5. Present a sequential outline of the training subject matter.
6. Explain how trainees will be evaluated, on both short- and long-term basis; tell how you will keep management informed of evaluations.
7. State the costs of the program and justify each aspect.
8. Restate the main points of your proposal and ask for approval.

---

how you will report that information back to them. Finally, detail your costs. Spell out the cost of each item and justify it.

The Conclusion

Close the proposal by stating, in one or two sentences, what you plan to do. Ask for immediate approval by restating your objective (to get approval) and giving your best argument.

If your proposal is not for a specific course but, rather, for a training thrust into a new area that will eventually evolve into several courses, describe your plan of action instead of providing an agenda for what will be taught. If the proposal is a repeat budget request with no new course or plan of action, state last year's performance, describe your planned activities for this year, and then justify both (see Chapter 12 for budgeting procedures). If the proposal is a request for money to acquire new audiovisual equipment, describe how you will use the new equipment, what advantages you will gain, and how, with those advantages, you will address management's problems with even better results.

Summary

The training function needs good public relations because it is usually on the wrong side of the corporate ledger. This chapter considered the role of training manager as a person marketing the advantages of training to the company. Too often training is considered only in terms of its cost. It was shown how training managers need to adopt a pro-active stance, and let the corporate world know what training can achieve. To do this, we examined how to put together a marketing plan and what channels are available for spreading the word.

Because much of the marketing is selling, we examined the art of persuasion, including the three types of persuasive appeal and some factors and tactics for persuading management. Since marketing also involves good writing, we looked at how to improve writing skills. We concluded with a discussion of a format for writing proposals.

CHAPTER 14

Negotiations and Training

GERARD I. NIERENBERG, often called the father of modern negotiation, defines it as "any interaction to change a relationship." [1] As a trainer, you are in the business of change. You bring about changes in behavior through your classes. While marketing your services, you are engaged in changing other people's perceptions of your function. You sometimes need to convince your boss to accept your budget, plan, or proposal, and that involves a change, too. Most often, it is relationships that are changed. For example, training managers need to develop their staff, and they change their relationships with subordinates as they do so. Of course, as you buy services or equipment you change your relationship from being a sales rep's prospect to that of a vendor's client. Everyone is constantly engaged in changing situations, and many of these changes require negotiation. Let's look at a few pointers and procedures for negotiating.

Three Variables of Negotiation

No matter what is negotiated, there are always three variables that influence that negotiation: time, information, and power. If you put these three variables to work for you, you'll be in a strong position.

Time

Ecclesiastes says, "To every thing there is a season." Timing your negotiation efforts properly is paramount. The best time to ask for a budget increase is during an excellent year when senior management has just expressed concern about employee training, not during a loss period when employees are being laid off. Notice that labor contracts nearly always expire just at the most difficult time. Vendors have sales with limited-time offers or upcoming price increases, which if you order immediately you can just avoid. The time you choose (or are compelled) to negotiate greatly influences the dynamics of the negotiation.

A second aspect is that negotiation is not a single event. It is a process that takes place over time and is never really completed. In my negotiation seminars people sometimes respond to this with, "But once you sign the contract it's over. You've agreed." True, you've agreed, but it's not over. The negotiation has just begun. Now comes the stage of negotiation in which both parties comply (or fail to comply) with the provisions of the contract. A mortgage, a purchase order, a disciplinary hearing, a court case, an employee assessment session, parent and child agreements, marriages — every one is an example of a negotiation that doesn't stop when agreement is reached. For example, a difficult participant may agree to attend a seminar session but may remain a problem participant for the whole time. Failure to live up to an agreement causes a renegotiation of the relationship, thus no negotiation is ever complete.

If these two points are combined you can see that it is much easier to wait for the right time to concede a point or make an offer when you realize that the whole process is an ongoing negotiation rather than a final event.

The third point about time is the most common one: The person who feels under the gun is more likely to concede or deal than the person with no time pressure. It is the nature of our culture to feel the pressure of deadlines. Most of our laws are passed just before Congress recesses. What student ever turns in a term paper early? Why do we rush to catch a plane? People get more things done when they have deadlines; they need a defined time frame to make their task an event. Negotiation is not an event, so we set time limits to make it one. The time limits are, however, arbitrary, and recognizing this fact will allow you to gain an advantage. Set the deadlines for yourself and for those with whom you negotiate, and at the same time, keep free of other people's deadlines.

As a rule, never let the other side know your real time pressures. Instead, set deadlines that pressure them. In addition, defer the toughest issues to last because, by then, time is pressuring both of you and there is stronger motivation to compromise.

Information

Professional negotiators agree that the single most important step in successful negotiations is to prepare thoroughly. The more you know about those with whom you will negotiate, the better. This includes both technical background (past history, prior negotiating behavior, goals, social or economic status, and so on) and personal attributes (office politics, emotional needs, personal foibles, and the like). The more you know, the stronger your position becomes because you can address what they know, what they want to know, and what they need to know. If that sounds familiar, it should. Both needs analysis and the Socratic Method provide this kind of information. And, indeed, training is a form of negotiation, a contract to learn.

Probably the single most important thing you need to know is how badly the other party wants what you have. Do you go into a negotiation knowing your own needs and pressures? Are these foremost in your mind? Naturally, you are worried about getting what you want from the negotiation, but thinking this way puts pressure on you. To ease that load and give yourself leverage, ask yourself, "How badly does he or she want what I have?" Instantly, your position is stronger. If the answer is that the other party doesn't want what you have at all, then perhaps this is not the time for a negotiation. Or find a way to create a desire for what you are offering. This is why you must provide a management rationale for every proposal you make. It gives management something to buy into — a reason to create (or change) a relationship with you — to give you approval or support.

Power

A negotiation can also be defined as a power struggle, certainly in cases in which either or both parties perceive it as a win–lose situation. A negotiation is not a win–lose situation, however, if for no other reason than because there is no reason to comply with the contract if either party fails to gain enough of what they want. Because a negotiation is never really ended, you must always be sure that the other side has enough of what it wants to continue to supply you with what you want. Both parties must *win,* or both will lose together.

Unfortunately, managers who have not learned to examine the needs and wants of the other side play to win because they are afraid to lose, and they see only those two mutually exclusive outcomes. They create a power struggle by viewing a win only in terms of making someone else lose. Your job as a trainer, then, is to see that management benefits from the training you provide, that supervisors and others for whom you train have enough input to your training to make them feel it is beneficial to them to support you, that trainees see the value in learning from you, and that vendors and consultants recognize your training expertise and strive to truly satisfy your needs rather than just sell their products and services to you.

Negotiating power, therefore, is not a flexing of muscle. Far from it. It is exerting subtle control over the negotiating climate. As with training (in which, for example, you are negotiating a learning contract with your trainees), the environment in which you negotiate is a major key to success. You can create a win–win climate by being open and frank about what you want. Be honest and ethical. Do not accept what is unacceptable to you but explain why the unacceptable is so. Make your offer in good faith. Appeal to the other side's sense of fairness (more on this later), and remain calm and unruffled. Remember, you only lose when you allow the other side to win without winning anything for yourself. When you get much of what you want and the other side gets much of what it wants, you've both won.

There are several other quite subtle ways of assuming power in the negotiations, which you can then use to reach a mutually satisfactory conclusion.

- *Precedent.* It is nearly impossible to strike out on a new path when precedent stands in your way. "Things are done the way they are done because that's the way they are done." If you align your negotiating appeal with the way things have always been done, or company policy, or an ongoing company-wide thrust or program according to procedures and guidelines, you'll gain tremendous authority.
- *Legitimacy.* A negotiating appeal based on a demonstrated need will always appear as a legitimate position. In any negotiation, you need to have credibility, a contributor to such legitimacy. Establish your expertise if you feel those with whom you are talking are unfamiliar with it (see Chapter 4). In addition, anything in print gains legitimacy; a written proposal is considered legitimate merely by being printed. Use forms, contracts, documents, and computer printouts to enhance your power by holding a legitimate position.

- *Risk.* Everyone who has ever played poker with a skilled bluffer knows the power that can come from taking risks. Every time a union calls a strike, it is taking a risk to make a bid for power. If management can't run an equal or greater risk, the union will win. If management can risk having the strike run indefinitely, however, the union will lose. Unfortunately, a strike is a win-lose situation. Once the union goes on strike, everyone loses and the situation for both sides becomes one of minimizing losses. As in the stock market and in the gambling casinos, however, the high rollers — those who risk the most — command the greatest respect, have the potential for earning the highest rewards, and gain the greatest power.

- *Persistence.* There is power to be gained merely by continuing to ask for what you want. I can recall very successful negotiations that came about after years and many tries. By realizing the nature of the negotiating process and treating it as a part of a long-range process, you gain leverage from persistence. If you've ever been called on repeatedly by the same sales rep, you know it gets harder to keep saying no.

- *Patience.* Closely related to persistence is patience. In fact, patience on your part may be the best antidote for persistence on the part of the other party. If you can wait patiently for the right time to ask (proper timing, remember), you can get most things you want.

- *Decisiveness.* In contrast to patience, when opportunity presents itself — when the time is right — you must seize it. Merely being patient allows the world to pass you by. Be patient with a purpose, but move when it is right to do so. Decisiveness at the right time gives you power and commands respect. This is particularly true when dealing with trainees. As shown in Chapters 2 and 4, decisive leadership in the training room is vital.

- *Morality.* To reject an ethical appeal is to risk being thought of as unethical, and few of us would do that. By announcing that you are seeking "fairness" or a "mutually equitable" or an "ethical" solution, you force the other side either to agree to do so also or to deny that it is fair, equitable, or ethical. Use phrases like "doesn't that seem fair?" to call your offer equitable.

- *Space.* As was shown in the material on training techniques (see Chapter 4), where you place yourself in the room and how you use the space around you reflect power. Sitting behind a desk lends a feeling of authority; sitting away from it, or to one side, creates a friendlier, equal-to-equal image. When each side of a negotiating team sits facing each other on opposite sides of a long table, there's an atmosphere of confrontation rather than cooperation. You gain power by meeting with people in your office or sitting at the head of a table, but you soften your authority by meeting with them in their office or sitting alongside the table. You also can exercise authority by taking over someone else's office or using all the space in their room. This is why negotiating sessions are often scheduled in neutral territory at round tables.

These three variables — time, information, and power — are at play in every negotiation. Recognize them as your first step, then use them to your advantage for more successful negotiations.

Negotiation Skills

There are three skills for effecting negotiations. They are the ability to (1) understand the other person, (2) plan your strategy, and (3) apply appropriate tactics. The consummate negotiator is expert at all three. Most of us are better at one than the others, consequently we do one part of our negotiating very well and hope we'll get by for the other phases. This may have been enough in the past, but your negotiations will improve greatly if you develop your skills in each of these areas.

Understanding the Other Person

This is such a vital skill that, in my two-day seminar on negotiating, I devote an entire day to discussing how to read and influence the behavior of others. Unfortunately, this is not a book about negotiation, and we cannot take the space here to delve into this all-important aspect. Throughout this book, however, are suggestions that you will find useful. For example, the ten principles of Adult Learning apply to negotiation because, after all, you are teaching the other person your position and learning his or hers. Check yourself on Chapters 2 and 4. These address aspects of human behavior. In particular the material on active listening, question-asking, and uniqueness will help you. You can also benefit from the discussion of nonverbal communication, especially semantics, in shaping the perceptions of those with whom you deal.

In the context of negotiations, the purpose of understanding others is to motivate them to work toward a mutually satisfactory goal. To be successful at this, you should acquire a background in motivation theory. Start with my cassette workbook series, which covers the topic in detail.[2] Good follow-ups to this are books by Abraham H. Maslow, in particular his *Motivation and Personality* (Harper & Row, 1970). Check also *Games People Play* by Eric Berne (Ballantine, 1978); *I'm O.K., You're O.K.* by Thomas A. Harris (Avon, 1982); *Transactional Analysis at Work: A Guide for Business and Professional People* by Maurice Villeré (Prentice-Hall, 1981); *TA and the Manager* by Dudley Bennett (AMACOM, 1976); *The Presentation of Self in Everyday Life* by Erving Goffman (Doubleday, 1959); *Work and the Nature of Man* by Frederick Herzberg (Crowell, 1966); and *Leadership and Decision-Making* by Victor H. Vroom and Philip W. Yetton (University of Pittsburgh Press, 1976). You will find these books fascinating reading, and you will come away with a much deeper understanding of why people do the things they do and how to change their behavior.

Planning Your Strategy

In any negotiation, your strategic plan is the basic approach you intend to take. In effect, you draw up the plan simply by doing your homework and preparing to negotiate. Of course, your plan is a *preliminary* one. I have seen many professionals give up strong negotiating positions because they locked themselves into plans that became out of step with the negotiation. A strategic plan is only good so long as it reflects the reality of your negotiation. As soon as the circumstances change, you must re-evaluate and revise your strategy.

Here are seven questions to consider when preparing your strategic plan. Once you have the answers, you can use them to create your plan.

What Are the Power Bases?

Ask yourself how badly you want what they have. Then ask how badly they want what you have. If you don't know the answers, find out. In addition, ascertain what the time pressures are and what sources of power (if any) they are most likely to use. What sources of power are likely to work for you?

What Are the Causes of the Problem Being Negotiated?

Often, removing a cause of a problem eliminates the need to negotiate. Track the situation back to its roots so you'll understand it thoroughly. Get a grasp on its cause and you may turn up more creative alternatives, especially if both parties can't agree on some issues.

Are there any other solutions available besides negotiation? This question is also important. Investigate whether there is a better way to safeguard against spending time and energy negotiating something better solved another way. For instance, if you have an employee with a drinking problem, negotiation will not solve it. An alcoholic will agree to anything but cannot be held to it; he or she cannot control the addiction on the

---

Seven Questions for Planning Your Strategy

1. What are the power bases? How badly do they want what I have?
2. What causes the need to negotiate? Are there other solutions?
3. What personal and corporate needs are involved?
4. What are the other party's dominant behavior characteristics?
5. What is your minimum–maximum range?
6. What strategies are available to address the problems?
7. What tools will you need?

---

strength of a negotiation. Answering this question also gives a different slant on the pressures at work. If alternatives to negotiation are unacceptable, then both parties will feel pressured to negotiate. The more unacceptable, the greater the pressure. For example, ask yourself what the alternatives are to negotiating an arms control agreement with the Soviets. Your answer should explain at least one reason why the United States continues, despite sometimes unsatisfactory results.

What Personal and Psychological Needs Are Involved?

Here's where your study of motivation theory pays off. Regardless of what business matter you are negotiating, people are deeply affected by their personal needs. Major corporate decisions are often based on whims and pet projects or are made out of spite and for childish reasons. People are psychological beings, and we function within our mental and emotional networks. Understanding the other party's needs as well as your own is essential for an effective conclusion. Of course, you must also know what his or her corporate needs are and address them in the negotiation. But answering this question about less obvious factors is a tremendous help in reaching a win–win negotiation. If you don't know the other party's needs, you can't work to help achieve them.

What Are the Other Party's Dominant Characteristics?

How does he or she behave? Ask around if you don't know. Find out if the other person is a hard-driving, success-oriented overachiever or more analytical in style, weighing alternatives and delaying decisions until all the facts are in. Your approach with these two types is completely different. The hard-drivers seldom care about all the facts; they want results — action now. They are always pressured by time. The analytical types use time to their advantage; they don't want to make snap decisions and balk when pressured.

There are several personality inventory systems, and all are about equally effective. Choose one and figure out how you should respond to each personality type. I recommend David Keirsey and Marilyn Bates' book *Please Understand Me: Character and Temperament Types* (Prometheus, 1978).

Transactional Analysis is another tool for categorizing behavior, especially useful because it provides directions for handling each personality type.[3] Analysis of the other parties involved in a negotiation pays off handsomely in the end.

What Is Your Minimum–Maximum Range?

Have you known people who gambled away more money than they could afford to lose? Or who got carried away at auctions and bought things they couldn't afford? These are fairly common occurrences, but they shouldn't happen to you. Prevent this by setting maximums for yourself and don't exceed them. For negotiations I recommend three lists: (1) the things you have to have, (2) the things you'd like to have but could live without, and (3) the things you can afford to give away. These are your minimum–maximum limits.

Here's how the lists work. You will have already determined your objectives and decided what you must have and what you cannot compromise. You will have listed some key items for which you will fight but could compromise if pressed hard. And you will have a list of negotiables —things that, if others fight for them, you can give up without losing. Develop these three categories with thought and you'll have more successful negotiations.

What Strategies Are Available to You?

Using your three minimum–maximum lists, decide what concessions you can make and draw up a tentative sequence in which to make them. Decide what you will do and how you will respond when the other party asks for concessions you cannot give. At this point, think through your alternatives and decide on several possible approaches. Use "what would probably happen if . . ." questions.

At this stage also weigh your credibility. If you think the other party may try to take advantage of you (either because he or she feels you don't know enough to spot it or you don't know enough about the business), you need to plan how you will gain credibility. There was a southern senator who used to say, "As far as I am concerned, the negotiation is over when the small talk ends." He used the introductory small talk to measure his opponent. Make your first moments count by establishing your credibility early on.

Your final step in answering this question is to consider what forms of resistance you are likely to meet when asking for each of the things you want. Consider also how you'll respond to the resistance; this is a form of cost-benefit analysis, and the format answers the following questions:

1. What are your requests?
2. What are the likely responses to each?
3. What will each of these responses cost you (in concessions, climate, relationship, and so on)?
4. Is it worth it to you?
5. If not, what less costly alternatives are there?

Again, remember at this point that you are only examining alternatives.

What Tools Will You Need to Implement Your Strategies?

There are three "tools": language, skills, and tactics. To begin, what language — what words and maps — will you need to shape your point of view? Are there any language or word barriers that you will need to work around or that will cause you to re-define your terms? What you must do is decide how to present your arguments in terms that will be understood by all involved.

With regard to skills, we've already mentioned the power of asking good questions and the corollary skill of active listening. One week before the negotiation, practice your question and listening skills, and brush up on reading nonverbal behavior. When the meetings begin your skills will be tuned to performance pitch.

Applying Appropriate Tactics

Consider which tactics you need for your negotiation to best influence the individuals involved. The pages that follow describe some standard tactics. Some you will have already used often or you will recognize as having been used on you. See how they work for you and choose those that get you the best results. Every time you negotiate with a new person, come back to this list and consider which tactics might work this time.

For more information on negotiating tactics in general, read Gerard Nierenberg's *The Complete Negotiator* (Nierenberg-Zeiff, 1986) or his earlier book, *The Art of Negotiating* (Cornerstone, 1981). Both are excellent, with the best coverage of the subject. For more of a "how-to" approach, consider Steven Samuels's cassette/workbook program *How to Negotiate,* available from AMACOM.

Salami Slices

Large issues sometimes are so monolithic they seem impossible to resolve. Slice large topics into pieces (like a salami), and they become manageable.

Trial Balloons

Couch your suggestions or offers in terms of "What if. . . ." This allows both sides to consider an idea without really deciding on it. It's an exploratory statement rather than a crystallizing one. And, as you explore, you can learn a great deal about the other person.

Deferred Issues

To engage in an up-front struggle on the biggest issue usually means you'll never get past that issue. Let both sides start on what is easily agreed upon. Then, as the list grows longer, it gains momentum and begins to pressure both parties to compromise (if need be) on the big issue. Furthermore, the longer the negotiation process takes, the more those huge issues start to shrink. With success, everyone gains confidence that they can be solved too.

First Concession

Many negotiators won't agree with me, but you gain several important advantages when you concede first. For instance, you establish yourself as a "good guy"—someone who is ready to deal to work out a solution. It gives you a moral edge. Also, fair is fair. You've given one, now the other side owes you a concession. You have a right to it. Lastly, you establish the turf. By making the first offer, you set the direction for the entire negotiation.

Straw Issues

This is a sneaky ploy, in which you make a large issue of an unimportant point. You make it seem important by fighting hard for it, only to give in at last and then demand a large concession in return.

Feinting

This is a variation on straw issues, whereby you make an issue of one aspect to hide a weaker point, in the hope of slipping that weaker point by unnoticed while everyone is upset about the false issue.

Fall-back

Plan your retreat. If you anticipate having to concede, don't do it easily. Make them work for it. Don't give in without demanding concessions in return. They will value something they had to work for far more than an easy victory. By the way, when you concede, pay them a compliment. Give credit for good negotiating; it may lull them into early satisfaction.

Trade-off

This is an offer to trade one-for-one so as to avoid or break a deadlock.

Deadlock

This is usually regarded as a negative result but can be an excellent tactic to use when you need more time or if you suspect the other side is pushing too hard because of time pressures.

Bland Withdrawal

I have seen this tactic used most effectively by simply agreeing with the other side and moving on. If the other party is anticipating tough opposition or a denial from you, by simply giving in, you completely throw them off base.

Reversal or Turnabout

This one is a very tough defensive ploy. I advise using it *only* when you perceive the other side has or is taking advantage of you. Simply say "I've changed my mind. I don't agree to anything we've agreed on so far. Let's start over from the beginning." The usual response is to cater to you and make an important concession to avoid risking the entire agreement so far. But to use it for any reason other than a defensive one is unethical and predisposes a win–lose situation.

Temper Tantrum

In my experience lawyers are fond of throwing temper tantrums to intimidate others. Many managers keep employees in line this way, too. I deplore it as a management tool because it intimidates some and antagonizes others. The best response to anger is to remain calm and logical, and to thank the person for being honest with you. Or calmly remark that the person seems very upset, that you don't understand what's so upsetting, and ask for an explanation of the outburst. This forces them to discuss the issues rationally, in a win–win manner.

Walkout

A walkout is when you draw a line — you say you can go no further — and then walk away. It doesn't have to be done in anger, though it often is. A walkout is a way of implying you can't concede more, that you're not getting what you want, and that you're leaving. If the other side has invested time and effort, it will concede rather than give up all that's been invested. On the other hand, if the other side can't give anything more, then your walkout is appropriate because there is nothing more to negotiate. If someone walks out on you, it implies that the next move is yours, but you don't have to do anything about it. If they still want to negotiate, sooner or later they will come back. When they do, you have an advantage — they are coming to you. If they don't come back, of course, that is the end of that round of negotiation.

Fait Accompli

This is a frequently used and powerful tactic. In fact, much of our legal system is built on it. The term is French and means "the thing is done." In a negotiating sense, it is when one side takes some unilateral action and then presents the other with a finished event, take it or leave it. A subpoena is a *fait accompli;* so is a traffic ticket, a court order, a police raid, and many other such events. This is also what hijackers and terrorists do, what suicides do, what nations often do when they invade another country. You do it first and ask questions later, but there really is no answer. You must respond in some manner, either weak or strong. Because the tactic is so manipulative, use it with great care, if at all. If it is used on you, respond as calmly and rationally as possible.

Some Negotiating Situations

Now let's look at several direct applications of these negotiating principles to situations involving training managers.

How to Negotiate with the Boss

Working out an agreement with your boss brings us back to the three variables: time, information, and power. Usually the boss controls time by preempting it or by terminating interviews. You can gain control of the

Negotiations with the Boss

(Be a team player with company's best interests at heart.)

Time	Controlled by the boss. Minimize your use of time. Use time the way the boss does—slow, fast, and so on. Wait out the decision; bide your time.
Information	Your strength; do your homework. Phrase your appeal in terms of company goals or benefits.
Power	In the boss's hands. Use precedent and support from others. Align your proposal with the boss's pet project. Back up your appeal with facts; demonstrate the need for what you suggest. Use *fait accompli*—if it is not too risky.

Answers for the Seven Questions

1. Clearly define your strengths and weaknesses. Find something the boss wants badly and offer it in *exchange*.
2. Clearly define the real problems. Show how your solution is better than any others.
3. Analyze your boss's personal, political, and organizational needs.
4. Determine the boss's personality type (using TA, Maslow, or some other system) and work out your best way of dealing with it.
5. Make a list of your minimum needs and your maximum desires.
6. Show the boss how he and the company will gain from your proposal.
7. Be prepared to justify the maps you have chosen.

situation by using your time well. Be prepared, and express your arguments in crisp, concise language. Use time as the boss does. If he or she is a driver, be brief, factual, and action-oriented; if the boss has a slower style, cover *all* the issues and help guide his or her thinking.

In this negotiating arrangement information is your strong suit. If the boss has more or better information, you are not likely to win. Your information should point out company or personal benefits for him or her. Make them tangible benefits, on the lowest rungs of the ladder of abstraction (see Chapter 13).

Overt power is largely in the boss's hands, so you'll need to be as subtle as possible. Align yourself with precedent (if possible) or with larger ongoing campaigns. Write a persuasive proposal. Gather political support. If you have a boss who respects a "can do" attitude, try a *fait accompli* for part of your proposal. Use statistics and computer printouts, but don't take the time to go over them in detail; just submit them as backup evidence and summarize them if need be.

The Seven Questions

Present your appeal in terms of what your proposal can do for the company. Avoid appeals to what you want, but emphasize those that produce results for the company. Work on this win–win approach. In short, follow the guidelines for marketing to management in Chapter 13. Become thoroughly familiar with the problem and *all* other possible solutions. Have indisputable reasons why the other solutions are less effective than yours.

Define for yourself what your strengths and weaknesses are. What are your psychological needs? What "face" do you have to save? Ask yourself how badly the boss wants what you are offering, then find something he or she wants and offer it. Analyze your boss's personal and political needs, too, and structure your negotiation to appeal to them. Define, on paper, what kind of person your boss is. Decide on a distinct personality type, then structure your approach to complement those characteristics.

Create a minimum–maximum range for your appeals. Assuming you want to keep your job, it's hard to maintain a "must have" position, but go for it because that's what you want. Look persuasive; you should be committed to your idea. Include your "must haves" in your "would like to haves" and then work to get them all.

In planning your strategies, remember that you are both on the same side. You'll gain credibility by:

1. Understanding the boss's point of view.
2. Having a successful track record or showing how what you want has been successful elsewhere.
3. Aligning your proposal to his or her current interests.
4. Demonstrating real benefits to the company rather than personal benefits.

One of the problems in presenting proposals to management is that it is often an either–or situation. They either approve or disapprove. Period. If yours is such a situation, then you will need to build concessions into your proposal. Create two or three alternate plans, with separate budgets and separate results. Have one plan at a "must-have" level; it would be least costly but would also produce minimal results. Have another at a "like-to-have" level, which would produce much better results for a marginally increased budget. Finally, have yet another at an "even-more-like-to-have-but-can-live-without" level, for an ideal budget producing still more benefits. Present all three and let management choose. The key is to scale the benefits and make them real. If the first plan, which addresses the problem but doesn't solve it (merely holds the line), is accepted, at least you'll be able to maintain *status quo*. The second plan can then solve the problem but will cost more, and the third can solve it and provide additional benefits. By tying your costs into the boss's goals, you'll gain greater leverage.

Of course, you must anticipate any resistance. For best results, answer questions before they are raised. Do your political homework and speak with those who may oppose you. Give them what they want, if you can; deal before you present your package.

Choose your arguments carefully and be prepared to justify them. Practice your negotiating skills, and plan which tactics will be most effective. Obviously, high-handed methods are out of place here because they encourage win–lose situations. Since you're dealing from a subordinate position, you lack the leverage to keep them win–win situations.

Over the years I have successfully used the following tactics in negotiating with superiors:

> Trial balloons
> First concession
> Straw issues
> Feinting
> Fall-back
> Deadlock (to wait for time and events to prove me right)
> Bland withdrawal
> *Fait accompli*

I've also made the first concession in negotiations with management to gain higher pay, acceptance of programs, promotions, and budgets, including an expanded staff. Whatever tactics or approaches you use with management, make sure you are a team player, with the company's best interests at heart. You will come out ahead.

How to Negotiate with Subordinates

Again, let's begin a review of this negotiating situation by examining the variables of time, information, and power. In this instance time is officially in your hands, but be careful. There are subordinates who will waste a good deal of your time by begging to have their hands held.

Negotiating with Subordinates

(Create a win–win situation.)

Time	You control it.
	Beware of stalling and hand-holding ploys.
Information	Be fully informed.
	Know the people involved and the circumstances of the negotiation.
Power	Be subtle, not overt.

Answers to the Seven Questions

1. What power do your subordinates have? What are the real limits of your power? What things can you offer easily that they want?
2. Why are they negotiating? Is this a serious problem or is it routine? Are there any other solutions?
3. Define their corporate and personal needs, and your own.
4. What is their dominant personality type?
5. Define your minimum–maximum range of what you can give them.
6. Anticipate resistance and plan a response to it. Keep negotiations on a friendly, relaxed basis.
7. Use verbal maps.

Remember that negotiation is a process, not an event. You need to give them enough time to ensure that their performance doesn't waste your time. Review Chapter 12 for ways to do this.

Be informed. The more you know about the subordinate and his or her job performance, as well as what he or she wants to negotiate with you, the greater your leverage in getting what you want and, if need be, in arguing against giving too much.

Use the subtle forms of power. Choose the location to suit the individual and your intent, and prepare documents, if need be, to legitimatize your position. Show your knowledge of the facts — be a source of information. Show parental concern for the individual's well-being, and approach the subject from his or her point of view.

The Seven Questions

When dealing with subordinates, ask yourself what their power bases are. How badly do they want what you have and vice versa? What are the *real* limits of your power? Begin by giving them something they want. It doesn't have to be something they are asking for at this time, but it must be something they want and appreciate.

Ascertain why they are coming to you to negotiate. Are there other, better options? Is this a problem or is it merely routine? If it is a problem, what are the causes (not the symptoms)? Can negotiation solve the problem? If not, what else is needed?

Define what their personal needs are. Do the same for yourself. This will give you the opportunity to be personal, to discuss the situation informally. It also will prepare you to save face, both theirs and yours, if need be. Also, what are their dominant characteristics? This step, coupled with the last one, will tell you what your subordinate's "hot button" is (an expression used by salespeople for the thing that gets a prospect excited and ready to buy).

Define your minimum–maximum range. Unless you are an autocrat, be prepared to give something. Know what you must have from your subordinates, what you'd like to have, and what you are willing to give in on. Never give more than you can afford, and gain something from every concession you make. To anticipate what they will ask, examine what you know about them and decide how much more you need to learn. Then ask yourself how you can use that information to gain personal credibility and support. Anticipate what they will resist and prepare to deal with that resistance. Work up a scenario for each anticipated resistance, detailing your tactics for handling it.

Finally, decide on the approach you will use and which negotiating skills, if any, you will need to practice ahead of time. In considering tactics, here are a few more to consider:

1. Look at the record. Examine both your past performance and that of the subordinate. A sense of what has happened in the past will put the present negotiation into perspective.
2. Needs search. Both parties should specify their needs at the outset. Agreement is nearly always possible on several items and the tougher issues become more defined.
3. Ultimatum. Never make an ultimatum right at the start. It is meaningless then and can lock you into a position that you later might want to shift. When you make one, do it gently and with empathy. Allow the other side to save face and withdraw with dignity.

In summary, the recommended tactics for negotiating with subordinates are:

salami
trial balloons

first concessions
bland withdrawal
anger (only if needed)
look at the record
needs search
ultimatum

How to Negotiate with Outside Vendors

Time is on your side. It is a buyer's market, and even if you are pressured by your own deadlines (budgeting, for instance), you can set an artificial deadline that puts pressure on the vendor. Anticipating your needs and early planning helps, too. Most vendors create time pressures by forecasting price increases or offering special deals for a limited time. If you feel pressured by them, either ignore them or turn them down flat. If the pressures are real you will have to pay more later, but you'll know it's fair. If the limited offer was just a hype, they'll make another one. With salespeople, get them to invest time and effort in you. It puts pressure on them to close the sale, and you can gain concessions. With consultants, however, this usually doesn't work because they have only time to sell. If you take that time, they will charge you for it; you may get some concessions, but you'll pay a higher fee overall.

Information is vital. Always ask for lists of current and satisfied subscribers, then check them. Network with other trainers to find out how good the service is, or see consultants at work, or try packages before you buy them. Remember that catalogues and salespeople, while required by law to be honest, take great pains to present their wares as favorably as possible. To a lesser extent this applies to consultants, too. You can hire them for one job to see how they work, and if you like what you've bought, hire them for more. If you have a lot of work for them, after the trial project offer them a retainer. Remind yourself that vendors need your business probably more than you need what they offer. In the case of a consultant whom you really need, this situation is lessened but there are always other consultants, possibly many who are better than the one with whom you are dealing.

Power is always in your hands; they are coming to you. True, you have a need, but you have identified that need and they need you, too. Use all the tactics discussed earlier, not in a high-handed way but in a confident manner. Refer to precedent, be decisive, and use space to your advantage. Be prepared to risk not closing the deal, but persist on the points you need and stress fairness and ethical conduct. As a rule, have a higher power who must approve whatever you negotiate. This enables you to postpone requests for instant commitments.

Negotiating with Outside Vendors

(This is a win–win situation.)

Time	Make it your strength.
	Allow enough lead time to avoid feeling pressured.
	Ignore offers designed to hurry a decision.
	Be realistic.
	Book consultants early, not at the last minute.
Information	Know exactly what you want.
	Ask for information—successful customers and references.
	Network with other trainers.
	Try before you buy.
Power	Use it subtly.
	Always have a power out—a higher authority to check for approval.

Answers to the Seven Questions

1. They need you more than you need them.
2. Be prepared to drop negotiations and try another solution.
3. Needs are paramount in these negotiations. Identify yours specifically and consider vendor's needs for more business and for more time to deliver.
4. Vendor will probably tailor his behavior to yours.
5. Know your minimum–maximum range and be creative in what you can offer them. Work to get what you want at a fair price.
6. Establish your credibility and prepare for resistance to strong demands.
7. Pay special attention to word maps—theirs as well as yours.

If the negotiation is not going well, it is good to be able to shift to other solutions. Know what your options are before you begin to negotiate.

The Seven Questions

Needs are of particular importance in this type of negotiating situation. Aside from your training needs, whatever purchase or contract you make reflects back on you. Good consultants or sales reps are aware of this and do everything in their power to make you look good. You can measure their interest and confidence in their wares by their attitude toward you.

On the other hand, the vendors have needs as well. They look for sales that can be enlarged or expanded to cover several wares or services. Salespeople are concerned mainly with sales volume; consultants are concerned mainly with time. Both have egos and both respond to compliments. Consultants, for example, need to know they are the best and that their advice is acted upon. If money is a problem, very often a package can be worked out at a lower fee in exchange for more work, commitment to future work, or expense packages that include families. For salespeople, almost the only cost reducer is a volume purchase which lowers the cost per item.

Look at your vendors' work needs and personal needs. To warm people up, take them into your confidence, listen attentively, take their advice, and treat them with respect. Take them to lunch and return their phone calls. Give them tough problems to solve and let them show you how good they are; give them a reputation to live up to. By speaking to their ego needs, you'll gain leverage in negotiations.

When dealing with vendors, remember that dominant behavior characteristics are less important because, as good salespeople, they are usually willing to match your behavior. Still, if you want to influence them, give some thought to how they behave. If you can accurately predict their behavior, you can better plan your negotiations.

Know your minimum–maximum range. This is vital when you are negotiating with a consultant. Most are independents and have flexible fees. If you know what you need, what you'd like, and what you can give, you can afford to be flexible as well. As a consultant, I've found that some of my most satisfying arrangements have been negotiated around unusual perks, payment formulas, business partnerships, royalties, or barters. If you really know your needs and limits, you can afford to be free within them.

To negotiate effectively you will need to demonstrate your competence and knowledge of what you are buying. Research the subject. Being knowledgeable will give you credibility. Review Chapter 9 for the questions or demands you can make of outside vendors. Be prepared for resistance, of course. Try to predict the responses to your demands and then ask yourself what that response will cost you. Can you afford it? If not, don't make a demand that provokes that response. If you can, then you are free to demand.

Pay special attention to your words — and theirs. All vendors will be happy to talk, but you will need to ask questions that probe to prevent deception or misunderstanding. What an off-the-shelf package sales rep means by "tailoring" his or her material is completely different from what a consultant means. Demand specifics. Keep the discussion on the lowest rungs of the ladder of abstraction. Define your meanings and be sure that you both understand. Saying exactly what you mean is important, as are listening and reading nonverbal behaviors.

Remember that vendors are not enemies. They are folks who need to work with you to make a living. Your negotiations with them should frame a partnership that: (1) gives you the service you need at a cost you can afford, and (2) allows the vendor to enjoy a livelihood commensurate with his or her abilities. All of the positive negotiating tactics are appropriate, but the confrontational ones usually are not.

How to Negotiate with Political Peers

Time is a factor in this negotiating circumstance only in that it is wise to recognize the other people's pressures and stay out from under any yourself. In essence, you both have infinite time. Do remember, however, that whatever engagement you develop, you will both have to live with for that infinity. The negotiation is a process, so take it easy. Aim small, but build for the future.

Information is vital in this situation. It is often beneficial to have subordinates who have friends who work for your peers. Of course, this smacks of a spy network, and if you are not comfortable with such an arrangement, don't do it. Otherwise, monitor the performances of your peers so you can know their positions and be aware of how you can help them when you need to work together.

Power is a treacherous element in negotiations with peers. Because of the insecurity of interoffice politics, neutrality is usually the best stance. To exercise power is to make political enemies. On the other hand, to give your power away seems foolhardy. Work at neutrality. Guard yourself against power plays, not to win them but to maintain a mutually winning stance.

The Seven Questions

You must know how badly your peers want what you have. If they don't want it, bide your time; one day they may. If you need their support, devise something that they could want from you. Otherwise, you negotiate without a position.

As you talk, listen for their solutions. If possible, go along with their ideas—it puts your peers in your debt. Perhaps you can align yourself with someone so powerful that you can bypass them, eliminating the need to negotiate at all. In other words, analyze the political climate before you offer to negotiate (see Chapter 1).

The heart of peer negotiation is needs satisfaction. You need not love your peers, but both of you have ends to achieve and personal needs to fill

Negotiating with Political Peers

(Remember, you both work for the same organization.)

Time | Infinite.
Don't let time pressure you.
Use others' pressures to your advantage.
Build to gradually gain what you want.

Information | Set up spy networks if possible.
Keep track of others' activities.

Power | Can be treacherous; try to be neutral.
Maintain a win–win stance.

Answers to the Seven Questions

1. You must know how badly they want what you have. Be prepared to exchange something they want for something you need.
2. Give their solutions a try. Perhaps you can leapfrog over them.
3. Need satisfaction is the key consideration. Strive for a win/win result.
4. Define their personality types and strive to complement their style.
5. Minimum–maximum ranges are not a key issue, but don't set a firm limit on what you can give.
6. Make sure you get something in exchange for each concession and anticipate resistance. If there is nothing for you to gain, don't negotiate.
7. Maps may be the key to success. Use your diplomacy and language skills.

for affiliation, support, esteem, recognition, and so forth. Finding your peers' needs and helping to achieve them put you in a strong bargaining position. This is a win–win approach; it is a "how can I help?" not a "how can I get back at you?" attitude.

Because, as peers, you are working together for the same organization, you should strive to complement each other's styles. Psychologist Jard DeVille presents interesting approaches to peer struggle in his book, *The Psychology of Leadership: Managing Resources and Relationships.*[4] DeVille suggests ways of matching and complementing behavior patterns to minimize friction.

Your minimum–maximum range is probably less important in peer negotiations than other forums, but you should still list exactly what it is you want and precisely how much you are willing to pay for it. Then stick to your decision. Be careful of the price you pay, and set strict limits for yourself to prevent others from taking advantage of you.

As advised, guard your concessions. Give them generously, but only if you get what you need in return. Don't worry about credibility or identification unless the problem comes up. Your position gives you the credibility and identification, but if others have a mistaken view of either, you can demonstrate (don't tell or inform them) the truth. Don't rub it in — let it be discovered. Remember, also, that no one willingly switches position 180 degrees. Be patient and prove your points a little at a time. Resistance will be a problem, but recognize that most is personal and should be resolved at that level. If you anticipate very strong resistance, you have a few choices: (1) offer something irresistible; (2) negotiate only for the moral purpose of having made the effort; or (3) postpone the negotiation until a better time.

The words and expressions you use can be the key to success with peers. Nearly all disagreements with peers usually stem from how each party perceives the other's intentions or behaviors. Perceptions are nearly always controllable by your choice of words. Choose the expressions that both parties can accept and many difficulties will disappear. Of course your approach must be accurate, too, or the agreement will be temporary and future disappointments will cause even more friction.

Chief among the negotiating skills to practice with peers is diplomacy. Good listening ability and an empathetic response are helpful, too. So are reading nonverbal behaviors and asking good questions. Some useful tactics include:

> Trade-off
> First concession
> Trial balloons
> Straw issues
> Feinting
> *Fait accompli*

In addition, use two tactics mentioned in regard to negotiating with subordinates: needs search and looking at the record. At all costs, however, avoid ultimatums.

Summary

Negotiation is a blending of desires for a mutually satisfying result. It is an interaction to change a relationship. Three variables are always at play in a negotiation: time, information, and power. Each shapes the outcome of any negotiation.

Many people regard negotiation as a win–lose situation, but it isn't. Both parties must be satisfied for a contract to be enforced. This means you should always take care that other parties win at least some of what they need and want. This is also why no negotiation is ever really concluded.

One crucial element that influences the outcome of any negotiation is the preparation you put into it. To help, this chapter outlined seven questions for preparing a negotiating strategy. It also discussed common negotiating tactics. The chapter concluded by showing how to apply these negotiating principles to four common situations for a training manager: negotiating with the boss, with subordinates, with outside vendors, and with peers.

Notes

PART I

Chapter 1

1. Lewis Carroll, *Through the Looking-Glass,* in Martin Gardner, *The Annotated Alice* (New York: Clarkson Potter, 1960), p. 191.
2. Marshall McLuhan, *Understanding Media: The Extensions of Man* (New York: New American Library, 1973).
3. Based on "Mapping the Corporate Culture," a handout from Career Strategies seminar in Evanston, Ill.; and Beverly Hyman, *How Successful Women Manage* (New York: AMACOM, 1981), Chapter 7, "Managing Change."

Chapter 2

1. Edward L. Thorndike, *Human Learning* (New York: Century, 1931).
2. Beverly Hyman, *How Successful Women Manage* (New York: AMACOM, 1981), Chapter 7, "Managing Change."
3. Edward DeBono, *New Think* (New York: Avon, 1971).
4. Jard DeVille, *The Psychology of Leadership: Managing Resources and Relationships* (Rockville Centre, N.Y.: Farnsworth Publishing Co., 1984).
5. Solomon Asche, "Effects of Group Pressure upon the Modification and Distortion of Judgment," in *Groups, Leadership, and Men,* ed. H. Guetzkow (Pittsburgh, Pa.: The Carnegie Press, 1951).

Chapter 4

1. Stanley Milgram, *Obedience to Authority: An Experimental View* (New York: Harper & Row, 1956).

2. Based on Stanley L. Payne, *The Art of Asking Questions* (Princeton, N.J.: Princeton University Press, 1980); John McConnell, *AMA Conference Leadership Manual* (New York: AMACOM, 1973); and "Effective Strategies for Platform Speaking," a manual from a 1981 AMA course.
3. Ray L. Birdwhistell, *Kinesics and Context: Essays on Body Motion Communication* (Philadelphia: University of Pennsylvania Press, 1970), and *Introduction to Kinesics* (Louisville, Ky.: University of Louisville Press, 1952).
4. Paul Watzlawick, et al., *Pragmatics of Human Communication* (New York: Norton, 1967).
5. Albert Mehrabian, *Nonverbal Communication* (Chicago: Aldine-Atherton, 1972).
6. Edward T. Hall, *The Silent Language* (Westport, Conn.: Greenwood Press, 1980), and *The Hidden Dimension* (New York: Doubleday, 1966).
7. Beverly Hyman, "The Dominant Models and Metaphors with Which Teachers Report They Function in the Classroom Environment," Ph.D. thesis, New York University, 1980.

PART II

Chapter 6

1. Elton Mayo, *The Human Problems of an Industrial Civilization* (New York: Macmillan, 1933).

Chapter 8

1. Joseph Weizenbaum, *Computer Power and Human Reason: From Judgment to Calculation* (New York: W. H. Freeman, 1976).
2. Beverly Hyman, Trainee's Manual from "Training the Trainer," a 1987 AMA course, © 1980 Beverly Hyman, Ph.D., and Associates.

Chapter 9

1. Karl R. Popper, *The Open Society and Its Enemies* (Princeton, N.J.: Princeton University Press, 1966).
2. Based on Beverly Hyman, "Advanced Training the Trainer," a 1987 AMA course.

Chapter 11

1. Based on Chris Dean and Quentin Whitlock, *Handbook of Computer-Based Training* (New York: Nichols Publishing Co., 1982).
2. This treatment of equipment is based on the working operations of Uniforce Temporaries, New Hyde Park, N.Y., and on research conducted by Beverly Hyman for "Advanced Training the Trainer," a 1987 AMA course.

PART III

Chapter 12

1. Section on budgeting based on Paul E. Guilmette, "Budgeting," a 1987 Dun & Bradstreet seminar, and Grover M. Clark and Jeanette Pearlman, "Budgeting for Human Resource Systems," in William R. Tracey, ed., *Human Resources Management and Development Handbook* (New York: AMACOM, 1985), pp. 111–122.
2. Section on staffing based on David W. Brinkerhoff, "The HR Professional Staff," in William R. Tracey, ed., *op. cit.*, pp. 174–178.
3. Based on Richard W. Beatty and Craig E. Schneier, *Personnel Administration: An Experiential Skill-Building Approach* (Reading, Mass.: Addison-Wesley, 1981).
4. George S. Odiorne, "Management by Objectives for HR Managers," in William R. Tracey, ed., *op. cit.*, pp. 101–110.
5. Beatty and Schneier, *op. cit.*
6. Odiorne, *op. cit.*
7. Frederick Herzberg, *Work and the Nature of Man* (New York: Thomas Y. Crowell Co., 1966).
8. Paul Hersey and Kenneth H. Blanchard, *Management of Organizational Behavior: Utilizing Human Resources*, 4th ed. (Englewood Cliffs, N.J.: Prentice-Hall, 1982).

Chapter 13

1. Jerome Brunner, "Credibility in the Media," paper delivered at Media Ecology Symposium, Saugerties, N.Y., April 1984.
2. Lorraine Hansberry, *A Raisin in the Sun* (New York: New American Library, 1961), Act II, scene iii.
3. Beverly Hyman. *Writing,* course offered by Beverly Hyman Associates.
4. S. I. Hayakawa, *Language in Thought and Action*, 4th ed. (New York: Harcourt Brace Jovanovich, 1978).

Chapter 14

1. Gerard I. Nierenberg, *The Complete Negotiator* (New York: Nierenberg-Zieff, 1986).
2. Garry Mitchell, *How to Motivate for Superior Performance*, cassette/workbook series (New York: AMACOM, 1982).
3. Dudley Bennett, *TA and the Manager* (New York: AMACOM, 1976).
4. Jard DeVille, *The Psychology of Leadership: Managing Resources and Relationships* (Rockville Centre, N.Y.: Farnsworth Publishing Co., 1984).

Appendix

Training Resources

Associations

American Society for Training and Development
1630 Duke Street
Box 1443
Alexandria, VA, 22313

American Management Association
135 West 50 Street
New York, NY, 10020

Publications

"Training and Development Journal"
(included in ASTD membership)

"Training"
50 South 9 Street
Minneapolis, MN, 55402   (612) 333 1471

"Bulletin on Training"
The Bureau of National Affairs
1231 25th Street N.W.
Washington, DC, 20037   (202) 452 4200

Evaluation Service

Seminar Clearing House International (formerly Mantread)
630 Bremer Tower
St. Paul, MN, 55101   (612) 293 1044

Off-the-Shelf Resources

*The Trainer's Resource: a Comprehensive Guide to Packaged Training
Programs:* Leonard Nadler and Eugene Fetteroll, Eds. (Amherst, Mass.:
Human Resource Development Press, annually)

Video Resources

Almanac/Catalogue of Video Equipment and Video Services: MPCS Video
Industries, Inc., Bill Daniels Company, 1984

Index